volume 1

METROPOLITAN SCHOOL ORGANIZATION:
Basic Problems and Patterns

edited by Troy V. McKelvey
State University of New York at Buffalo

McCutchan Publishing Corporation
2526 Grove Street
Berkeley, California 94704

Library of Congress Catalogue
Card Number: 72-14045
ISBN: 0-8211-1223-6

Contents

Foreword

In many cities across the land the imposing structures of schools built early in this century symbolize both the past and present in education. These structures and the architecture that shaped them remind us of the pioneering and glorious days of urban education; they and the conditions surrounding them also highlight the pervasive and sweeping changes of recent decades that have helped create the current crisis in urban education.

The conditions of educational crisis found in almost all of America's major cities are relatively well known. These conditions stem in part from far-reaching changes in the environment of schools. The racial mix of student populations, for example, has changed substantially. Even two decades ago school populations in the large cities were largely white. Today, however, student populations in these cities are largely black. Accompanying the change in racial mix and contributing to it has been the flight of citizens and businesses from the cities to the suburbs. The flight of citizens has resulted in lessened leadership in the urban settings; business transfers have cut needed tax revenues.

The spiraling costs of education and diminished resources have created a severe crunch and deficit financing in a number of urban school systems. Wayne King, writing in the *New York Times* (18 February 1973) about the Philadelphia school system projected a deficit of $35 million for 1973 and estimated that the deficit for 1974 would range between $46 and $125 million. Consortia of banks in different cities are seeking to keep the schools afloat through loans in the face of growing deficits. That such consortia are restive is suggested by the fact that four of the eleven banks providing support for the Philadelphia schools withdrew recently and others were considering the same course of action. It is understandable, then, that one of the bankers associated with the consortium in Philadelphia remarked: "Other cities—New York, Chicago, Detroit to name a few—are in the same boat, being swept down the same river to the same waterfalls."

The conditions highlighting the urban educational crisis are better known than the solution to the crisis. At the same time an increasing number of observers are saying that a portion of the solution can be found in the concept of "metropolitanism." More scholars and leaders are making the case for metropolitan government generally and for metropolitan educational government specifically. In both cases, metropolitan government would span the city and its suburbs.

Some urban communities have already chosen the metropolitan approach to educational government. This volume, as the first of two volumes, chronicles the progress made in these communities and sheds light on particular operations and processes within the context of metropolitan government for education. The volume also presents a range of concepts gleaned from studies of metropolitan approaches used in different areas.

We congratulate Professor McKelvey on his initiative in bringing this volume and its companion to fruition. We are grateful to those at the State University of New York at Buffalo who cosponsored, with the University Council for Educational Administration, the seminar at which the papers in this and its companion volume were originally presented. We hope that the papers will provide useful clues to leaders interested in turning the urban educational crisis into opportunity and progress.

Jack Culbertson

Executive Director
UNIVERSITY COUNCIL FOR EDUCATIONAL ADMINISTRATION

Preface

The major purpose of this anthology is to describe and discuss the study and development of metropolitan educational delivery systems. This is accomplished through the introduction of substantive works focusing on the forces presently surrounding the problem of metropolitan educational reform and the present state of operating systems for education in metropolitan areas.

This volume explores the underlying concepts of metropolitanism by examining both its quantitative and humanistic aspects. The problems of scale brought about by large and increasing numbers of people concentrating their living patterns within regional boundaries, the barriers increasingly being raised between the central city and the suburbs, the thin veneer of complacency that surrounds the explosive inner city, and the volatile and emotional trauma of racial unrest raise many problems for which solutions are not readily available. It is hoped that the sharing of knowledge about metropolitan school organization will motivate and increase research and development. It is timely to bring together current thinking and baseline data in order to explore solutions to educational problems produced by inadequate systems and the shifting values and populations of our society.

Volume I is intended for scholars and practitioners engaged in the improvement of education. Students and professors of educational administration, as well as their counterparts in the behavioral sciences at colleges and universities, should find ideas and concepts for research and development. Planners and systems designers in a variety of settings should find this material useful. Administrators, school board members, and state legislators will find this material beneficial as they debate and formulate policy decisions about metropolitan structures designed to solve metropolitan problems. Anyone interested in improving education and wishing to participate as an informed citizen should find this volume an important resource.

The provision of high quality equal education for our society has been accepted as a common purpose, but we are still struggling with the means to accomplish such a goal. History points to the consequences of lingering confrontations between affluence and poverty, and the conflicts between belief systems and the process of surrounding rising expectations with barriers, be they of brick or the attitudes of those at such an interface. Many believe that broadening the structure of education to the metropolitan area would decrease the problems of the cities and the suburbs and improve the human condition for metropolitan areas.

It is to this purpose that this volume is dedicated. Its distribution should increase our awareness of present operating regional education structures, provide the opportunity for individuals and groups to study the appropriateness of metropolitanism for their region, develop new structures by finding new relationships using the appropriate elements of existing structures, and promote support for such study and development. It is only through such effort that any new and exciting model for the organization of education can become a reality.

Papers included in this book were supported by an ESEA Title III subcontract to the Faculty of Educational Studies, State University of New York at Buffalo, under the grant number OEG-0-8-0634304568, project number 68-06343-0, Project 1990, directed by the Western New York School Development Council.

Troy V. McKelvey

Acknowledgments

In order to acknowledge the many individuals and organizations contributing to these volumes, it was necessary to review almost five years of notes. During the summer of 1967 Dr. Robert Heller and I were privileged to visit metropolitan areas throughout the United States. We were interested particularly in gathering information concerning metropolitan progress in Nashville, Tennessee and Louisville, Kentucky and comparing this progress with developments in the Bay Area surrounding San Francisco, and in Greater Seattle. This interest was further stimulated by pioneering authors in the field of metropolitanism such as those contributing to the National Society for the Study of Education Yearbooks, and the scholarly efforts of Dean Alan Campbell and his colleagues of the Maxwell School of Citizenship and Public Affairs at Syracuse University. Given this interest, I was motivated by Jack Culbertson, Executive Director of the University Council for Educational Administration (UCEA), who assisted me in the development of a UCEA Career Development Seminar entitled "Alternative Models for Organizing Education in Metropolitan Areas." Papers prepared for this UCEA seminar provide the major input for both volumes of *Metropolitan School Organization*.

The basic financial support for this overall effort came from the Western New York School Development Council, through the leadership of its Executive Secretary and Director, Robert Lamitie. This organization, with the assistance of Austin Swanson and Robert Heller, had submitted a proposal under ESEA Title III to the Office of Education for a metropolitan study of education on the Niagara Frontier. This project, known as "Project 1990," had three major components: a middle school study for the City of Buffalo, a financial component, and an organizational component. The organizational component of this study, using funds provided by a direct grant to the Faculty of Educational Studies, State University of New York at Buffalo, supported both the baseline data papers developed for Project 1990 and the papers developed specifically for the UCEA Career Development Seminar. This was an opportunity to bring together the Project 1990 organizational component, the interests of the University Council for Educational Administration, and the State University of New York at Buffalo in a combined effort to present knowledge on how educational delivery systems might be formulated better to serve the people in metropolitan areas. The efforts of authors contributing papers to this combined endeavor is greatly appreciated. The contribution of Thomas Laverne, former New York State senator and chairman of the Joint Committee on Metropolitan and Regional Areas Study, is also appreciated.

I am indebted to the secretarial staffs of the Department of Educational Administration, State University of New York at Buffalo, and the University Council for Educational Administration; Harriet Ferrell, Margaret Tossi, and Marilyn Host who ably served the staff at the University Council at Columbus, Ohio, and Marilyn Del Nagro, Eunice Garey, Ellen Glaser, and Roslyn Pronik without whom the department at Buffalo could not exist.

Several others deserve plaudits for their assistance during the tenure of this project—Lenora Cole, Dick Podemski, Bill McGee, Orville Harris, and Fred Frank from the Department of Educational Administration, and Bill Harris from the Policy Science Program, State University of New York at Buffalo; and Jack Blough from the Department of Educational Administration, Ohio State University. There are many individuals whose names have not been mentioned but who deserve an expression of gratitude: the staff members of the Department of Educational Administration, State University of New York at Buffalo, who covered my absence while on special assignment as a UCEA Fellow at UCEA headquarters during the 1969-70 academic year; members of the Faculty of Educational Studies at the State University of New York who assisted with the UCEA Career Development Seminar; Assistant Provost Nancy Broderick, for her financial wizardry; and Provost Rollo Handy, for allowing it all to happen. Special appreciation should go to the UCEA headquarters staff, Jack Culbertson, Robin Farquhar, Alan Gaynor, and Mark Schibles, for their inspiration and thoughtful guidance. Most gratefully I thank my wife Alice, who endures my continued forays into such projects.

Contributors

S. Theodore Berg (ED.D., State University of New York at Buffalo) —Currently Assistant Superintendent of Schools for the catholic school system of the Diocese of Buffalo and part-time lecturer in education at Medaille College in Buffalo.

Joseph A. Caligiuri (M.S., Canisius College)—Presently Director of Special Projects for the catholic school system of the Diocese of Buffalo, New York. He has taught in secondary schools and at Rosary Hill and Medaille Colleges in Buffalo.

Alan K. Campbell (Ph.D., Harvard University)—Formerly Director of the Metropolitan Studies Program; now professor of Political Science and Dean of the Maxwell School of Citizenship and Public Affairs, Syracuse University. A specialist in urban affairs, Dean Campbell has written numerous articles for political science, scholarly, and business journals. He edited the series, *Education in Large Cities* (Syracuse University Press, 1967 and 1968) and wrote (with Seymour

Sacks) *Metropolitan America* (The Free Press, 1967) and *Financing Equal Educational Opportunity* (McCutchan, 1972). He has served on Governor Rockefeller's Council of Economic Advisors.

Daniel E. Griffiths (Ph.D., Yale University)—Dean of the School of Education, New York University. His contribution to education administration goes without question—both in text books and monographs focusing on administrative theory and its practice. His contribution to this volume is the result of a year spent in England where he studied the organization of the Inner London Education Authority.

William Harris (B.S., Stroudsberg State College, Pennsylvania)—Graduate work in rehabilitation counseling at Springfield College, Massachusetts and for the Policy Science Program at the State University of New York at Buffalo. Formerly Director of Personnel Development and Training for the Southern Railway system.

Robert Heller (Ed.D., Pennsylvania State University)—Professor of Educational Administration at the State University of New York at Buffalo. Heller has done considerable research on informal organizations and their influence on perception. His current interest and research are in the areas of urban school administration, organizational theory, and school integration. He contributed "Desegregation, Integration, and Urban Schools" to Frank W. Lutz's *Toward Improved Urban Education* (Jones Publishing, 1970).

Clifford P. Hooker (Ed.D., Indiana University)—Chairman, Department of Educational Administration, University of Minnesota. Hooker has long been a contributor to the literature of educational administration and, with Van D. Mueller and Donald E. Davis, contributed "Cooperation among School Districts in a Metropolitan Area" to the National Society for the Study of Education's 1968 Yearbook, *Metropolitanism: Its Challenge to Education,* edited by Robert J. Havighurst.

Henry M. Levin (Ph.D., Rutgers University)—Associate Professor, School of Education and Department of Economics, Stanford University. Levin has specialized in the economics of education, urban economics, public finance, and the economics of human resources.

He edited *Community Control of Schools* (Brookings Institution, 1970) and was one of the authors of *Schools and Inequality* (MIT Press, 1971).

Troy V. McKelvey (Ed.D., University of California at Berkeley) —Associate Professor of Educational Administration, State University of New York at Buffalo. He has research and development interests in both macro- and micro-organizational structures for education. A former fellow at the Center for the Advanced Study of Educational Administration, University of Oregon, and the University Council for Educational Administration, Ohio State University, he was one of the editors of *Urban School Administration* (Sage Publications, 1969), and of *The Monroe City Simulation Materials* (UCEA, 1971).

Mike Milstein (Ph.D., University of California at Berkeley)—Associate Professor of Educational Administration, State University of New York at Buffalo. Milstein's major interest and research is in the politics of education. With Robert Jennings he wrote *Educational Policy-Making and the State Legislature: The New York Experience* (Praeger Publishers, 1973) and is one of the editors of *Educational Administration and the Behavior Sciences* (Allyn and Bacon, 1973).

Van D. Mueller (Ed.D., Michigan State University)—Associate Professor of Education and Assistant Chairman of the Division of Educational Administration, College of Education, University of Minnesota. Mueller has served as school finance consultant and chief school officer in Michigan. His recent research and publications have been concerned with the metropolitan area and its problems of staffing, cooperation, and financing. Among his most recent publications is "Equal Treatment to Equals, a New Structure of Public Schools in Kansas City and St. Louis Metropolitan Areas."

Raphael O. Nystrand (Ph.D., Northwestern University)—Chairman of the Department of Educational Administration, College of Education, Ohio State University. Nystrand has served as a member of several study groups, including a consortium of professors from five universities studying school policy making in big cities. Nystrand's publications deal primarily with the development, impact, and implications of community action programs for educational change and decision making. "Organizing Schools to Develop Humane Capabilities," written with Luvern Cunningham, appears in *Developing Human Characteristics,* the 1970 yearbook of the Association for Supervision and Curriculum Development. His latest work deals with student unrest in the public schools.

Theodore L. Reller (Ph.D., Yale University)—Formerly Dean of the School of Education, presently Professor of Educational Administration, University of California at Berkeley. Reller's major interests are educational administration, including the historical development of administrative organization and practice, organizational structure, administration of personnel, community development, and comparative educational administration. His articles and books have had a noticeable impact on the study of educational administration. Recognized as an early proponent and student of regionalism, he is currently studying the decentralization of power and decision making in selected large cities of the world.

Brock Rideout (M. Ed., University of Toronto)—Professor of Educational Administration at the Ontario Institute for Studies in Education. Rideout has been associated with school finance studies in Ontario and metropolitan Toronto. His work on the Ontario School Foundation Program is well known. An experienced school finance man at both the local and provincial levels, he has long studied the development of the Toronto metropolitan school system.

Michael D. Usdan (Ed. D., Teachers College, Columbia University)—Formerly Associate Professor of Educational Administration, Teachers College, Columbia University and presently Chairman, Graduate Program in Educational Administration, City University of New York. He has been active in various projects involving urban school administration and the author of several articles and reports on topics such as desegregation and teaching the disadvantaged. With David Minar and Emmanuel Hurwitz, he wrote *Education and State Politics* (Teachers College Press, 1969).

Bernard C. Watson (Ph.D., University of Chicago)—Formerly Deputy Superintendent of the Philadelphia Public Schools, and presently Professor of Urban Education, Temple University. Watson has written several articles dealing with problems of the metropolis. He made an early contribution to the analysis of the principal's role and the staff negotiation process. Known to be devoted to change and innovation, Watson will continue to make a major contribution to the solution of problems in the urban setting. He is a member of the National E.P.E.A. Advisory Committee.

Albert H. Wheeler (Dr.P.H., University of Michigan)—An Associate Professor of Microbiology and Dermatology at the School of Medicine, University of Michigan. Wheeler is a past president of the Michigan State Conference NAACP and has served as chairman of the Equal Opportunity Board of Washtenaw County. He has served on state advisory committees to study the financing of public schools in Michigan, the Governor's Educational Reform Committee, and the State Committee on Title I of the Higher Education Act. His other activities include a study of racial imbalance in the Ann Arbor schools and the development of a black studies program.

Introduction

Present school organization patterns in our metropolitan areas have been brought about by population expansion and the lack of planning for such growth. The existing fragmentation of school systems is maintained most often through competitive rather than through cooperative efforts. Prior to World War II, the best school systems in this country were thought to be in the central cities. Soon thereafter, we saw a decline of city systems and beginnings of lighthouse school systems in the suburbs. Thus the locus of good quality educational systems was reversed. This situation is linked with the shift from the cities to the suburbs of more affluent families and the migration of the less fortunate into the cities. Within a few decades this population shift brought into stark reality a decided inequality of educational opportunity. We now face the problems arising from these shifting populations and a changing value system that demands a more adequate system of education. Many feel that the metropolitan unit would help solve present problems and be a more effective system.

To understand the concept of metropolitanism fully, it is first necessary to differentiate the meanings of *metropolitanism* and *urbanization*. After World War I, urban centers began growing rapidly. Our agrarian society was moving to the city. Agricultural technology was rapidly replacing the need for human labor and the city became the work place of our formerly agricultural work force. The decades between 1940 and 1960 were certainly a period of urbanization. During this same period, shortly after World War II, the move to the suburbs began. This population movement, both from the city and rural areas, created a population distribution that cannot be expressed adequately by the term *urbanization*. The term *metropolitanism*, which includes the central city and its surrounding population, now becomes more appropriate. The 1970 census reports that 68 percent of the total population of the United States live in metropolitan areas: 31 percent live in central cities, 37 percent live in the adjacent area. We now have approximately the same percentage of population living in urban, suburban, and rural areas with the majority of citizens living within metropolitan areas. Some cities in recent years have grown in population, but in most cases this increase can be attributed to annexation policies rather than real growth. Compounding the effects of this population shift are the problems of race and the white flight from the central city. Integration and the busing issue have provided such fervor that a political candidate is careful not to take strong positions. Busing now is attached to all change, even metropolitanism. Integrationists state that central cities will have a totally black population if present segregation trends continue. The most striking example is provided by the city of Washington, D.C., which now has a black population of over 90 percent. Some would say that the metropolitan structure would defuse the political power of the black population. However, the consequence may well be that black cities would be left with a tax base so narrow that public services would be impossible. In any case, the problem of affluent white suburbs and predominantly poor central cities presents a complex of social and educational issues confounding to most observers.

The militancy of teachers and the negotiation process mandatory in many states have both become time-consuming and perplexing problems. The present strength of professional teachers' organizations and the range of what is to be negotiated vary considerably. Such variations can contribute to unequal distribution of good teaching staffs. Many now feel that such negotiations should shift from the local district to combinations or collectives of districts. Education on a metropolitan basis would make regional negotiations a reality.

Two old issues are again coming to the surface and will receive increased attention in the future: the politicalization of education, and public support for parochial schools. Large cities have always had partial politicalization, but the relationship between the superintendent of schools and the mayor may well become closer in the future. Unfortunately, the marriage of the schools and politics may come about through efforts to survive rather than to improve. The case for increasing partisan responsibility for quality education may very well become stronger.

The separation of state and religion is an old issue indeed, but scarce resources and bankrupted cities forced to accept students from parochial schools that have closed for lack of funds may change the views of many on the support for and even inclusion of parochial schools in a state system.

The problem becomes even more complex with the introduction of recent court decisions. The *Serrano* v. *Priest* decision found that no longer can the education of children be determined by the wealth of their parents, and that present methods of financing education cannot withstand constitutional challenge. Similar court cases in several states have strong implications for the organization of education. Pending court cases on the integration of city and suburban schools point out the inequity of the present educational organization and the lack of an adequate support system to meet new circumstances in our society. The United States Supreme Court could, within the near future, hand down a far-reaching decision that would affect every metropolitan area in the nation. We have always lacked a national policy for reform in education. Such a policy may very well be provided by the courts.

Some metropolitan systems are presently operational. All are associated with the delivery of educational services. They do, however, differ in scope and scale, from the general to the specific, and from the public to the parochial.

The historical development of operating metropolitan school systems in the United States is relatively brief. Beginning in the late 1960s, local governments and school systems, mostly in Florida and Tennessee, began, through enabling legislation passed by the state legislatures, to develop charters for metropolitan government. The Nashville-Davidson County merger came some six years after such efforts began. Miami-Dade County and Jacksonville-Duval County in Florida have been highlighted because of their progress toward metropolitan government. However, it must be remembered that Florida already had a county school system, while Tennessee, for the most part, had city and county school systems. Tennessee represents an interesting case in the development of metropolitan school systems. For instance, animosity toward an annexation policy in

Nashville was one of the forces that made the voters approve of its metropolitan charter, although Knoxville, with a completed charter, has been unable to obtain the approval of voters. Memphis, operating quietly under state annexation laws, is incrementally merging the boundaries of the city and county.

The adoption of metropolitan government and school organization has been extremely difficult. Voters face one another across an abyss created by differing value systems. Neither the suburban or the urban voter has been enlightened about such an inevitable union. Will such mergers, unions, and reforms come about by referendum, mandate, or litigation through the courts?

The success of present metropolitan systems has still to be determined. However, we need a greater understanding of the process of development, implementation, and operation of these systems. The examination of present operating models provides some insight into the current organization of education in metropolitan areas and provides a base for future study and development. We need to increase our knowledge of such existing organizational patterns and, to do that, we need to understand the factors that underlie the concept of metropolitanism. We need a greater understanding of the present political and economic forces that, in some cases, simultaneously maintain the present structure of school organization and point to its reform.

Since some organizational change has taken place in various regions of the United States and in foreign nations, this change needs adequate description and rigorous analysis. Such analysis should provide insight that would enable the development of structures more appropriate to the changing educational needs of this nation.

This anthology is volume one of two volumes on metropolitan school organization. Part one of volume I describes the setting of education in the metropolitan context, presents the black perspective, and proposes a solution for financing education. Part two examines the relationships between the central city, the state, and the federal government, and identifies the political forces requiring change. Part three describes current operating models for the delivery of educational services on a metropolitan basis and an analysis of the operating models that proposes some concepts for future consideration. Part four outlines some options for the development of metropolitan schools and leads into the second volume.

In volume two, *Metropolitan School Organization: Proposals for Reform,* both the philosophical and the practical issues surrounding the concept are presented. The articulation of a clear set of goals for education is followed by discussions of the fragmentation of knowledge about organizational change, internal change, and communication. These theoretical perspectives are intended to assist in the understanding of superstructures and subunits in a general system. Selected conceptual frameworks are proposed, described, and rationalized in detail as models for metropolitan schools. Volume two closes with a consideration of the problems of marshalling the resources to implement such changes.

part I

Factors Underlying the Concept of Metropolitanism

Since 1950 there has been a decided shift in the population of the United States that has brought to crisis proportions social, economic, and educational problems within metropolitan areas.

Chapter one points out that our society has failed to meet the fiscal requirements of our cities and provide equality of educational opportunity. Alan Campbell describes the present setting of education in metropolitan areas. His population statistics point to the scale and scope of the issues between the city and the suburbs. He states that some encouragement might be found in presently pending court cases but is not encouraged about the integration of schools. The evidence seems to be that our present system of education is not fulfilling the expectations of our democracy.

Chapter two focuses on the black experience in education. Albert Wheeler, a professed social dermatologist, presents the case of unfulfilled expectations for good quality and equality in education. He denies that equal justice exists for blacks in this society and notes that racism is our greatest human problem. From the black perspective the elimination of poverty could lift the dignity of man. He suggests that the numbers of black staff members in schools of education be increased, and that blacks be elevated to positions of power within the educational bureaucracy. He presents several problems including the lack of awareness of the black perspective on the part of teachers, testing programs with cultural bias, the discipline practices, and the tracking of students in schools. This chapter makes a plea for a model of change influenced by a black bias for equality and justice.

Through the application of economic theory, chapter three proposes the caveat that metropolitanism may not be the answer to the social and economic problems facing metropolitan areas. Henry Levin challenges the assumption that cooperation necessarily has spillover costs and increased benefits, and the assumption that attitudes and behavior can be changed by changing geographic boundaries. He states that the elimination of present school boundaries will not necessarily change the equity factor between the city and the suburbs. A strong case is made that metropolitanism is but a dream until adequate strategies for implementation can be developed.

Part one describes a population distribution highly associated with the distribution of racial and socioeconomic factors. It explores this unequal distribution for in the confrontation of these problems is the challenge of metropolitan school organization.

1

Education in Its Metropolitan Setting

Alan K. Campbell

The redistribution of population and economic activity since the end of World War II—from countryside to city and from city to suburb—has been accompanied by difficulties (some have called it a crisis) in the delivery of government services. The population and economic shifts have produced metropolitan areas that are socially and economically interdependent while they are governed by a fragmented system. The logic of the situation has led to many suggestions for local government reform, the most common being one or another form of metropoliswide government.

Many of the recommended reforms for general government organization have their counterparts in changes advocated for the government of education. Students of educational organization, examining the same evidence as students of general government, in many instances have come to the same conclusion—the necessity for metropoliswide government for education.

Standing behind these recommendations are both the population movements and the redistributions of economic activities. Not only has there been a migration of people from the countryside and small towns to urban areas, but also there has simultaneously been a "sorting out" of population within metropolitan areas from central city to suburbs. This redistribution has been neither random nor neutral. Rather, it has produced a residential pattern of people at the lower end of the income scale living in the cities and people in the middle and upper ranges of that income scale overrepresented in the suburbs. The redistribution has concentrated the black population in the central cities while the suburbs have become increasingly white during the decades between 1950 and 1970.

While this population redistribution was taking place, economic activities were also shifting. Manufacturing employment grew rapidly in the suburbs, while it just barely held its own or, in some instances, declined, in central cities. Retail activity followed its customers to the suburbs, slowing the growth rate for such activity within cities. The result was more rapid growth in economic activity in the suburbs than in the cities.

Zoning and other practices often made it impossible for workers at the lower end of the wage scale to follow jobs to the suburbs because housing was not available for them. It was a particularly difficult problem for blacks who faced both economic and social difficulties in acquiring suburban homes. This situation contributed to large-scale unemployment within the ghettos and, in other instances, produced a difficult and awkward reverse commute for those who did find employment in suburbs but were unable to live nearby.

Impact of Shifts on Education

All these changes had significant impact on the delivery of educational services within the central city. *De facto* segregation resulted in actual increases in segregation in many large city schools. In addition, central city schools became characterized by increasing income homogeneity—most pronounced among children of low-income parents.

The movement of economic activity also weakened the tax base needed for the support of educational services. With competition from increased demands for other traditional municipal services, and a declining income source, schools found themselves at a double disadvantage. The fiscal problem, added to the educational difficulties caused by the student mix, made it no exaggeration to describe the problems facing many central-city schools as approaching crisis proportions.

Proposals for Integration

To meet this crisis, many solutions were proposed and some were even tried on a small scale. Most of the suggestions and actual changes were made within the framework of the current government structure of education.

For example, in order to deal with the problem of increasing segregation, various busing schemes were proposed. In some instances, proposals were even implemented, although rapid increases in the proportions of black students in most cities made genuinely integrated education unlikely. There was stiff political resistance in many white neighborhoods to such busing. Also suggested, but never moving beyond the drawing board, were proposals for educational parks that would draw students from a wide area within the city, thereby producing at least some integration. A recommendation implemented in a few places was that of paired schools—a black school and a white school combined in such a way that students would be distributed between the two schools in somewhat equal proportions. None of these schemes has made a substantial contribution to integrated education and, in nearly every large city, segregation continues to increase.

Overcoming Fiscal Inadequacies

Efforts were also made to overcome the fiscal disadvantage of the central city school. A few cities attempted to tap the more prosperous suburban tax base with commuter income taxes. Some revenues were gained, but their contribution to closing the fiscal gap has been relatively small.

Another means of attracting resources for the cities was to push hard for increased federal and state aid. State aid was furnished, at best, very slowly and, in most of the states, suburban schools continued to receive more aid than did their central-city counterparts. The passage of the Elementary and Secondary Education Act did move some resources from the federal government to schools with disadvantaged students, but the increased resources seldom amounted to more than another 4 or 5 percent of what was already being spent. The result has been very little improvement in central city education.

Community Control

Frustration with the quality of education in many ghetto areas led to demands for decentralization and increased community control of central-city school districts. Although such moves could not have contributed to integration, or increased resources for central-city schools, they were based on a belief, held particularly in many black neighborhoods, that stronger community involvement in the schools would, even with current resources, improve the quality of education. These efforts continue and there is some evidence that a new spirit has emerged in some city neighborhoods—a spirit that is at least improving the relationship between school and neighborhood. However, the underlying need for increased resources remains and, until this problem is solved, it is unlikely that community control will make any major long-run contribution to the improvement of central-city ghetto education.

Metropolitan School Districts

Moving beyond the efforts to improve the quality of central-city education within the confines of the present educational system, a good number of people have advocated some form of metropoliswide school district. The proposals vary in the degree of decentralization they would permit, but all are designed to increase local resources for education, while simultaneously improving the possibility for integrated education. Although moves to metropolitanize education have had substantial professional support, they have not been carried out except in some places in the South where some form of metropolitan government has been adopted in Nashville (Davidson County), Tennessee; Miami (Dade County), Florida; and Jacksonville (Duval County), Florida. Even there the transitions were facilitated by peculiar circumstances. In Florida, the two systems were organized as county school systems prior to metropolitanization and, in Tennessee, a city school system and a county school system merged. With these exceptions, there have been no major changes in the government of education in metropolitan areas. Some consolidations of districts continue, but these occur more in rural than in metropolitan areas.

New Trends for the 1970s?

While educational problems become increasingly severe, and as students and practitioners within the field advocate changes—using the statistical evidence of the 1960 and 1970 censuses to justify their recommendations—economic and social changes continue.

It is clear that the population movements of the 1950s have persisted through the 1960s into the 1970s, with some significant differences. The central city population has continued to decline and suburban population to grow, but the movement from countryside and small towns to metropolitan areas has been slower. As a result, population within metropolitan areas has increased during the 1970s at a much slower rate than during the 1950s.

Manufacturing is still growing more rapidly in suburbs than in cities, with some cities losing manufacturing jobs within their boundaries. The same is true of jobs in the retail sector, with retail jobs in metropolitan areas increasing within suburban areas and declining in the cities. These phenomena are more pronounced in the larger, older metropolitan areas than in the newer and/or smaller ones. The pattern, however, is relatively consistent across the country.

Growth of the Service Sector

The central city is showing economic strength in the service sector—the most rapidly growing segment of the national economy. Consequently, the greatest economic strength of the cities exists in the sector that is also showing the greatest overall vitality. The situation offers some encouragement.

Within the service sector, the category of activities that the census defines as *other services* shows the greatest strength. These services constitute 13.4 percent (or did in 1963—since when no comparable data appear to have been produced) of all central city jobs for eight major cities: Baltimore, Denver, New Orleans, New York, Philadelphia, St. Louis, San Francisco, and Washington, D.C. Between 1948 and 1956 the annual growth in this category was 4 percent a year; between 1956 and 1967 it jumped to 15.7 percent a year. Although not carefully defined by the census, this category includes jobs in medical, legal, educational, nonprofit organizations, and miscellaneous business services. In the other service sectors—finance, insurance and real estate, and government—the growth rate has been less substantial, but still shows considerable growth potential within cities.

Apparently what is occurring economically in the cities is an increasing specialization of central-city functions. This specialization will probably result in a continuing decline in manufacturing activities inside cities and a growing emphasis on the service activities for which a central location makes economic sense. It is possible, but by no means certain, that there will be a slowing down at a fairly high level of central city economic activity as the manufacturing redistribution plays itself out and the growth in the service sector provides a base for increasing the economic viability of the city.

Changes in City Population

The population pattern of the central city has been undergoing substantial change too. The 1970 census indicates that most central cities are continuing to lose population. In fact, it was in the mid-1960s that the evolutionary distribution of American urban society reached the historic point when suburban population passed central city population in total numbers. This change does not bode well for the political strength of cities in either state legislatures or Congress.

Nevertheless, there are patterns within this decline in central city population that do indicate some improvement in their overall situation. As would be expected with a decline in population, density is also decreasing. Perhaps more interesting is that this thinning is greatest within the poor areas. The density of the white population in such areas declined, between 1960 and 1967 at an annual rate of 2.9 percent, while the nonwhite population for the same period declined by only 1/100 of 1 percent. Between 1967 and 1968, however, the population decline on an annual basis was 13.5 percent for the white population and 8.9 percent (a fantastic jump) for the nonwhite population. Apparently, as income levels make it possible, residents in poor areas find more satisfactory housing either elsewhere in the city or beyond the city boundaries.

While this movement out of the poorer areas of the city was occurring, there was a population shift taking place between city and suburb, shown in table 1:1. It appears that in 1968/69 the increase

TABLE 1:1. AVERAGE ANNUAL POPULATION CHANGES
FOR ALL METROPOLITAN AREAS

		1960-64	1964-68	1968-69
White population	Central cities	0.1%	-1.1%	-0.6%
	Outside central cities	2.9%	2.6%	2.1%
Black population	Central cities	3.8%	1.9%	3.6%
	Outside central cities	2.0%	2.6%	3.7%

Source: U.S. Bureau of the Census, *Current Population Reports: Special Studies, Trends in Social and Economic Conditions in Metropolitan and Non-metropolitan Areas,* Series P-23, no. 33 (Washington, D.C.: U.S. Government Printing Office, September 1970).

of the black population of the suburbs reached approximately the same percentage as that of the white. It is probable that the middle-income black is following his middle-income white counterpart to the suburbs as soon as his income makes that move possible and as the discrimination barriers to such a move gradually come down.

Age Distribution

Changes in the age distribution of the population between cities and suburbs may point to an actual decline in central-city school population. For example, between 1960 and 1970 there was a 29.6 percent decline in the population under the age of five in the central cities, while this sector of the population decreased by only 1.3 percent in the suburbs. Although the growth rate in the suburbs was slower than it was in the earlier decade, it appears that the younger portion of the central city population is growing much more slowly than had been true between 1950 and 1960. The general pattern of growth by age category is given in table 1:2.

TABLE 1:2. PERCENTAGE POPULATION GROWTH BY AGE CATEGORY FROM 1960 TO 1970 FOR U.S. METROPOLITAN AREAS

Age	Central Cities	Suburbs
Under 5	-29.6%	- 1.3%
5-15	- 7.9%	+39.3%
16-19	+12.7%	+80.9%
20-24	+30.1%	+90.3%
25-44	-20.9%	+19.5%
45-64	+ 0.1%	+37.9%
65 +	+19.9%	+50.0%

Source: U.S. Bureau of the Census, *Current Population Reports: Special Studies, Social and Economic Characteristics of the Metropolitan and Non-metropolitan Areas: 1960 and 1970*, Series P-23, no. 37 (Washington, D.C.: U.S. Government Printing Office, June 1971).

Income Changes

There also seems to be some improvement in income distribution within central cities. For example, between 1959 and 1969 the percentage of the population in central cities with incomes below $4,000 (stated in 1969 dollars) declined from 20 percent to 15 percent. Even more significant is the percentage of the population earning over $15,000 a year (again stated in constant dollars). In 1959, only 9.8 percent of the central-city population was in that category; by 1969 it had increased to 18.9 percent.

Although the income of the black population continues to lag behind that of the white population, even at the same educational levels, the gap is slowly closing. For example, in the central city the black high-school graduate in 1959 earned an income equal to 69 percent of the white high-school graduate's. By 1969, the black worker was earning 75 percent as much as his white counterpart. Table 1:3 indicates the pattern of this relationship between black and white income at similar education levels. The size of the current gap is still a national disgrace.

TABLE 1:3. BLACK MEDIAN INCOME AS A PERCENTAGE OF
WHITE MEDIAN INCOME FOR MALES 25 TO 54 YEARS OF AGE
IN METROPOLITAN AREAS: 1959 AND 1969
(IN 1969 DOLLARS)

		1959	1969
Central City			
Elementary:	8 yrs. or less	67	79
High School:	1 to 3 yrs.	67	76
	4 yrs.	68	75
College:	1 to 3 yrs.	68	79
	4 yrs. or more	*	72
Suburban Rings			
Elementary:	8 yrs. or less	51	63
High School:	1 to 3 yrs.	*	69
	4 yrs.	*	68
College:	1 to 3 yrs.	*	*
	4 yrs. or more	*	*

*Base less than 75,000.

Source: U.S. Bureau of the Census, *Current Population Reports: Special Studies, Social and Economic Characteristics of the Metropolitan and Non-metropolitan Areas: 1960 and 1970*, Series P-23, no. 37 (Washington, D.C.: U.S. Government Printing Office, June 1971).

Implications for Schools

From the viewpoint of education, these data present a mixed picture. The central city remains the home of the low-income family, a situation that presents a major challenge for the educational system and one that cannot be met unless those schools educating the children from low-income homes receive resources commensurate with the educational services required.

It does appear that there will be a decline in central-city school population and, to the extent that this decline is not accompanied by a significant decline in tax base or a vast increase in costs for educational salaries, maintenance, security, and the like, it may make available more resources per student than are now available. The improved income distribution of the central-city population may improve the fiscal base on which the schools may draw for those needed resources. Although the pattern of economic activity does not suggest a substantial increase in the property tax base of the city, it does indicate that, if the city uses a retail sales and an income tax, there may be some improvement.

The movement of blacks to the suburbs may be robbing the city of another stabilizing element, the significant middle-income group. Nevertheless, the increase in the proportion of central city population earning over $15,000 a year does indicate that perhaps there is some movement from the suburbs back to the city that will introduce a larger middle-income group into the city's population.

The new data do not present much encouragement for the integration of central-city schools. The decline in the population of poor areas may bring about some integration in the lower-middle- and middle-income areas of the city, but certainly not for those remaining in the ghetto. Concurrently, although the increased movement of blacks to the suburbs may bring about some integration of education there, it is quite possible that the movement to suburbia is simply creating some black school districts, or black schools, within suburban school systems.

All in all, the new evidence does not fundamentally change the arguments that have been used to favor some degree of metropolitanization of at least school finance. In fact, the argument for this has now extended itself to demands by many for complete state financing of education. Most important are recent court decisions. Beginning with *Serrano* v. *Priest* in California in 1971, courts in several states have found the current system of education financing to be in violation of the equal protection clause of the federal and some state constitutions. Even if the plaintiffs lose their cases in the United States Supreme Court, prevailing circumstances and state constitutions will continue a movement toward state financing that has only begun. The political climate in a number of states may reinforce the court pressures for these changes.

Such financing changes, however, will not automatically contribute either to integration or to the improvement of ghetto schools. It is possible, though, that either metropolitan or state financing would put more resources into ghetto and poor area schools. The argument in favor of either of these approaches remains as sound now as it was when first made by James Conant in 1968.

The demand for more community control of schools may well be encouraged by the new evidence. Both in suburbs and cities the shifting population pattern may be creating more self-conscious communities. The major exception is to be found in those low-income communities characterized by population instability, where social organization is already being badly disrupted by the continual movement of people.

These structural issues are only indirectly related to the quality of educational services provided. This question must receive more and more attention if the delivery of educational services to various parts of the population is to be substantially improved. Structural changes are important but cannot substitute for direct improvements in the service itself because of their possible relevance to community attitudes and resources. Significant performance breakthroughs may dictate changes in structure and financing. Certainly the advocacy of such changes would be vastly strengthened if they could be clearly correlated with improvement in the quality of educational services.

2

Human Needs in Metropolitan Areas: A Black Perspective

Albert Wheeler

In contemplating the writing of this chapter, I faced an uneasiness because I have no professional knowledge of current or future developments of metropolitan educational systems, and a sense of not belonging because I am neither a scholar nor a practitioner of education. My varied experience in school systems does, however, account for some qualifications. One is related to my professional work. I am not a clinical dermatologist; I am a social dermatologist concerned with skin color in urban society. Another is my role in society, which may be illustrated by an anecdote about the late Martin Luther King, Jr. Dr. King and the white manager of a large washing machine manufacturer in Birmingham, Alabama, had just completed negotiations for hiring and training blacks. Just as Dr. King was leaving, he said to the manager, "There's one thing that bothered me throughout our discussions. Can you tell me why all of the hundreds of washing machines that you have on display here are white?" The manager thought for a moment, scratched his head, and replied, "Dr. King, you have your problems and I have mine. Inside each one of them is a black agitator." I hope that I can be the kind of black agitator who works inside the white machinery of government and society to eradicate the racism that threatens the very foundation of American democracy.

I suspect that my third qualification is possibly the fact that black students in the public schools and colleges of Michigan have repeatedly called upon me to give counsel, to assist them, and to persuade the educational establishment to listen and act on black demands for a good quality education and for a full and relevant school experience. In my community, I have been engaged during past years in four school administration conflicts that reached serious proportions. In several colleges in Michigan, I have been called by the students to help. I consider this a great honor because young people do not usually waste much time with people who have passed fifty: they consider us irrelevant. Until the last episode with our own local school system, the administration and the Board of Education did not want me in. When this conflict reached the point where the Board of Education said, "Come in! Come in!" I said, "I will not come in, because you intend to have police on the scene." The board was ready to bring in the police because certain community leaders would not cooperate with them in quelling the disorder in the schools. I had to challenge this notion, because I did *not* say I would not participate. I simply said I would not participate in the presence of the police. Finally we kept the police out and we settled the issues; at least, we resolved the most tense situations.

It is my sincere hope that these varied experiences inside the school system over the past two decades will enable me to clarify some of the human needs in metropolitan areas. I should like to make some preliminary comments for the record. First, I really am not a very moderate man and, I suspect, many people will say that I am not a very nice man. Some of my statements may be abrasive and not very complimentary about professions or about the professionals. However, in addition to my own personal opinions, I think it is important that I express the views of some young blacks who are currently in and out of high schools, public schools, and colleges. To do less would be a disservice and waste your time. I hope you will not be turned off if I do become somewhat abrasive. I recognize that, in all generalizations, there are exceptions and so I include my readers in the exceptions and among those who are qualified for and dedicated to making significant changes and reforms in urban education. Second, I will focus primarily on the black experience, recognizing that, in some communities, Spanish-speaking Americans and other nonwhite minorities, including Orientals, are victims of similar frustrations, deprivations, and superficial solutions to their problems. Third, I will generalize about white racism and white racists, yet I know not all whites are insensitive, nor are all whites conscious, active racists. I am aware also that some blacks are opportunists who use the racial issue to further their own economic ends, their social aggrandizement, and their professional or political ambitions. Finally, I do not profess to speak for all blacks nor do I have the black solution to any racist problem in this society. I am writing as an individual and drawing upon my personal involvement and assessment. If you were to hear from twenty other blacks on this subject, each would use different words and different rhetoric; each would have a different orientation, but I venture that at least fifteen of them would agree with my evaluation of the racial problems in America.

THE CONTEXT OF HUMAN NEEDS

I view the central city as an island of poverty in a sea of affluence. Most people in the central city are black; they are poor, they are uneducated, they are unskilled, they are frustrated and, above all, they are currently powerless. They are dissatisfied with the mere pittance of democracy, justice, and hope that is their lot. Suburbia is white; it is middle class, and its people have political and economic power, skilled jobs close to home, good schools, better hospitals, and a fair measure of legal justice. Youth, in both the inner city and suburbia, is becoming more and more disillusioned with the ever-widening gap between the promises and expectations of democracy and the actual deeds and fulfillment of the democratic process. This is part of the hippie, white, student revolution. Recent situations suggest that this group of disillusioned whites is joining forces with Black Panthers, Puerto Ricans, and others in our urban areas who are also disillusioned. The potential for conflict grows. It requires no special genius to see that, unless massive, compensatory remedial or preventive programs are initiated or expanded immediately, our metropolitan areas will foment even greater conflicts of poverty, race, and disillusioned youth. The central city will be the eye of the hurricane. The unhappy alternatives to a society in which every person enjoys a full measure of citizenship and sufficient economic security to live a useful and happy life are these: either a metropolis plagued with violence among races, classes, and generations, or a metropolis in which the blacks, the poor, and the dissident youth are restrained by more stringent laws and increasingly powerful police agencies, or, possibly, both. However, if we can perceive our common problems clearly and truthfully, and if we use our ingenuity and resources now to eliminate and to prevent the recurrence of those problems, we may be able to escape the inglorious fate of other great nations that have died in the past.

THE PROBLEMS THAT DIVIDE AMERICA

What are some of the problems that divide Americans along racial and class lines, and how do they relate to education? I would make the overall issue white attitudes and commitments. Both black and white Americans are now fully aware that white racism is the major racial problem in America today but, until very recently, white Americans would not acknowledge this.

Racism

In the first half of the 1960s, the black freedom riders, the black youths who marched through a human gauntlet of hate into the schools of Arkansas and Alabama, the blacks and whites who marched in Montgomery, Birmingham, and Selma ripped off the thin veil of legality and respectability that cloaked the violent, inhuman, white racism in the Deep South. Thousands of white northerners participated in exposing to this nation and the world the social cancer that possessed the white South. Millions of white northerners supported the president and Congress in enacting the laws on voting rights and the several civil rights laws and in creating government bureaus to develop and implement equal opportunity in jobs, education, and housing. The white North was self-satisfied and self-congratulatory. It was a short-lived happiness.

The blacks of the North, particularly the young blacks, knew that in California, New York, Michigan, New Jersey, and Illinois their lot was not significantly better than that of their black brothers in the South. Unrest and hope stirred in their breasts, but their problems were different. The white southerner was an overt racist who made no secret of his individual or institutionalized racism; in fact, he placed signs on toilets, water fountains, in elevators, parks, schools, churches, and in public buildings to separate blacks and whites. He enforced this separation by unconstitutional local and state laws, by police given unlimited license to kill any black person who disregarded these laws, and by intimidation or murder of the black trespasser.

In the north, the white racist was covert and subtle. He passed laws forbidding racial discrimination in education, employment, housing, and public accommodations. Yet, schools are racially segregated. Blacks are both unemployed and underemployed at anywhere from two to five times the national rate. They have no money. They have no power. Blacks were and still are the victims of an unjust legal system. The racism in the north was institutionalized and cloaked in reasonable and logical requirements, such as high school or college diplomas, prior relevant experience, good credit ratings, no police records and, in good middle-class tradition, the requirements of promptness, reliability, responsibility, honesty, and cooperation.

The police, the prosecutors, and the courts—not the Klan and the white Citizens Council—were the protectors and the enforcers of this northern status quo. But black unrest in the North grew; conflicts between blacks and the police increased, both in frequency and intensity. I think it is important to realize that, in the South, the movement was a nonviolent movement and brought about through the leadership of Martin Luther King. But in the North, there was a different set of people. There were young people, young leaders. There was Malcolm X and Stokely Carmichael, and their message or sermon was not nonviolence. Their sermon—their message—was "Hit, if you're hit. Destroy. Tear down." This militant influence of young blacks in the North made part of the difference in the way the revolution moved in the two parts of the country.

More recently, we have had Rap Brown, Eldridge Cleaver, and others—all overt, aggressive, "let's attack the system" teachers. The North experienced its riots and rebellion in both large and small communities. There were the confrontations and conflicts in Watts, Harlem, Cleveland, Newark, Washington, D.C., and Detroit. White property was destroyed and black people were killed. The president finally appointed a commission on civil disorders, the Kerner Commission, to determine the causes of and possible solutions to racial conflict in the North. The findings are known to all: white racism permeates American society and is rapidly turning us into a nation of two unequal societies, one white and one black. The original Kerner Commission report identified what black Americans believed to be the most significant demonstrations of white racism: the well-known problems of employment, money, housing, education, police injustice, legal injustice, and health services. It is indeed a sad commentary that a follow-up report entitled "One Year Later" suggests that no significant progress has been made nationally to eliminate the previously identified root causes of conflict. It is my opinion that in 1973 racial polarization, black frustration, and white resistance are more severe than they were in 1967 after the great riots. It is frightening and ominous that the present administration in

Washington, unlike the administrations of Kennedy and Johnson, appears to be totally unresponsive to this situation. Black Americans today expect more "law and order" but less legal and social justice under the Nixon administration.

The Attitudes of Individual Whites

During the past several years, I have spoken to about ten thousand whites in suburban Michigan and five or six hundred young white college students in Michigan and the following observations are crystal clear to me:

1. Most white adults still believe that blacks are genetically inherently inferior, and that most blacks are criminals, rapists, murderers, robbers, and have a markedly limited intellectual capacity.
2. Most white youths admit that they hold the same attitudes to some degree because black inferiority and white superiority has been taught at home, both implicitly and explicitly.
3. White youths who wish to change their concepts about and relations with blacks cannot discuss these matters in a peaceful way with their parents.
4. Most white parents believe that the presence of black children in school classrooms, even if the percentage is small, will result in a deterioration in the quality of education.
5. I believe that there is now a new hero in thousands of homes: Dr. Arthur Jensen, an educational psychologist at the University of California at Berkeley. His findings, or the interpretations of his data, suggest that Negroes are about fifteen points below the average white IQ, that this works against the Negro in cognitive learning or abstract reasoning, and that blacks do well in rote learning and certain motor skills. I think that this information and the conclusion of this research heartens and strengthens those who hold racist ideas in education.

The Attitudes of Individual Blacks

It is indeed very difficult to express black attitudes because they are mixed, they are confused, and there is no pattern of black attitudes. By and large, adults are passive, almost all of them hopeless and frustrated. Most black adults are inclined toward integration in white society; most believe that the school administrator and the teacher are correct and that their children are always wrong; most are willing to accept or blend into white society. Black youths are quite different. They want to discard white standards as irrelevant. They consider integration as a secondary, or even an irrelevant, issue. Black youths are seeking self-identification, self-esteem; they are seeking what they see as survival in a racist society; they are working for the politicalization of the black masses. These attitudes are not limited to college students. In high schools and junior high schools, black youngsters are instilled with a new sense of black pride and black identity. They are demanding black history. They are demanding books that do not exclude the contributions of black Americans. They want to participate in the total school environment and, above all, are crying out for a meaningful, good quality education. I think it is important to suggest that the black athletes in America, in secondary schools and at college, are doing a yeoman's job in calling to the attention of white America the injustices and the racism that permeate this society.

Legal Injustice

If I were to be asked what I considered the most threatening racial problem in this country, I would say that it is the prevailing legal injustice for the black poor. It makes no difference what other attributes one may have or what material goods one may acquire. If one is denied legal justice in a nation of laws, one is stripped of the legal protection due and accorded a citizen of this country. I am not speaking of legal justice in the narrow sense of relations between the police and the community. These relations are a significant part of the problem, but the problem itself goes much deeper. It is not only the police, it is the injustice and the inequity in a racist prosecutor's office; it is the lawyer, the white lawyer, who gives inferior or even bad legal services to the black and the poor; it is the sanctimonious judge who permits racial injustice within his district and who tolerates excessive bail bond procedures and costs. Some judges, in my opinion, are today's counterparts to plantation owners. In many communities a judge may have anywhere from two hundred to two thousand young blacks on probation. He tells them where they can go, with whom they can associate, where they can work, and that they must report regularly. This is pretty much the situation we had a hundred years ago.

Once, at the request of the Chamber of Commerce of Michigan, I submitted for publication a paper on police and racial justice. It was discarded. They did not like it because it was the truth. I was protesting the consequences of a national organization of police unions, recalling what had happened in New York City in the late 1960s when the police Benevolent Association said to the Mayor and the Police Commissioner, "We will not obey any of those orders about going easy on demonstrators and these racial groups." This was turned around in about forty-eight hours. Shortly thereafter there was a meeting in Omaha, Nebraska, of the chiefs of the associations that were to form the national police union, the purpose of which was clearly stated: "To improve the conditions of work and for greater active participation in local politics." There are about four million law enforcement officers, who are armed and belong to a union, advocating that they themselves have more control in local politics. I say that this is a serious problem, not only for black Americans, but also for white Americans. With black youth in revolt, with white youth in revolt, it would be easy to resort to a militaristic, authoritarian police state.

Poverty

The whole question of employment, inflation, black employment, and underemployment leaves me disillusioned by the fact that the chairman of the President's Economic Advisory Committee said, upon taking his office, that we will fight inflation with greater unemployment. Now, I have this from a newspaper interview; I trust that it is correct. He said that the unemployment will be tolerated among the poor and the black who are accustomed to living in poverty. Current data suggest that the unemployment rate for black Americans is increasing while the unemployment rate for poor white Americans is decreasing. I think that this is a very ugly situation.

We do not believe in this country that there are hungry and malnourished people. In 1968 a Senate investigation committee suggested that there are hundreds of thousands, virtually millions, of Americans who are hungry and malnourished. The committee also suggested that prenatal diet and prenatal care may influence the ability to learn, and there does seem to be a discernable relationship between prenatal diet and a baby's intelligence. For the U.S. as a whole, the infant death rate is about twenty-two per thousand live births. For the city of Detroit it is about twenty-eight per thousand. In the inner city of Detroit, in two areas that have been measured, the infant death rate in one is forty-two per thousand live births and, in another, thirty-nine—almost twice the national rate. These data become even uglier when you move halfway out of the city, where the mortality rate is eighteen per thousand live births, and to the fringes of suburbia, where it is eleven per thousand live births. We can correlate with affluence and with whiteness the throwing away of human life because it is black and its preservation because it is white.

Another problem that educators and others ought to understand is that of money. Most whites can go to some bank or savings association and borrow a dollar. Depending on where you are and how you borrow, it may cost you six cents on the dollar or it may cost you eight cents on the dollar. Black people or poor people in the ghetto have to go to the local finance company on the corner, which, in Michigan is allowed to charge 30 percent interest on the dollar. Those who have no money must pay more to get it, and must in addition, if they own a television set or are buying one, sign that over to the loan company. I have seen several instances in which a $200 life insurance policy on a baby has been signed over as security to these corner loan companies. Without money, there is no flexibility and no mobility. There is no decision making. Most of their money comes from public sources, and they are told how to use it, or they are given a substitute, such as stamps, in the place of money. We all know the conditions of housing but I do not know if we realize how much inadequate housing affects one's dignity, well being, and motivation.

The Educational System

From my point of view, the principal problem in the educational system in America is that it is a racist educational system. This system is the cruelest of all because it has the most long term degrading effects on the human condition. Millions of dollars from the federal government have been allocated to sustain and support our educational system. When that system allows three-quarters of the black children to come up unprepared for college, unprepared for work, or unprepared for competition in society, that is a racist institution. We can take dumb white children and we can salvage between 75 and 80 percent of them. These are statistics that should shame us all.

The second problem in education is that I believe we have inadequate Schools of Education in the universities and that the faculties, staffs, and administrators need a revitalization. Most of these institutions are middle class or better. Most are insensitive to the problems of black education and have failed to meet the challenge of education for the black and the poor. That is where the focus ought to be. Administrators are largely unimaginative; the faculties are fossilized; the methods and curricula are traditional. They are irrelevant to the needs of the black and the poor. Administrators and teachers should go into the ghetto and ought to invite blacks to come into their schools. Blacks and whites should go through a sensitizing program. We should be able to see where racism really is—not direct, conscious, overt racism, but those kinds of things that we tolerate and that lead to such broad racial gaps in opportunity and progress. On my campus, a number of students and some young people say that the bright students do not go to the School of Education. They want to go where the action is. It appears that Schools of Education are unable to prepare teachers and counselors for ghetto schools, in spite of evidence suggesting that such counselors are extremely important.

A third problem as I see it with educational departments and Schools of Education is that they are unprepared, uncommitted, and that their programs are irrelevant to the needs of the black and poor. This means that we have to find and train new kinds of teachers and counselors. Have we tried to pick people from the Peace Corps and Vista programs? They may have long hair and funny clothes, but they also have the kind of experience with poor and with blacks that gives them a different view and a different outlook on life. There ought to be some real black administrators, teachers, and counselors in our Schools of Education. One of the problems here is that generally we go out and look for the most uncommitted, timid kind of black person. We bring him in and will not even permit him to express a moderate approach. We want to channel him into areas where we feel safe, where the white community feels safe. If you are going to get black people in, get black people in and then give them the freedom to suggest, to recommend, and to implement. Not all blacks can do this job, but they certainly cannot do it if they have on top of them the restraints of a power structure that says no.

The fourth problem I see in educational institutions and our public schools is caused by the practice of putting youngsters in tracks. The uninterested or alienated youngster has no place to go but down. Along with this tracking system is the whole problem of testing. IQ testing is a dastardly procedure to use on poor or black children in the ghetto. Even the language is unfamiliar and uninterpretable. If children in the sixth grade can only read at the fourth grade level and the test is written at the sixth grade or fifth grade level, they cannot even read the test, let alone interpret it. I suppose my IQ score was fifty because, when asked about Beethoven's Fifth or Tchaikovsky's Fifth, I knew only Jack Daniels' fifth and that was not on the list. I had had no exposure to the culture of the test, but I had to take it, and this is the kind of test that children have to take now. Let me suggest that you check the records in your public schools. Look at the third grade and the sixth grade achievement tests and then, covering up the names of the schools, read the scores. You can almost invariably pick out the schools that are all black or virtually all black, and those that are virtually all white on the basis of the test scores at the third and the sixth grade levels. That is a shame and, as shameful, the results for 1972, 1970, 1968, 1965, and 1960 will be the same. Black schools are always at the bottom of the list, which suggests that the quality of education and the commitment of the professionals who are supposed to teach black children is not there; and, probably, that the tests are totally irrelevant and meaningless to the children.

Discipline is another problem that is a cause of unrest in the public schools. School discipline is responsible for the pushouts and, in some measure, the dropouts. We have extended school controversies over the type of dress permitted and whether or not the children should be able to use their own press, their own school papers, or to say what they believe. We have questions about the language children use. We have had children thrown out of school for two months in the state of Michigan because they demonstrated in front of the building and called some of the faculty and staff "sons of bitches." We sit in the classroom and get upset because a black child or a poor child from the ghetto uses that kind of language. This is hypocrisy, because we all know these words. If you have ever served in the army or played with youngsters in a gang, you have used this language. The difference is that these children live where this is the language of the street. They have no playgrounds, so they play in front of the pool room and this language means nothing to them. Let me tell you of a young girl who came into a pool room one day when I was there and said to a fellow who was shooting pool, "Say, you better come on and get out of here. You've got something to do." He turned around and said, "Look, motherfucker, mind your own business." Two minutes later, after they had left, I asked somebody, "Well, who was the guy and who was the gal?" They were brother and sister. They did not mean anything by that kind of language. It was just common language, but we, with our middle-class values, are so shocked when we hear that kind of language that everything turns red.

The demonstrations of black youth, the raising of fists, the refusal to salute the flag, and the refusal to say the Pledge of Allegiance may upset you. I upset some children in Monroe, Michigan when I said, "The [black] kids raise a fist like this and do not salute the flag because, in a literal sense, the flag is a rag. It is a decoration. If the Chinese saw our flag, if the Japanese saw our flag, if the French saw our flag, it would not stir the great patriotism in their hearts that would their own flag. The flag has a meaning only when it says that everybody who lives under the flag enjoys the full citizenship that the flag proclaims. Young black people are saying that the pledge to the flag is irrelevant because it speaks of "one nation under God, indivisible, with liberty and justice for all." Honest young blacks ask, "Where is my liberty? Where is my justice?" They have the guts or the temerity not to say words that have no meaning to them. These are the kinds of things that get blacks thrown out of high school, and colleges. They are making a new demand for citizenship with real meaning.

Community control is a term that disturbs a lot of people and many are deeply concerned about it. There are all kinds of approaches to community control. I think there are only two or three major cities in the nation that are developing community control of education. I understand that the city of New York has divided its school district into thirty-two decentralized areas. Reorganization in Detroit may follow passage of a bill that permits the creation of eleven decentralized school districts. One man from Michigan said that it is really a diffusion of the central administration with power retained in different parts of the community. These are the games that people play. These are games that lead to further conflict, violence, and disillusionment. Black people, and especially young blacks, are not going to fall victim to the hypnosis of equal opportunity. Decentralization has no meaning without educational change at the community level, and those in a position to advise educators about community control would do well to say, "Let's not play games." If we intend to do it, let us do it meaningfully.

It has been said before: you cannot separate community control from money. I say to white society and to our politicians and legislatures that, if you are going to approve community control, let the people select their leaders and have enough confidence in them to let them handle the money. If they do not know how to handle the money, I think they have brains enough to go out and find some competent, sensitive, white people to help them learn. In the city of New York, it seems that the Ocean Hill-Brownsville district is going to be eaten up by a larger district created by the state or the Board of Education. Anybody in his right mind knows that that is going to lead to some terrible conflicts there. The residents are too well established, too powerful, and too intent upon what they intend to do to sit quietly aside while somebody else gerrymanders the district. These are the kinds of things that, it seems to me, intelligent people can foresee. When they do not foresee them and they do not act, I can draw only one conclusion: they are not stupid; they just thrive on any conflict that is bound to come. Because of conflicts, progress will be slow and delayed, and one can always say, "See, we gave *those* people an opportunity to do something and they didn't do it."

Again, the white majority is willing to act in a paternal way but it does not share its power. I ask you how many black superintendents of major public school systems are there in the United States of America? I think I know—only a few. But I will bet most big cities have at least one, and possibly three, assistant superintendents assigned to this pupil or that pupil. Such cover administrative positions are not where the power is—the power lies with the superintendent of schools. Why can a black man not be a superintendent of schools? How many Schools of Education have a black dean? How many colleges have a black president? How many Schools of Education have black professors? I am not going to chide you if they have been there only six months or a year because the situation is better than it was two or three years ago and a step forward. But the decision-making power for blacks is lacking.

TOWARD A SOLUTION

At this point I shall comment on some simplistic solutions. I call one solution the Wheeler Model because the London Model and the Toronto Model will be mentioned later in the book. I could not call it the Ann Arbor Model because the folk at the University of Michigan would get mad at me. So, facetiously, I call it the Wheeler Model.

If we know what the problems are, then we should begin to work at some kind of solution. White attitudes need to be changed through the home, the church, and the school. You pray and then you must be prepared to wait because attitudes have changed very, very slowly but that, at least, would be the direction in which to work. Administrations and faculties in Schools of Education need training in awareness. They need to be brought to the ghetto out of their towers so that they can see and feel the problem, not theorize about it. They ought to examine themselves in terms of: "What are my racist problems?"

I think that, when a superintendent of public schools is sought, every effort should be made to find a sensitive human being. It might not be a bad idea to give him the power to fire anybody in the administration and start hiring his own people. I think we all know that there is an entrenched, traditionalist status quo and even some bigots in public school administration. At present, when we find a decent human being to run a school system, we leave him with all of those anchors around his neck. If second level administrators cannot cooperate and do the job, the superintendent had better be able to pick his own people. I think that white teachers and counselors are going to have to work in the ghetto and have some supervision from semi-militant or militant blacks. I think that white teachers and counselors are going to have to take psychological tests for prejudice. I think we would do well to suggest that teachers and administrators, as well as the black children and poor children in the schools, be disciplined. This is one of the knottiest of problems. The children in my school system in Ann Arbor have asked that demonstrable overt racism be a condition for the dismissal of a teacher, black or white. This of course, would void the tenure provisions of a contract. Now, you know that no administration is working on that, and there will probably have to be a few more demonstrations before anything happens. The children, the parents, and the faculty are going to have to join forces in creating discipline policies. I believe that, if I participate in developing a plan, I will respect that plan more; if such a plan were imposed upon me by someone else, I would disregard it.

I think we must get rid of those so-called special classes where the antisocial and the disturbers are placed. Such classes are nothing but vegetable bins in which children vegetate for the next few years and finally get thrown out because they continue to be disruptive. We must substitute a retrieval system for the dropout and the pushout. We need to determine what these children can do, what their problems are, and attempt to rehabiliate them.

We ought to develop what might be called an urban loan. This country has had a farm loan program for fifty years. The farmers borrow money to do a lot of things; they have money in their pockets and can use it. We ought to create urban loans so that anybody who lives in a city, just the simple residents of a city, who want to do something about the health or education of their children, to buy a home, or obtain legal justice may have access to a loan program. Such a plan would tend to get rid of all of this welfare junk and play on paternalism. I think that our financial plans for public education need reforming. I am not really happy with Michigan's program to reform the distribution of money to districts. It is an effort to collect money through an income tax, a reduced property tax, and a uniform state property tax, and distribute it on the basis of need in an attempt to equal the amount of money available to the various districts. This proposal divides the state into fifteen districts. The governor will appoint the State Superintendent of Education and fifteen regional directors. I do not accept this feature because it moves the control further and further away from the local area. The governor is also talking about money for the support of compensatory services. This statewide distribution of funds may provide money for some of the problems that are occurring in suburbia as well as in the inner city.

I would like to see a school or school system experiment with dual educational programs, one of which would parallel the current routine school system. We have the Board of Education as it now exists with the present education program; we would also have an experimental or special program. I would like first to see the preschool classes in this experimental system, followed by divisions of grades kindergarten through three, four through six, seven through nine, and ten through twelve. At the end of the sixth year, an evaluation and some modifications should be made. This special program should require excellence irrespective of ethnic and economic conditions. I would start services for pregnant women. I would give them prenatal care and nutritional supplements. For the infants, I would provide well-baby clinics and make available nurseries and day care centers for babies between the ages of one month and two years. I would like to suggest a preschool program that takes children from the age of three through kindergarten. I would also have a powerful education control board, with money, to control the program from preschool through high school.

In the regular system we would have a similar pattern. One-eighth of the children would be transferred from the special program to the regular school program, and one-eighth of those in the regular school system to the special school program. This transfer process would take place along all grade levels. This means that we would transfer half the children from the special school to the regular school and vice versa. Transfers could take place at one or two year intervals. It seems to me that, if we can do this in multiples of 400—400, 800, 4,000—at every level in the educational process, we would then be able to measure some of the effects of prior exposure in either the special or the regular school systems. Thus we might begin to determine what is happening to children.

For such a dual system to operate, we would have to do something about teachers, classes, tutorial services, the decision-making roles of the students, the discarding of IQ tests, and the inclusion of special remedial programs. I think we have to provide for those children between the tenth and twelfth grades who, in spite of everything, are dropping out of the education system. Instead of throwing them out, we are going to have to do something useful for them: teach them the politics of the ghetto; teach them the economics of the ghetto; teach them the socialization of the ghetto; teach them to· survive where they are going to have to live and struggle. We do a lot of research and spend a lot of money on education, which to date have not produced anything. I have suggested only an approach. It will take a long time and require a lot of money, but this is a long and costly problem. We *can* better our efforts to provide creative programs to improve the human condition in metropolitan areas.

3

Financing Schools in a Metropolitan Context

Henry M. Levin

The problems of both city and suburban schools are serious indeed. The danger of concentrating on metropolitan approaches to these problems is that metropolitanism may not be the answer; even the best planned approach to organizing education in metropolitan areas may be an invalid one. I begin with the sharp *caveat* because of the enormous and often blind faith that advocates of metropolitanism share. In many ways, metropolitanism has become a cliché that has prevented a clear and penetrating analysis of the deep failings of urban education. In the process, many straw men have been constructed and deposed, and this kind of intellectual assassination has surely provided a greater potential source of material for broom factories than it has for those who must design solutions to some of society's most intransigent problems. The point is that metropolitan problems might not yield to answers provided in a metropolitan context.

It is useful to ask: "What kinds of problems should be solved in a metropolitan framework?" The usual case for metropolitan consolidation of the planning and production of government services is made on two bases: economies of scale and spillover costs and benefits. In the first case, the level of output that is necessary to foster efficient production of a public service is so large that a regional approach is required. That is, one unit of local government can not sustain the demand for an output sufficiently large to produce the service efficiently, while many cooperating local governments can.

In the second case, the benefits or costs from any one unit of government providing (or not providing) a public service spill over to surrounding communities. Thus, if one local government pours raw sewage into a common body of water (such as Lake Erie), all of the surrounding localities suffer. Therefore a metropolitan approach to sewage disposal becomes necessary. Transportation networks are characterized by both economies of scale and by spillovers among local governments within metropolitan regions; therefore coordination of transportation on a metropolitan basis is imperative.

Where the economy of scale argument, or the spillover one, applies, services should be produced or coordinated by a larger government unit. In some cases the metropolitan unit will be the appropriate one and in other cases it will not be, depending on the extent of both scale economies and spillovers. But how about the case for education? Are there economies of scale or significant spillover effects that justify the production of education on a metropolitan basis?

Certainly, economies of scale do not seem to characterize urban school systems. If anything, it appears that the city school districts are too large and cumbersome to be administered efficiently. Statistical studies of the relationship between cost and size find no evidence of economies of scale once moderate enrollment levels are reached. (See, for example, Swanson [1961], pp. 28-30; and also the review of studies examining economies of scale in James and Levin [1970].) Moreover, the recent move to decentralize the large city schools is a testimonial to the failures of largeness. Clearly, the case for metropolitan districts cannot be made on the basis that the present urban school units are too small.

How about the spillover argument? Indeed there are spillover costs and benefits associated with education. These result from the fact that the social costs attributable to poor education are often shared by units other than just the school district that was derelict. Undereducated or poorly educated citizens become a burden of the larger society and are disproportionately represented among the unemployed, those committing crimes, and those on the welfare rolls.

Yet, this type of spillover effect is interesting because it is not attributable to the production of the good by local school districts; it is attributable to underproduction of the good. A higher level of output by the underproducing school district would ameliorate the spillover costs of its neglect. The important point to note is that leaving local school districts intact, while increasing the spending of those that are undereducating their students, is the implied solution. If somehow the financing were substantially separated from the local tax base, spillover costs could be stemmed without creating metropolitan school districts. Later we will consider this remedy, but first we must denote specifically the reasons that prompt intellectuals and practical men of affairs to trumpet the clarion of metropolitanism.

THE EQUITY ARGUMENT

It appears that the call for metropolitan school districts is not an issue of scale or spillovers as much as it is a strategy for equalizing the distribution of educational resources, both human and fiscal. In short, metropolitan areas are characterized by large inequalities of population and wealth between cities and surrounding suburbs. Many large cities have less taxable wealth than their suburbs, and the disparity is increasing, with concommitant shifts in the tax base, as commercial enterprises and middle-class families move to the suburbs (see Netzer 1966, pp. 117-25). Moreover, the cities face higher prices, greater educational responsibilities, and greater demands for other social services than do their suburbs. Thus the cities are placed at a severe disadvantage relative to their suburbs in financing educational needs. (For a more extensive description of this problem, see Levin [1971].) Recently the Fleischmann Commission of New York State recommended full state funding: an effort to provide equity in financing education (*The Fleischmann Report on the Quality, Cost, and Financing of Elementary and Secondary Education in New York State,* vol. 1, 1973, chapter 2).

Paralleling the distribution of fiscal resources in metropolitan regions is the division of human resources. Increasingly, the cities have become the receptacle for the poor and black, while their surrounding suburbs have become the growing enclaves of the white middle class. Housing discrimination, low incomes, and job opportunities have all combined to enjoin any substantial movement of disadvantaged populations to the suburbs. (Even as jobs move to the outlying areas, the lack of similarly situated housing for low-income and nonwhite persons limits severely their ability to opt for suburban jobs [Kain 1968].) Moreover, the distribution of the general population along socioeconomic and racial lines between city and suburbs is mirrored by their respective schools. As far back as 1966, of the twenty cities in the largest metropolitan areas, nine had black majorities among their elementary school enrollments, and fifteen had enrollments that were over 30 percent black. Since it is widely accepted that racial integration of the schools is a desirable goal, the boundaries that separate cities and suburbs prevent the racial heterogeneity of school population required for meaningful integration (U.S. Commission on Civil Rights 1967).

In summary, two factors work against equality of educational opportunity in metropolitan areas. First, the distribution of fiscal resources shortchanges the city schools while enhancing the suburban ones, and second, the racial and socioeconomic distribution of the population between city and suburbs prevents meaningful school integration. In addition, present patterns of state financial aid do not begin to equalize the educational support of city and suburban schools. In fact, many cities receive fewer dollars from the states for each pupil than do their wealthier suburbs (ibid., p. 29).

Solving the Equity Problem

The view of the metropolitanists is that, if the arbitrary boundaries between city and suburb could be broken down by the formation of metropolitan governments and school districts, a more equitable distribution of fiscal and human resources would take place (Brazer 1962; Campbell and Jacks 1967). In my view, the application of this approach to solving the problems of the schools is exceedingly naïve. It presupposes that a geographical area or territory is essentially the prime motivator of behavior. That is, it assumes that changes in boundaries are the key to changes in political, social, and economic behavior. (This is strikingly similar to the views of ethnologists who see social behavior as being territorially ingrained: Ardrey [1966] and Lorenz [1966].) It is based tacitly upon a political strategy so improbable that it is unlikely to come about in the forseeable future. Finally, there are alternatives for at least providing fiscal equity that are both superior to the metropolitan plan and politically may be implemented in the near future.

First, what if we were to create metropolitan school district boundaries? Would the creation of larger territories improve dramatically the distribution of human and fiscal resources? One way of answering that question is to examine the distribution of students and school support within the smaller territories: the individual school districts. All the evidence suggests that schools *within cities* are stratified along racial and socioeconomic lines and that schools attended by poor and black children receive less financial support than those attended by middle-class white students.

The U. S. Commission on Civil Rights found that in seventy-five cities, ". . . 75 percent of the Negro students are in elementary schools with enrollments that are nearly all-Negro (90 percent or more Negro), while 83 percent of the white students are in nearly all-white schools (1967, p. 3)." Moreover, studies of expenditures per pupil on a school-by-school basis show that more is spent on students in middle-class schools than in lower-class and black schools. (For more details, see Levin [1971].) Even federal aid that is specifically designated for children from low-income families, such as that received under Title I of the Elementary and Secondary Education Act of 1965, appears to be used to support services for those who are not poor (Martin and McClure 1969). If such fiscal disparities and racial stratification take place within the city school districts, how will metropolitan districts change such behavior? If anything, the fact that many suburbanites have fled the city, in part, to obtain more expensive school services in a middle-class setting suggests that suburbanites will wish to redistribute neither their wealth nor their children for the benefits of equitable and integrated education. Inequality in the allocation of school resources and human resources is a reality in the smaller territories, and in no way have the metropolitanists shown that such behavior would reverse by shifting to metropolitan school districts. All the evidence suggests that we could expect continued discrimination against poor and nonwhite students.

At the same time, it is peculiar that, just as the disadvantages of large school districts are being recognized, the metropolitan approach would increase the size of the overall administrative unit. The cumbersome and highly bureaucratized behavior of the large-city school districts is responsible for many of the failures of the city schools. Increasingly, it appears that good educational decisions are made at a level that is close to the individual child (see, for example, Fantini [1970], pp. 40-75). Despite this recognition, the movement to metropolitan school districts would centralize further the level of decision making and buttress that centralization with an even greater opportunity for bureaucratic mindlessness. Consistent with this factor is the finding that school districts with an average daily attendance of more than between ten thousand and twenty thousand pupils experience higher economic costs due to inefficiencies. (For evidence, see James and Levin [1970].) Thus metropolitan government would conflict with a strong case for decentralized decision making (see Levin [1970] for an extensive discussion of this issue).

Moreover, just as black Americans in the large cities are beginning to attain political efficacy in city government, there are intellectual demands for moving to a metropolitan government that would include both city and suburbs. Such a move would clearly dilute the increasing ability of blacks to affect their destiny within the cities. Since black cohesion seems to be important to black political strength, one must question whether a movement toward metropolitan government would not retard substantially the developing political strength of urban blacks (Maynard 1970; National Advisory Committee on Civil Disorders 1968, p. 400).

Perhaps the most unrealistic aspect of the metropolitan school district approach is the lack of a strategy for attaining it. "If wishes were horses, then beggars would ride." Even if one were to assume that metropolitan school districts were the answer, they have been discussed in the context of wishes rather than horses. How does one obtain an effective coalition between middle-class whites in the suburbs and poor blacks in the cities whereby the whites would share their wealth and their children with the neglected populations from which they have fled? How can we achieve metropolitan school districts for such metropolitan regions as Philadelphia and New York whose boundaries cross state lines and divergent education codes? Where are the mechanisms, political coalitions, and legal structures that will create metropolitan districts? Strangely, the designers of metropolitan school districts are silent on strategy. Yet, without a *modus operandum* the metropolitan school district is no more than an intellectual plaything.

An Alternative

Probably a more productive approach to solving the inequitable distribution of resources between city and suburb is to ask what kind of strategy presently exists for redressing metropolitan inequalities. It appears that such an alternative already exists within states because the present method of financing the schools seems to violate the equal protection clause of the Fourteenth Amendment. Legally, the schools are the responsibility of the states, and most state constitutions call for a "uniform system of schools." Accordingly, the large inequalities in school expenditure within states due to differences in local wealth suggest that students in poorer localities are not being given equal protection of the law. (For greater detail, see Wise [1968]; and Coons, Clune, and Sugarman [1969].)

On this basis, many school districts are in the process of suing their states in order to achieve a greater measure of equality of school support. While some of the suits argue for equal expenditure per student—perhaps adjusted for differences in price levels—others seek unequal expenditure in favor of the poor. In either case the impact of these cases, if they are won, would be to redistribute the tax burden and school expenditures more equitably among school districts within a state. Such a redistribution would equalize fiscal resources among metropolitan regions and between rural and urban areas as well as within metropolitan regions, an action that is far more pervasive and consistent than that suggested by the formation of metropolitan districts. According to constitutional scholars, the equal protection strategy shows great promise. (See, for example, Kurland [1968] and McKay [1968].) The *Serrano* v. *Priest* case (1971), holding that property tax financed school systems in California are in violation of the Fourteenth Amendment, supports the view that the quality of a child's education cannot be a function of the wealth of his parents. The important point is that this approach can achieve fiscal reform by applying pressure where both the power and leverage exist. Clearly, such an effort should be made at the state level because the states are responsible for the schools, and the equal protection suits represent the lever by which the states can be forced to put their houses in order. In contrast, no legal or political provisions exist for forcing the suburbs to accept metropolitan finance of school districts.

Moreover, the same reasoning might be applied to the distribution of student resources. School districts are quasi corporations that exist only at the pleasure of the state. The states have the power to modify school district boundaries and to bus children across traditional ones. Yet, at this time there is no obvious legal strategy to force the states to alleviate *de facto* segregation between districts. Thus, for the present, the possibility of fiscal redistribution within states and metropolitan areas is much closer to attainment than the redistribution of human resources. Whether any strategy can achieve the latter goal in the near future is an open question.

PERSISTENCE OF THE METROPOLITAN MYTH

If the metropolitan solution to urban school problems is just a set of empty wishes, why does its popularity persist? I believe that the tenacity of this approach is at least partially attributable to a desire for simple answers to complex questions. Inequalities of human and fiscal resources exist between two territories. If only we could join the two, we could obtain a better distribution of the resources. It seems all that simple. Yet, when one looks beneath the argument, one sees no way of joining city and suburban school districts; nor does one see how the present patterns of fiscal, racial, and socioeconomic stratification among schools within school districts will be alleviated by increasing the size of the district.

A second reason for the popularity of the metropolitan school district concept is what I call the *aesthetic package approach.* Many public goods should be produced and coordinated at the metropolitan level, including transportation, police services, and environmental quality. Those who advocate better metropolitan planning for these goods often call for complete metropolitanization of all local public services despite the inappropriateness of putting schools in this category. They see true metropolitanism as a reality only when the schools are included in the scheme, and the reason that they put schools in the package is obvious. The schools represent the preponderant share of local public expenditures and public employment. Therefore, many advocates of metropolitanism include schools in their metropolitanism without thinking properly about how the new organization will solve the problems of urban education; for without schools, the metropolitan package is closer to empty than it is to full.

Let me conclude by drawing a metaphor. In the marvelous autobiographical work *Land Without Justice* (1958), the Yugoslavian author, Milovan Djilas, tells of the classic struggle between beauty and usefulness. It seems that his father had the choice of building the family home in a sheltered glen or at the top of a hill. If the home were built on the hilltop, it would have a commanding view of the countryside and could, itself, be seen from miles around. Yet, the bluff was a very windy place with apparently shrill and powerful gusts that would be troublesome for any who might dwell there. If his father were to build in the sheltered glen, the house would be more livable, but less accessible to beauty. Beauty or functionality? That was the dilemma, and I believe that it is the dilemma that we face here. Djilas's father chose the hilltop and, while the house was beautiful, it was not very livable.

That is my view of the metropolitan solution—beautiful but not very livable. It is not likely to come about if its birth depends crucially upon the mutual cooperation of city and suburb, and it is not likely to change political and social behavior if it were to come about. Worst of all, while we stand around and admire the beautiful sketches of the metropolitan dream, we are ignoring the legal responsibilities of the states and the festering condition of urban education.

REFERENCES

Ardrey, Robert. *The Territorial Imperative.* New York: Atheneum, 1966.

Brazer, Harvey. *Some Fiscal Implications of Metropolitanism.* Brookings Institution Reprint 61. Washington, D.C.: Brookings Institution, 1962.

Campbell, Alan, and Jacks, Seymour. *Metropolitan America.* New York: The Free Press, 1967.

Coons, John E.; Clune, William H.; and Sugarman, Stephen D. "Educational Opportunity: A Workable Constitutional Test for State Financial Structures." *California Law Review* 57, no. 2 (April 1969): 305-421.

Djilas, Milovan. *Land Without Justice.* New York: Harcourt, Brace, 1958.

Fantini, Mario. "Quality Education in Urban Schools." In *Community Control of Schools,* edited by Henry M. Levin, pp. 40-75. Washington, D.C.: Brookings Institution, 1970.

The Fleischmann Report on the Quality, Cost, and Financing of Elementary and Secondary Education in New York State, vol. 1. New York: Viking Press, 1973.

James, H. Thomas, and Levin, Henry M. "Financing Community Schools." In *Community Control of Schools,* edited by Henry M. Levin, pp. 250-74. Washington, D.C.: Brookings Institution, 1970.

Kain, J. F. "Housing Segregation, Negro Employment, and Metropolitan Decentralization." *Quarterly Journal of Economics* 82, no. 2 (May 1968): 175-97.

Kurland, Philip. "Equal Education Opportunity or The Limits of Constitutional Jurisprudence Undefined." In *The Quality of Inequality: Urban and Suburban Public Schools,* edited by Charles U. Daly, pp. 47-72. Chicago: University of Chicago, Center for Policy Study, 1968.

Levin, Henry M., ed. *Community Control of Schools.* Washington, D.C.: Brookings Institution, 1970.

Levin, Henry M. "Financing Education for the Urban Disadvantaged." In *Resources for Urban Schools,* edited by Sterling M. McMurrin, pp. 3-22. Lexington, Mass.: D.C. Heath, 1971.

Lorenz, Konrad. *On Aggression.* Harcourt, Brace and World, 1966.

McKay, Robert. "Defining the Limits." In *The Quality of Inequality: Urban and Suburban Public Schools,* edited by Charles U. Daly, pp. 77-88. Chicago: University of Chicago, Center for Policy Study, 1968.

Martin, Ruby, and McClure, Phyllis. *Title I of ESEA, Is it Helping Poor Children?* Washington, D.C.: Washington Research Project and NAACP Legal Defense and Educational Fund, Inc., 1969.

Maynard, Robert. "Black Nationalism and Community Schools. In *Community Control of Schools,* edited by Henry M. Levin, pp. 100-114. Washington, D.C.: Brookings Institution, 1970.

National Advisory Committee on Civil Disorders. *Report.* New York: Bantam Books, 1968.

Netzer, Dick. *Economics of the Property Tax.* Washington, D.C.: Brookings Institution, 1966.

Serrano v. Priest, 5 C3d 584, 96 CR 601 (1971).

Swanson, Austin. *Effective Administration Strategy.* Institute for Administrative Research, Teachers College, Study no. 13. New York: Columbia University, 1961.

U.S. Commission on Civil Rights. *Racial Isolation in the Public Schools.* Washington, D.C.: U.S. Government Printing Office, 1967.

Wise, Arthur. *Rich Schools, Poor Schools.* Chicago: University of Chicago Press, 1968.

part II

Political Forces Requiring Change in Metropolitan Communities

The complex relationships of local school systems, their respective state governments, and the federal government continue to confound complete understanding. The pervasive parochial nature of most local government units seems to have a tax rather than a programmatic orientation. A preoccupation with funding programs for which there is little hope of substantial payoff seems to describe present local, state, and federal politics of education. Confusion, dilution, and disappointment seem to be the order of the day.

Part two examines the relationships of the federal, state, and urban governments and looks within a large urban center. These political relationships highlight required change. Reform is the plea. Local, state, and federal units of government must be more responsive to metropolitan educational needs.

Mike Milstein reviews the intervention of the federal government in education. Drawing upon his knowledge of government, its history, and its practice, he analyzes the role of the states as they struggle to carry out their responsibilities for education in an arena of overlapping competition for resources. He proposes that the case for state government lies in its ability to provide more adequate educational support, to reform school organization, and to provide for regional planning. Strengthening state leadership will increase the state's ability to monitor federal dollars directed to support sound, well planned programs.

Chapter four is a realistic look at the interface of the states and the federal government. The problems seem to be even more complex when the idea of revenue sharing is fragmented to get votes rather than to combine resources to solve metropolitan problems.

Chapter five reviews relationships between the cities and the states. Again the cry for strengthening state government is made. Mike Usdan, knowledgeable in the politics of education, presents an interesting dilemma. He elaborates on the striking potency of localism on the part of individual education units on one hand and, on the other, the reluctance of state governments in most cases to exercise their authority. Suggestions are made to improve state legislative practice, state education leadership, and to bring the federal share of educational support to a more appropriate level. The case is made for nonpartisan leadership while some realists are presenting the opposite point of view. The question may be asked: What kind of state and local leadership is needed when there is little likelihood that state legislatures dominated by the suburbs will promote the concept of the metropolitan school system?

Watson looks within the metropolis and finds education with broken promises to whites and no promises to be broken for blacks. Chapter six makes the point that traditional values are sometimes supported by both black and white constituents. However, the display of bigotry and fear within the city is frightening. Though unionism and professional conservatism are viewed as barriers to change, there seems to be an opportunity for cooperation between industry and education to solve urban problems. Many groups are pressing for change but there still does not exist a constellation model to harness the resources and influences of such groups. The battle between the forces for change and those for maintaining the status quo continues against the backdrop of bankrupt local governments. Current solutions for such a grim situation remain drastically inadequate.

4
_____

Roles of the States and the Federal Government

Mike M. Milstein

The focus of this chapter will be on problems and potentials of the states and the federal government in dealing with issues of metropolitan educational organization. This will include an exploration of ways they might cooperate, given the resources at their disposal, to come to grips most effectively with the problem. It might be well, at the outset, to ask why the states and the federal government should be concerned with metropolitan educational organization. If we can focus on questions of need and justification for a moment, we will be better equipped to examine present and future possible modes of state and federal involvement in metropolitan educational organization.

THE NEED

There are many more demands in metropolitan areas than in nonmetropolitan areas upon the taxpayer's dollars for such

Reprinted from *Urban Education* 5, no. 2 (July 1970): 179-98, by permission of the publisher, Sage Publications, Inc.

government functions as health and hospital care, police protection, fire protection, parks and recreation facilities, housing and urban renewal, waste treatment, and libraries. Thus, in 1966/67, while metropolitan and nonmetropolitan areas spent about the same per capita on education—$143.19 in metropolitan areas and $132.30 in nonmetropolitan areas—total direct, general, local government expenditures differed sharply. Metropolitan areas spent $330.32 per capita compared to $245.11 per capita in nonmetropolitan areas for general local governmental purposes (U.S. Bureau of the Census 1969, p. 222). There are clearly greater demands for fiscal resources in metropolitan areas than there are in nonmetropolitan areas. Local fiscal ability, based heavily on the overburdened property tax, is not sufficient to meet these demands. As a result, local government officials look longingly to the greater resources available to the states and the federal government.

This problem has become all the more visible because of the imbalances in resources and needs between the cities and their suburbs. Simply stated, the suburbs today have more taxable wealth and less need for high-cost-per-pupil programs than do the central cities. This disparity is growing larger and, at least for the foreseeable future, will not be alleviated at the local level because of the number of school districts involved and the negative attitudes held by many suburban residents toward regional cooperation. As Dyckman (1966, p. 36) notes, "Local politicians confronted with the market choices of economically able households who vote with their feet and march to the suburbs, must appeal to state and federal agencies who have some power to alter the market terms." The present fractionalized jurisdictional division in metropolitan areas is, in Gunnar Myrdal's terms (1966, p. 9) "nothing but a legalized superstructure of the inegalitarian residential segregation."

There are other boundaries besides those that exist between municipalities. There are boundary maintenance systems between government functions *within* single municipalities. For example, school districts and parks and recreation departments often have overlapping functions, yet they are treated as completely separate government domains. Rather than coordinate their mutual objectives, local officials must compete with one another for resources. Often the result is program duplication and resource imbalance on a grand scale.

Regional planning cannot possibly be approached through local governments that are isolated by municipal boundary lines and functional barriers. Most problems are metropolitan in scope, yet "no more than a handful [of local governments] possess jurisdictions defined in metropolitan terms (Martin 1965, p. 181)." Consolidation of all government functions in one massive, regional policy-making body, a solution that has often been recommended, might create as many problems as it resolves. At any rate, it is highly unlikely to occur at this time.

How else then can we hope to achieve regional coordination? The very extent of metropolitan educational problems and the apparent inability of local officials to deal with them makes it eminently sensible that we look to the states and the federal government for help. In an environment in which citizens make increasingly greater demands for public services while politically antiquated systems foster unrealistic, parochial loyalty to municipalities, only the states and the federal government have the potential leverage effectively to promote regionwide cooperation. As Danielson notes:

> In the American federal system, no metropolitan area constitutes a self-contained political system. Fiscal and jurisdictional inadequacies, the monopoly of the formal powers of government by the higher levels, and the local base of the American political system combine to involve the polycentric metropolis in a complex web of relationships with the state and federal government (1966, p. 299).

THE JUSTIFICATION

What rationale, other than that of needs, can one provide for state and federal involvement in metropolitan affairs? There are various constitutional, jurisdictional, political, and financial grounds for state and federal concern and activity. State responsibility has been clearly established. State constitutions normally require state legislatures to establish and maintain systems of free public education that provide for uniform and efficient educational practices throughout the state. Thus, while local in operation, school districts remain the responsibility of state government. To be sure, the states have varied in their interpretation of this responsibility. For example, while Hawaii and Delaware maintain strong state control, centralizing administration of field operations and resource collection at the same level, Nebraska and South Dakota have maintained weak state control, contributing the minimum of funds from the state level for educational purposes and leaving most administrative decisions to be made at the local level. Most states lie somewhere between these two extremes, providing broad parameters for operational practices and contributing significant portions of capital and operating resources from state treasuries. The average state contribution in 1970/71 was 41 percent of all local public elementary and secondary education expenditures (National Education Association 1971). More than any other local government function, education, as a state responsibility, is susceptible to state intervention. The school district consolidation movement, which has reduced the number of school districts from 127,531 in 1931/32, to 17,995 in 1970/71, bears witness to the potential for state action (National Education Association 1971; U.S. Department of Health, Education, and Welfare 1968, p. 30 and 1971, p. 7).

The role of the federal government, less clearly justified on legal grounds and thus more controversial, is today approaching wide acceptance. There is not space, nor is it the purpose of this chapter, to review this controversy. (For several good reviews, see Sufrin [1962] and Munger and Fenno [1962].) Suffice it to say that many of the objections to federal aid have been overcome or sidestepped for the present.

The United States Constitution omits specific reference to education. However, Article I, Section VIII, often referred to as "the general welfare clause," has opened the way to federal support of education. Actually, support began even before the founding of the Republic when the Congress of the Confederacy passed the Land Ordinance of 1785, granting one of thirty-six lots in each township for the maintenance of education. This grant, supplemented by the Morrill Act of 1862, which led to the eventual establishment of sixty-nine land-grant colleges and universities, constituted the total extent of federal involvement in education until the twentieth century. In this century, the federal government has expanded its support of education with categorical grants-in-aid for such diverse concerns as vocational education, veterans' training, national security manpower needs, compensatory education for the "educationally disadvantaged," and most recently, the upgrading of the education profession itself.

Comments by former U.S. Commissioner of Education, Francis Keppel (1965) indicate how far national objectives for education have come. They are no less than to

> raise the quality of education in our schools, bring equality of educational opportunity to every child, provide vocational and technical training geared to the needs of today and tomorrow, make college and university study possible to any young people who

could benefit from it, and gear educational resources
to community problems.

Soon after being installed as U.S. Commissioner of Education,
the late James Allen made it clear that he saw the federal role in
education as broadly as did Keppel. He advocated that the federal
role, presently residual in nature, must be converted to that of an
"advocate of change." He went on to state that, "If this new advocacy role is to be effective, what is now essential is strong Federal
commitment to assume *full partnership* in renewing the public school
system (1969)." His successor, Sidney Marland, continued to support
this expanding role for the federal government.

Such a view makes sense if one visualizes the federal structure as
a system in which functions logically overlap rather than as three
distinct and separate levels of government. Grodzins depicts such a
system as a marble cake.

> Wherever you slice through it you reveal an insepa-
> rable mixture of differently colored ingredients.
> There is no neat horizontal stratification. Vertical and
> diagonal lines almost obliterate the horizontal ones,
> and in some places there are unexpected whirls and
> an imperceptible merging of colors, so that it is diffi-
> cult to tell where one ends and the other begins. So it
> is with federal, state, and local responsibility in the
> chaotic marble cake of American government (1963,
> pp. 3-4).

This view has not always been generally held in Washington. In
1955 President Eisenhower, concerned that a growing federal government might do great harm to state and local governments, formed
the U.S. Commission on Intergovernmental Relations (usually referred to as the Kestenbaum Commission, after its chairman). The
commission concluded that functions that are primarily state and
local should be administered and financed by these government
bodies. But it also established guidelines upon which it felt that the
federal government might justifiably become involved in intergovernmental activities. The commission felt that the federal government
should be concerned with state and local affairs when:

1. It is the only government that can bring sufficient
   resources to bear on a problem;
2. Geographical and jurisdictional limits of smaller
   governmental bodies make it necessary for a higher
   governmental body to play a role;

3. Uniformity of policy on a nationwide basis is required; and
4. The states, either through action or omission, do injury to people in other states.

Educational government in our metropolitan areas, it can be argued, meets the criteria set by these guidelines. The recent increase in federal aid focused on urban centers indicates that federal policy planners agree with Martin, who argues that metropolitan problems are

> *public* in nature, and the public involved is nothing less than the American people. They are therefore national problems; and if their place of origin is the metropolis they remain nonetheless national in both scope and significance. . . . The expanded federalism reflects recognition of the need to match public problems with public resources (1965, p. 172).

It is time to stop asking whether state and federal governments should be concerned with metropolitan educational organization. Instead we must ask how they can best focus their vast resources on this problem. Therefore, the remainder of the chapter will be devoted to a survey of their present activity, the consequences of this activity, and probable cooperative state-federal ventures that will be focused on urban education in the future.

STATE GOVERNMENTS AND METROPOLITAN EDUCATION

To a large extent today's metropolitan problems have been created by past actions (and inactions) of state governments. The states have used their power dysfunctionally, encouraging geographic and functional proliferation. State functions performed at the local level have hastened the process of separate and fractionalized communities within metropolitan regions. For example, the proliferation of state highway systems, which ring metropolitan areas, has increased urban sprawl and rendered mass transit a mortal blow in many cities. State aid for education, favoring suburbs over cities, accelerates the outflow of middle-class citizens, the cities' largest tax resource, to the suburbs. (For an expansion of this argument, see Danielson [1966], pp. 299-304.)

Why have the states been so inept in dealing with metropolis-wide problems? High on the list of villains are restrictive state constitutions, nonrepresentative state legislatures, and inadequate resources. State constitutions, written in an agrarian era, usually favor rural areas over urban areas. In addition, most are excessively detailed, focusing on what state and local governments may *not* do, rather than providing them with sufficient latitude to deal with problems of government that were not anticipated at the time of their writing. In an attempt to free state and local governments of archaic constitutional restrictions, several states have held constitutional conventions in recent years. Included in this group of states are Tennessee in 1966; Maryland, New Jersey, New York, Pennsylvania, and Rhode Island in 1967; and Hawaii in 1968 (Bebout 1968). These conventions have been less than totally successful in achieving constitutional reform, but they are important indicators that the states may be coming to grips with the problem.

State legislatures, notoriously overrepresented by rural areas, are finally being reapportioned. In the *Baker* v. *Carr* case (1962), often referred to as the "one citizen, one vote" rule, the United States Supreme Court moved the states toward new and more equitable representative state legislative bodies. The irony for the cities is that they are still minority groups in state legislatures, having traded rural domination for suburban domination. As a result, it is unlikely that state aid formulas will change in favor of the cities. Legislators from metropolitan areas view themselves as representing particular municipalities, not total regions. It could hardly be otherwise as long as local governments must compete for the states' limited resources and there is no effort to develop regionwide governmental functions. Without leadership from *within* metropolitan areas, it is unlikely that resources will be forthcoming from the state, or the federal government, to "save the metropolitan areas." Reapportionment is a necessary, but not sufficient factor. It will facilitate metropolitan approaches to problem solving only if representatives from these areas come to see such efforts as mutually beneficial.

Finally, the states have found that their resource needs are fast outstripping their resource bases. Though less limited in options for resource collection than local governments, the states have been spending at an accelerating rate. In fact, their debt level has increased at a rate even faster than that of the local governments. Between 1950 and 1970, for example, state debt went up from $5 billion to $42 billion while local government debt went up from $19 billion to $102 billion (U.S. Department of Commerce 1972, p. 406). But resources, by their very nature, will always be scarce. While state governments should direct their limited resources to meet their citizens' most pressing needs, in actual fact they rarely do. The need for resources is greatest in urban areas, but state aid patterns still favor rural and suburban areas. New York state's urban education program, which began in 1968/69 with an appropriation of $26 million to the state's urban centers and is now funded at approximately $100 million, is noted as an exception that may be an indicator of better things to come. (For information about this program, see New York State Education Department [1967 a]; and New York State University [1968].)

With all of their inadequacies, the states can still be a powerful force in redressing educational problems in metropolitan settings. They have the power to modify state aid formulas; to assume a major role for regionwide planning; and to encourage, through various means, the reorganization of school districts into more efficient and equitable units.

State Aid Formulas

With per pupil expenditure levels differing by ratios of two and sometimes three to one *within* single states, one can hardly refer to state aid formulas as resulting in an equalization of resources among school districts. Most present state aid formulas hardly provide enough support to assure even bare adequacy, let alone equalization. Although equalization is rather an "idealistic goal . . . because of a limited knowledge of what is equal (Alkin 1968, p. 137)," state aid formulas should take into account the cost of educating different youngsters. The cities, with more specialized program needs, which require sophisticated equipment and highly trained specialists, with great pools of educationally deprived children, and with obsolete school plants, have a justifiable claim to a greater share of state aid.

Despite this reality, suburbs receive far more state aid for education than do cities. For example, in upstate New York, the suburbs received $443.2 million and the cities received $115.7 million in state aid for schools in 1969/70 (New York State Commission 1972, pp. 20, 26). Without raising their contribution one penny, the states could have a major impact on metropolitan educational problems by simply putting new priorities on present state resources. There are, as usual, political issues involved, but the very magnitude of the problem may force the states to reconsider their present priorities.

Regional Planning

In promoting regional planning, the states can guide local municipalities toward developing cooperative metropoliswide objectives. The states are in a strategic position to collect information across municipal boundaries to help local governments develop benchmarks for progress, state governments integrate their metropolis focused activities, and the federal government take local and state development activities into consideration in its metropolis focused programs.

The states appear to be moving in such a direction. In fact, by 1967, sixteen states had established offices for local affairs (New York State University 1967, p. 53). These offices, to varying degrees, gather information that permits local decision makers to take into consideration those consequences that transcend individual municipalities or single government functions. Often providing technical assistance, they encourage local municipalities to seek cooperative solutions to urban problems. For example, because the construction of the new campus of the State University of New York at Buffalo, among the most ambitious single construction projects ever attempted in this country, will change western New York, economically, socially, and demographically, the state's Office of Planning Coordination is helping the region to plan for this impact. After extensive consultations and sessions to gather information from many sources, including local and state officials and community leaders, this planning office has been able to present the region with long-range estimations for such needs as new transportation networks, school facilities, and commercial outlets. Projects such as this indicate that regional planning by the states is a rich area for further exploration.

School District Reorganization

The states have it in their power to bring about more equitable and efficient regionwide educational units. This process, replete with political hazards for governors and state legislators in the era of rural school consolidation, would be even more of a problem in attempts to consolidate school districts in urban areas.

Reorganization by mandate has had little success in most states. One recalls the attempt of the 1917 New York State legislature to abolish all school districts in favor of education organized on a township basis. Only one town in the entire state complied, and the legislation was later repealed (Herman 1963, p. 118).

There are other means by which the states can encourage reorganization. They can, as they did during rural school district consolidation, offer fiscal incentives, but even without such lures they could do much by removing restrictions on local initiative to pursue cooperative efforts. This might be done by passing enabling legislation that would free cities of fiscal dependency, ease restrictions on local property taxation limits or permit local governments to tax sources presently closed to them, ease statutory and constitutional barriers to the extension of municipal boundaries, and authorize optional forms of municipal and county government that can meet metropolitan educational needs. Positive evidence from metropolis-wide operations that are underway in such places as Dade County, Florida and Nashville-Davidson County, Tennessee, indicates that the states should do all that is in their power to open this last alternative to their urban centers.

In the past the states have been very reluctant to play a major role in metropolitan affairs. But, as Beckmen notes,

> With no sign of metropolitan government in sight, the governor's office and the legislatures will increasingly serve as a place of arbitration and as a medium for developing understanding among suburban and city dwellers of their common interest in meeting the wide-ranging and disparate educational needs of citizens (1968, p. 198)."

THE FEDERAL GOVERNMENT
AND METROPOLITAN EDUCATION

Most federal activity in urban areas has occurred since the end of World War II, when the great metropolitan areas of our nation began to come of age. State inactivity and increasing evidence of urban needs have encouraged the federal government to provide required technical assistance and fiscal resources for the support of local functions that have repercussions for the entire nation. These local functions include such diverse concerns as airport development, low-rent housing, urban renewal, and assistance to schools in federally affected areas.

The federal government has recognized that, in the long run, many local functions have national implications. For example, although highways that link communities and airports that serve metropolitan areas are of immediate concern to specific regions, they also represent links in the vast network of highways and airports that serves the entire nation. When local functions have an impact on national interests, the federal government usually becomes actively involved with technical assistance and cash grants.

If the states choose not to participate, the federal government and the local governments often develop direct relationships. One might assume that this could not happen in educational government, because education is clearly a state responsibility. Recent federal activity leaves this assumption in some doubt. The states were by-passed entirely in several major titles of both the National Defense Education Act of 1958 and the Elementary and Secondary Education Act of 1965. The latter act also presents direct challenges to state constitutions that prohibit aid to private schools.

The states have reacted to the intrusion of the federal government in its largest functional area of responsibility by applying pressure to Washington to return control of these programs to the state level. One early result of this pressure has been the strengthening of the states' decision-making role in federally sponsored Supplementary Educational Centers (ESEA III). This has been heralded by state-level educators as a significant victory, but it might also be viewed as a federal triumph. The federal government's objective was to promote innovative educational programs, with some assurance that resources would be properly employed toward this end. The states have had to upgrade their supervisory and regulatory activities to assure compliance with federal regulations and guidelines. Such vigorous state activities enhance the potential for achievement of federal grant objectives. It is to the federal government's advantage to have strong state governments to work cooperatively toward the alleviation of educational problems that affect the entire nation. Monies granted to state education departments for improvement of state-level leadership and regulatory abilities support this view.

It appears that federal activity in educational government is here to stay. But it is questionable whether such involvement will necessarily result in more rational metropolitan organizational patterns for education. Congress is hampered by the same rural dominance and divided metropolitan representation that shackles state legislatures as they try to deal with this problem. As a result, there is no coherent federal urban policy. As Cleaveland notes (1969, p. 375), "In comparison to established policy fields like agricultural policy, labor policy, or foreign trade policy, urban affairs policy appears vague and hopelessly diffuse."

As might be expected, without a comprehensive federal urban policy, federal programs usually reinforce state and local inadequacies. Present federal urban aid programs result in bureaucratic overlap at the federal level and facilitate division of effort at the local level. Few federal grants require local planners of one government function to coordinate their activities with other local planners carrying out similar functions. It is within the federal government's power to reverse this dysfunctionality by requiring coordinated planning as a prerequisite to the receipt of federal funds. To do so, however, the federal government will have to develop coherent urban objectives and policies.

The U.S. Advisory Commission on Intergovernmental Relations noted that (1966, p. 120), of the 120 federal grants-in-aid programs in 1966, most were carried out in metropolitan areas. These programs are spread across various functional areas with little coordination among them. Nor can it be assumed that there is coordination *within* single functional areas. As Wood notes (1966, p. 331), program supervisors "move off in different directions and at different times. Frequently their activities cancel each other out and work in one program negates the other." The singular exception to this bureaucratic nightmare is the Department of Housing and Urban Development. This agency's success indicates that, with clear objectives and administrative coordination, the federal government can effectively focus its resources on urban problems.

To bring federal resources to bear most effectively on urban problems, some critics have called for the establishment of an Office of Urban Affairs. But even without this office, the executive and legislative branches of our national government can find ways, as they have in other policy areas, of identifying purposes and appropriate processes to meet them. A variety of much discussed processes, including federal regulation, technical assistance, categorical grants-in-aid, block grants, and revenue sharing can be employed if objectives can be developed.

FEDERAL-STATE COOPERATION

Both the states and the federal government can do much to improve their participation in urban affairs. But in the final analysis, if they operate in "splendid isolation," their numerous resources will not be effectively marshaled to meet urban educational needs. It is reasonable to expect that they can develop cooperative approaches to maximize their various resources. This expectation is based upon the belief that, in our evolving federal system, functional division of responsibility has never been clearly determined and probably never will be. Government policy making at any level should be based upon pragmatic evaluation of abilities and needs. As social and economic conditions change, so must government response. It is unlikely that an adequate response to urban educational needs will be forthcoming at the local government level where resources are severely limited and competition, confusion, and parochialism reign supreme.

As the U.S. Advisory Commission on Intergovernmental Relations noted (1966, p. 115), "Although local government reorganization has received most attention in the literature dealing with urban problems, the use of the federal system is an equally valid approach." What can be expected of the states and the federal government in the way of cooperative ventures? It is risky to predict government directions because public policy is made in a political setting, but, if we are to be able to set directions rather than simply respond to changing conditions, we must go through the mental exercise. In my estimation, we can expect more equitable representation in legislative bodies, more equitable allocation of resources, mandated coordination of program planning at the local level, and the marriage of federal fiscal resources and state leadership potential to meet urban educational needs most effectively.

Reapportionment

As reapportionment of legislative districts in the states moves ahead, urban areas with more equal representation in state legislatures and Congress will achieve a larger voice in the allocation of state resources. This will not, however, automatically result in greater state efforts to meet metropolitan educational needs because representatives of these areas still suffer from geographical myopia. That is, they do not see advantages in regionwide cooperation.

A less direct, but more immediately relevant outcome of reapportionment will be an increasing demand for state constitutional reform. Prohibitive limitations on local governmental activities will be put to extensive scrutiny. It can be expected that many limitations on local government cooperation will be relaxed, allowing leadership to devise regional schemes not now constitutionally possible.

Equalization of Resources

As reform movements such as reapportionment and constitutional revision continue, there will probably be increased efforts by both the states and the federal government to reduce local resource disparities. Indications that such an objective will be pursued can be found in the federal government's programs for the educationally disadvantaged and such state efforts as New York's Urban Education program.

State aid formulas can be modified to meet the states' most pressing needs. Certainly they should guarantee that all young people within a state's borders will receive at least a minimum of educational resources sufficient to assure an adequate education. It is unlikely that state aid will be drastically increased in the near future, but we can probably look to an increasing emphasis on urban aid by state governments.

At the federal level, where legislative representatives demand a "fair share" for their states, at least two breakthroughs are apparent: first, the recent effort to consolidate federal categorical grants will probably continue and Congress might well approve the concept of block grants for education. With consolidated grants and block grants, the states would have more latitude to funnel federal dollars to meet their own needs. In most states this will mean increased aid to urban areas. Second, revenue sharing, launched in 1972, will begin to align federal resources with local education needs.

Coordination of Effort at the Local Level

Most present aid to urban areas promotes functional proliferation and weakens the potential for regionwide planning. Consolidation of federal categorical programs, establishment of block grants, and closer working relations between state agencies and federal agencies may mitigate this problem. There is also some indication that federal regulations, as a basis for awarding of funds, will require school districts to cooperate with other agencies in planning for programs. For example, regulations accompanying the ESEA require that Title I programs be coordinated with Community Action agencies, Title II programs be coordinated with private school officials, and Title III programs be coordinated with "persons broadly representative of the cultural and educational resources of the area to be served (Public Law 89-10, 1965)." States that have most conscientiously insisted that local school districts comply with these requirements have noted that initial resistance to shared planning can be reduced in only a few years.

It can also be expected that, as more states establish offices of local government planning, school district officials will be required to cooperate with one another and other government functionaries throughout the metropolitan area. If the federal government continues to consolidate its programs, the potential for regionwide cooperation across functional and municipal lines will be further enhanced.

As Beckmen notes (1968, p. 197), "The roles of the federal and state governments continue to grow. They are helping local school systems do what local school systems cannot do very well for themselves." We can expect the federal government, with its superior resource base, to increase its fiscal contribution. The present leveling off of federal dollars for education is best viewed as a temporary plateau that will soon be superseded. Even at this holding point, support for the schools in 1969/70 was provided by approximately 52 percent local funds, 40 percent state funds, and 8 percent federal funds (Grant 1969, p. 25). Further, many educational observers believe that the federal contribution may grow to 15 percent by the mid-1970s, while the states' share remains constant and the local share decreases.

Increased federal funding can only be properly harnessed if the state governments provide necessary state-level objectives, leadership, planning, regulation, and technical assistance. Where states have done so, much has been accomplished. Where states have played only a passive role, the federal government has been encouraged to deal directly with local school districts, a process that has detracted from long-range, regionwide cooperation.

The challenges presented by the multiplying problems of urban educational organization are unprecedented. They will require unprecedented responses at *all* levels of government. Reorganization of education on regional lines may be necessary but, without commitment by the states and the federal government to focus their many available resources on the problem, it is not likely that efforts made at the local level will be sufficient.

NOTE

This chapter was originally prepared as a paper to be read at the University Council for Educational Administration's Career Development Seminar on Metropolitan Educational Organization, 16 November 1969.

REFERENCES

Alkin, Marvin C. "Revenues for Education in Metropolitan Areas." In *Metropolitanism: Its Challenge to Education* (Sixty-seventh Yearbook of the National Society for the Study of Education), edited by Robert J. Havighurst, pp. 123-47. Chicago: University of Chicago Press, 1968.
Allen, James E., Jr. Address to the Annual Medalist Dinner of the New York Academy of Public Education, New York City, 20 May 1969.

Baker v. *Carr,* 369 U.S. 186 (1962).

Bebout, John E. "State Constitutions and Constitutional Revision, 1965-67." In *The Book of the States, 1968-69,* pp. 1-18. Chicago: Council of State Governments, 1968.

Beckmen, Norman. "Metropolitan Education in Relation to State and Federal Government." In *Metropolitanism: Its Challenge to Education* (Sixty-seventh Yearbook of the National Society for the Study of Education), edited by Robert J. Havighurst, pp. 173-98. Chicago: University of Chicago Press, 1968.

Cleaveland, Frederic N. "Legislating for Urban Areas: An Overview." In *Congress and Urban Problems,* edited by Frederic N. Cleaveland, and associates. Washington, D.C.: Brookings Institution, 1969.

Danielson, Michael N., ed. *Metropolitan Politics.* Boston: Little, Brown, 1966.

Dyckman, John W. "The Public and Private Rationale for a National Urban Policy." In *Planning for a Nation of Cities,* edited by S. B. Warner, Jr., pp. 23-44. Cambridge, Mass.: MIT Press, 1966.

Keppel, Francis, as quoted in *Education U.S.A.,* 18 November 1965.

Grant, W. Vance. "A Statistical Look at American Education." *American Education* 5, no. 8 (October 1969): 29.

Grodzins, Morton. "Centralization and Decentralization in the American Federal System." In *A Nation of States,* edited by R. A. Goldwin, pp. 1-24. Chicago: Rand McNally, 1963.

Herman, Harold. *New York State and the Metropolitan Problem.* Philadelphia: University of Pennsylvania Press, 1963.

Martin, Roscoe C. *The Cities and the Federal System.* New York: Atherton Press, 1965.

Munger, Frank J., and Fenno, Richard F., Jr. *National Politics and Federal Aid to Education.* Syracuse, N.Y.: Syracuse University Press, 1962.

Myrdal, Gunnar. "National Planning for Healthy Cities: Two Challenges to Affluence." In *Planning for a Nation of Cities,* edited by S. B. Warner, Jr., pp. 3-22. Cambridge, Mass.: MIT Press, 1966.

National Education Association, Research Division. *Rankings of the States, 1971.* Washington, D.C.: National Education Association, 1971.

New York State Education Department. "Urban Education." *Position Paper No. 1.* Albany, N.Y.: New York State Education Department, 1967 *a.*

———. Basic Fiscal Data in Major School Districts, 1967-68. Mimeographed. Albany, N.Y.: New York State Education Department, 1967 *b.*

New York State Commission on the Quality, Cost, and Financing of Elementary and Secondary Education. *Report,* vol. 1. Albany, N.Y.: The Commission, 1972.

New York State University. *1967 Metropolitan Area Annual,* edited by Joseph F. Zimmerman. Albany, N.Y.: V. B. Printing, 1967.

———. *Major Recommendations of the State Board of Regents for Legislative Action, 1969.* Albany, N.Y.: The Commission, 1968.

Public Law 89-10, section 304(a) (79 Stat. 41-43, 1965).

Sufrin, Sidney C. *Issues in Federal Aid to Education.* Syracuse, N.Y.: Syracuse University Press, 1962.

U.S. Advisory Commission on Intergovernmental Relations. *Metropolitan America: Challenge to Federalism.* Washington, D.C.: U.S. Government Printing Office, 1966.

U.S. Bureau of the Census. *Census of Governments: 1967,* vol 5 "Local Government in Metropolitan Areas." Washington, D.C.: U.S. Government Printing Office, 1969.

U.S. Commission on Intergovernmental Relations. Message from the President of the United States Transmitting the Final Report of the Commission on Intergovernmental Relations, Pursuant to Public Law 109, 83d. Congress. Washington, D.C.: U.S. Government Printing Office, 1955.

U.S. Department of Commerce. *Statistical Abstract of the United States, 1972.* Washington, D.C.: U.S. Government Printing Office, 1972.

U.S. Department of Health, Education, and Welfare. *Digest of Educational Statistics.* Washington, D.C.: U.S. Government Printing Office, 1968.

Wood, Robert C. "A Federal Policy for Metropolitan Areas." In *Metropolitan Politics,* edited by M. N. Danielson, pp. 327-36. Boston: Little, Brown, 1966.

5

Urban-State Relationships

Michael D. Usdan

Our tripartite federal system, in which powers and functions are divided among national, state, and local authorities, is in serious crisis and disarray. The Committee for Economic Development in its report, *Modernizing State Government* (1967), acknowledged that there was "some validity in the facetious comment that our three-level federalism leaves the national government with the money, local governments with the problems, and the states with the legal powers (p. 11)."

The crisis in federalism is particularly acute at the state level, which is theoretically at least, "the keystone in the arch of the federal system—the bridge between local governments concerned with community problems and a central government dealing with nationwide issues (ibid.)." The structural and functional weaknesses of the states have been a salient factor in precipitating the current crisis in interlevel governmental relationships. Many of the states for a variety of reasons have virtually abdicated responsibility for the nation's urban problems. As a result, the states have been bypassed by problem-plagued urban centers, which have been compelled to turn to the federal government for assistance.

Modernization

The immediate priority, if the states are to become responsive to the needs of a society in which three out of four Americans live in an urban environment, is to undertake on a national scale a massive and comprehensive revitalization and modernization of state government. It is perhaps easy to agree that Washington, D.C. is not the fount of all wisdom and that decision making in a large, heterogeneous nation with more than two hundred million citizens should be decentralized. A critically important concomitant of this view, frequently not enunciated explicitly, is the desperate need to strengthen state and local governments so that they have the capacity to discharge the responsibilities that President Nixon and many others want them to have. The strengthening of the states is of particular significance to urban areas, which will continue to attempt to bypass state capitols and go directly to Washington unless dramatic changes are made.

It is, of course, impossible to generalize about urban relationships in the fifty states. Some states have been more responsive to urban problems than others, but it is fair to state that the overall record is rather dismal. The weaknesses of state government are of particular importance in a policy area such as education where the state has the paramount legal responsibility and authority. Despite the plenary powers that the states legally can exercise, the tradition of local operational control of public schools in the United States is politically potent, and most states have been reluctant to impose their full legal authority upon local districts. This fact of school politics has certainly helped to perpetuate in many, if not most states, the "hands-off" attitude that has characterized relationships between rural, suburban, and urban school systems and state educational officials.

The state's legal primacy in education makes any lack of response particularly felt by hard pressed urban school systems. The weaknesses of state legislatures, where legal authority for education actually lies, are particularly salient for those who would advocate greater state initiatives in ameliorating urban problems (Hamilton and Reutter 1958, p. 2). James Bryce some seventy-five years ago was reported to have commented that the convening of the state legislature "is looked forward to with anxiety by good citizens" and "its departure hailed as a deliverance." These apprehensions unfortunately would still be well founded in more than a few states.

The low visibility and weak performance of state legislatures are manifold. The following extract succinctly enumerates some of their weaknesses.

Before 1962, state legislatures had become *increasingly unrepresentative in composition*—a condition that recent reapportionments have helped to correct.

Such factors as extremely low pay, severely limited legislative sessions, and lack of adequate staff or supporting research competence have led to low esteem for legislatures and loss of confidence in the resulting product.

Many legislatures are unwieldy in size, which detracts from the prestige of membership in them.

Few are well organized to discharge their responsibilities.

Legislative committees give less intensive examination to proposed legislation than Congressional committees commonly provide; preliminary staff work is often casual, and testimony from acknowledged authorities is rarely solicited.

Undue attention is often given to detailed examination of administrative operations, petty local issues, and financial aspects of minor state operations— diverting energies from major policy matters.

The influence of pervasive and powerful legislative lobbies is notorious, even though the frequency of bribery and unseemly revelry has been exaggerated.

Those who seek improper gain as members often obtain more public exposure than those who contribute dedicated public service at considerable personal sacrifice (Committee for Economic Development 1967, p. 34).

I have dwelled at such length upon the role and the woeful state of the states because a discussion of urban-state relationships can be conducted only if one realistically assesses the present condition of state government. The states undeniably have been strengthened in recent years, paradoxically, as the result of the infusion of federal dollars and programs. The introduction of revenue sharing will be helpful. The critical question, however, remains: can the nation, with its urban centers rotting, afford the luxury of waiting for the states to be tooled up sufficiently to cope with our society's complex problems? This, I believe, is the central issue of the role of the state *vis-à-vis* metropolitanism. With only a few exceptions, state governments have been singularly quiescent in providing leadership.

With the Nixon administration, the states may now have their last chance to become more assertive and substantive participants in the federal system. The decade of the seventies may well see either a dynamic renaissance of the states or, if they continue to abdicate their responsibilities, a continued centralization of authority in the federal government. The weaknesses of the states, which we have thus far described in rather general terms, are pervasive, extending into the executive and judicial as well as the legislative branches of government. Concomitantly, these weak government structures, not surprisingly, have been unable to generate effective functional leadership in key policy areas such as education, welfare, housing, transportation, and pollution control, all of which are central to the needs of an urbanized society.

State Governance of Education

We have already alluded to the politics of localism, which for so long pervaded thinking about the governance of education. Political and economic factors, however, in recent years have been precipitating much thought about the urgent need to reassess and perhaps basically restructure public education.

The Crisis of School Finance

One transcendent issue that is compelling a reassessment of the entire structure of public education is educational finance. The crisis in school finance profoundly affects urban-state relationships. With the federal government collecting two out of every three tax dollars and yet supporting only 7 percent of the bill for elementary and secondary education, the fiscal burden has fallen disproportionately upon local and state governments. While the federal government has preempted the more elastic graduated income tax, local governments, which still pay on a national average at least 50 percent of the cost of public education, are constrained by relatively static revenue sources.

The property tax, still the bellwether of school finance as it was fifty and seventy-five years ago when it truly reflected wealth in a more rural economy, has reached saturation point in many communities. In recent years an unprecedented number of defeats for school budgets and bond issues has dramatized the need to reform an anachronistic revenue structure. "American school finance is characterized by inequity, irrationality, and by the consistent denial of equal educational opportunity (Berke, Campbell, and Goetell 1972, p. 2)." The well-documented (see Committee for Economic Development 1966, pp. 20-32) fragmentation of local government authority in metropolitan areas deters such reform. The problems of implementing coherent fiscal reforms in eighty thousand separate and diverse local governments situated in fifty states are apparent. Equally perplexing would be the development of equitable tax and revenue reforms in the nation's scattered 223 standard metropolitan statistical areas,[1] each of which has an average of 87 local governments (ibid., p. 21). The Chicago metropolitan area alone had 1,060 local government units as far back as 1962.

The structural weaknesses of local governments, like the states that have created them, are legion. Most local units are too small, they overlap wastefully, popular control is weak, vested interests deter change, apathy runs rife, policy-making mechanisms and administrative organizations are frequently ineffectual, and technically trained staff are difficult to attract because of low salaries (ibid., p. 11-13).

The fragmented and ineffectual structures and rigid sources of finance that hamstring local governments make grass roots reform extremely unlikely. For example, the formidable political obstacles to imposing sales or income taxes on a metropolitan or regional area are apparent. Many feel that only state and federal governments have broad enough tax bases to implement much needed tax and revenue reform to redress gross fiscal inequities in education and other social policy areas. Indeed, there is substantial opinion that political configurations even at the state level preclude meaningful reform. State politics, like local politics some maintain, tend to be tax politics, while federal politics can more readily be programmatic (Campbell and Burkhead 1968, pp. 646-47). Federalism, some feel, can be revitalized most readily through the prestigious influence and executive authority of the president of the United States (ibid.).

Nevertheless, it seems certain that the states must play an influential role in the comprehensive structural, functional, and financial reform of local government that is so desperately needed (Beckmen 1968). A rational restructuring of local units of government will require action by the state. The Committee for Economic Development (1966, pp. 60-64) made a number of recommendations to the states to modernize the local governments that are their creations:

Each state should revise its constitution to modernize the forms and powers of local government.

Each state should create a boundary commission with continuing authority to design and redesign local jurisdictional lines, and to set time tables for consolidations and annexations.

Federal and state grants-in-aid should be carefully designed to encourage formation of larger, stronger, well-managed local units. Comprehensive local planning, as well as coordination of all functions and all units, should be a condition of such support.

Civic leadership of a high order must be exerted to overcome the predictable resistance of vested political interests.

The school finance crisis at the local level is being exacerbated by the rising militancy of teachers as well as by the inflationary spiral. Instructional costs constitute more than 70 percent of most school budgets, and the recent aggressiveness of once relatively quiescent teachers' organizations is rapidly pushing local communities beyond their fiscal breaking points. The time-consuming and strenuous demands of negotiation and the inadequacies of most local boards of education to cope with them may push negotiations with teachers to the metropolitan, regional, or state level faster than most observers imagine. Moreover, the possible movement of negotiations to a broader level of government finally may seal the casket on some of the myths pertaining to local control of education that have persisted long past their time. Once the largest portion of a school budget is not negotiated locally, what fiscal discretion will be left to the board of education and its staff? Already the percentage of school budgets that is truly at the discretion of local officials is often almost infinitesimal.

The Challenge to State Education Departments

In the past few years judicial, political, and administrative momentum has been slowly building up for the states to assume total financial responsibility for education. In a case of great import the Detroit Board of Education sued the state of Michigan for violating the equal protection clause of the Fourteenth Amendment to the U. S. Constitution. The plaintiffs argued that the state was not discharging its responsibility of providing equal educational opportunity because expenditures per pupil were so much less in the city of Detroit than they were in other Michigan school districts (Wise 1969). Similar litigation (*Serrano* v. *Priest* 1971) in California and elsewhere, holding that the "right to an education in public schools is a fundamental interest which cannot be conditional on wealth," has implications profound indeed for the entire structure of school finance and the role of the states in determining educational policy.

Several influential leaders have recently discussed the need for at least considering the possibility of eliminating locally levied school taxes. In the summer of 1968, United States Commissioner of Education, the late James E. Allen, Jr., while still serving as New York's chief state school officer, floated a controversial trial balloon: that the state assume the responsibility for financing education. In Dr. Allen's view (1968), local financing of elementary and secondary schools erects "serious barriers" to the solution of high priority urban issues such as racial integration and decentralization.

A few months before Dr. Allen elicited, as predicted, "a high mark on the educational seismograph" with his comments, Dr. James B. Conant, at the third annual meeting of the Education Commission of the States proposed a "radical new idea" in education—"that public education in the states would be greatly improved if educational decisions at the local level could be completely divorced from considerations of local taxes." He proposed that all authority to levy taxes for schools at the local level be eliminated and that the local share of school financing be transferred to the state (ibid., pp. 70-71). In 1969, Michigan's governor also suggested that the burden for financing education be assumed by the state (Flint 1969). More recently, the Fleischmann Commission in New York State recommended full state funding for elementary and secondary education (New York State Commission 1972). The radical change in school financing suggested would undercut dramatically two basic premises of the traditional theology of American public education: local control and local financing (Allen 1968, p. 71).

If at least a modicum of credence is to be placed in the adage "he who pays the piper calls the tune," it is blatantly apparent that a necessary corollary to the state financing of education would be the strengthening of state education departments to assume new, greatly enlarged responsibilities. Until recently most state educational agencies were notoriously weak and understaffed. Ironically, federal programs have not weakened state education departments, but have provided them with a large percentage of whatever staff they may have.

> In 1947-48 vocational education and vocational rehabilitation accounted for more than half the total department professional staff in at least thirty-three states. Only five departments had more than fifty professionals in other fields of education and nineteen departments had fewer than twenty.

New Federal programs begun during the 1950s accentuated the trend. By 1960 more than half the professional staff in all departments combined were assigned to federally subsidized programs; in thirteen states the proportion was over 70 percent (Fitzwater 1968, p. 49).

In 1962, only 10 departments had professional staffs that totaled more than 100, 21 departments had fewer than 50 professionals (ibid.).

Despite the considerable boost given to state educational agencies by congressional passage of Title V of the Elementary and Secondary Education Act of 1965, glaring weaknesses still abound. Most state departments of education are still understaffed and lack personnel with the expertise to discharge adequately newly assumed responsibilities of educational planning, evaluation, training, research, and development. Perhaps the greatest challenge to state agencies, which commonly have been staffed by rurally oriented educators, is the establishment of symbiotic relationships with large city school systems. A few decades ago, when the cities possessed the best financed schools and most innovative programs, they scoffed at bucolic and backward state educational agencies, which had little, if anything, to provide them with in the way of services or assistance. Now, with the cities in dire straits, greater financial and other assistance from the states is mandatory. If education departments are to discharge their responsibilities to all the children of their states, they must manifest greater concern for and understanding of the monumental problems confronting the big cities. Some state education departments have taken positive action such as earmarking top level staff to work exclusively on urban problems, creating new units to deal with city districts, undertaking special urban projects in areas such as finance, race relations, urban-suburban cooperative service programs, and designing new curriculum and facilities especially for urban areas (ibid.).

The modernization of state educational agencies will be a difficult and tedious job requiring superior leadership (ibid., p. 62). Chances for successfully converting these departments into dynamic instruments of educational change and reform will be largely contingent upon the quality of leadership offered by the chief state school officer. Selection of these officials thus becomes significant. Although in twenty-nine of the states chief school officers are appointed by either the state board of education (twenty-five states) or by the governor (four states), twenty-one states still elect their top educational official. In fifteen of these twenty-one states, the state superintendent or commissioner of education is elected on a partisan political ballot.[2] In some states there is no civil service status or protection for departmental staff, and it can reasonably be argued that top quality educators would be loath to have their careers determined by the vagaries of partisan politics. With more federal money being dispensed to the states in recent years, the advantages of a nonpartisan state educational agency require little elaboration. Indeed, a good case can be made for the immediate restructuring of state educational agencies that presently are linked constitutionally or statutorily to partisan politics. These agencies if they are to provide more effective leadership in the future than they have in the past must not be restrained by partisan political structures.

The Need for Comprehensive Planning

In addition to finance, other factors will inevitably be pushing state and federal governments into assuming more responsibility for major urban problems like education. Comprehensive, coordinated planning is of basic importance to any efforts to improve urban life. Public education must be viewed as but one major subsystem of a cluster of interrelated urban problems such as housing, health, welfare, higher education, location of jobs, transportation, air and water pollution, land use, recreation, commuter service, and so on. Improvements in education, for example, cannot take place in a vacuum, but must be linked with efforts to ameliorate the housing situation and to provide jobs for the poor in the inner city.

The comprehensive planning that is necessary cannot be carried out on less than a metropolitan, regional, or statewide basis. The financial and political resources to energize comprehensive planning simply do not exist at local government levels. Cities, for example, have no authority nor an iota of political leverage to compel more affluent suburbs to agree to a more equitable redistribution of the tax base in a metropolitan area. Everyone is aware that cities are in a fiscal bind and need more money, but taxpayers generally, and perhaps understandably, are not noted for their altruism. One does not have to be a political sage to recognize that the possibilities are virtually nil that suburban governments, themselves facing rebellions from property-tax-payers, will voluntarily equalize resources with central cities.

Political Domination

Only higher levels of government, state and federal, have the political and fiscal resources to do the necessary job. The states, however, as we have already indicated, have been virtually powerless to improve the chaotic state of local government. Although the re-apportionment of legislatures means that people and not cows are now being represented in state capitols, suburban areas where the great post-World War II population growth has occurred will domi-nate legislatures. It appears doubtful that politicians representing largely white and more affluent suburban communities will push for metropolitan arrangements with fiscally starved central cities com-posed of growing numbers of disadvantaged minority group mem-bers. These cities are already burdened by state aid formulas that favor suburban school districts and do not take account of their special needs (Ranney 1969). This situation continues in spite of efforts to equalize local property tax rates, halt the declining state share of costs per pupil, and reduce the dollar gap between high-expenditure and low-expenditure school districts (New York State Educational Conference Board 1972).

The polarization in the core cities and suburbs on socio-economic and racial lines is disturbing to contemplate. There seems to be little likelihood that suburb-dominated legislatures, for exam-ple, would support the creation of metropolitan school districts, with the implied redistribution of resources.

In addition to strong political deterrents, the role of the states in promoting the modernization of local government is limited by even less tractable geographical and international factors. We live in an interdependent tension-ridden world that, for more than two decades, has been on the threshold of nuclear holocaust. As a result, it is unlikely that there will be dramatic changes in priorities to divert public attention and resources from the most basic issue affecting us all, namely, war or peace. The tax and reve-nue structure likewise will continue to reflect the defense and foreign policy needs of the federal government. A concomitant of this con-tinuing fact of life is the great visibility of the federal government and the resulting, and perhaps unavoidable, subordination of state and local government units.

Metropolitanism and Multistate Cooperation

Geographical factors also delimit the capacity of the states to handle the complex problems of metropolitan areas. The geographical boundaries of many of the states serve no functional purposes. States are unable, in other words, to handle many regional problems, such as air and water pollution and transportation, that cut across state lines. For example, the metropolitan New York City area, as defined in the membership of the Metropolitan Regional Council, consists of nearly fifteen hundred separate county, city, and town political entities. A population of more than twenty million people, which is expected to reach thirty million by 2000, resides in an eight thousand square mile area in three states bounded by Trenton, New Jersey, Poughkeepsie, New York, and New Haven, Connecticut. Obviously, the states cannot unilaterally handle the comprehensive planning needed by this most densely populated of all metropolitan regions (which has within its boundaries some 10 percent of the nation's total population). Only the federal government can provide the requisite fiscal incentives and sanction the interstate compacts that would make comprehensive metropolitan planning possible.

The cities particularly are strangling in the balkanization of government responsibilities. James W. Rouse, the president of Community Research and Development, Inc., the developer of Columbia, a new city in Maryland, deplored the lack of adequate responsibility for coherent urban planning:

> The building of the city is nobody's business—neither government nor industry. We have assigned a vague responsibility to local government to provide for orderly growth but have given it neither the power nor the process with which it can fulfill that responsibility.

> Nor have we developed a capacity in American business for producing well-planned, large scale urban development. Although the business of city building is the largest single industry in America, there is no large corporation engaged in it. City building has no General Motors or General Electric—no IBM, no Xerox; no big capital resources to invest in the purchase of large land areas; no big research and development program unfolding new techniques to produce a better environment. There are no large corporations engaged in the end-product production of the American city (1966, pp. 7-8).

A Well-Documented Crisis

The cities are undeniably in a grave crisis. Indeed, our society itself may hang in the balance as our great urban centers struggle to survive. We live in an anomalous situation where cities, which are the vortices of growth in a booming urban economy, are so poor in the world's richest country. The problems of the decaying cities have been pointed out *ad nauseam* in recent years. Countless writers have commented on the causes of urban blight, such as the flight of major industry and middle-class taxpayers, municipal overburden, and the obsolescent physical infrastructure.

Urban problems have now been documented adequately. The studies have been made and are largely repetitive. President Johnson's National Commission on Urban Problems reiterated the need for the federal government to share its revenues with local areas (Herbers 1968, p. 1). The prestigious commission, chaired by ex-Senator Paul Douglas of Illinois, recommended that 2 percent of federal income tax revenues (estimated at $6 billion annually) be allocated for a system of incentive grants to encourage the formation and strengthening of larger government units. The commission reiterated the weaknesses of local governments and urged metropolitan or regional approaches to issues such as land use, building codes, zoning, tax laws, and racial and social class integration. It felt, moreover, that the states had a special role to play in mitigating the urban crisis:

> We believe the states have tended to become forgotten members of the governmental family. By using powers they already possess, by assuming appropriate new authority when necessary, and in providing funds, they occupy a unique position to help bring urban areas out of confusion. State governments are close to the people and to the problems, but bring enough perspective to bear to help release urban areas from the excesses of localism. State action of the kind we recommend, where the states are willing to help pay a significant amount of the costs as well as exercising their authority, can help restore a genuine sense of community to our cities and their surrounding areas (ibid., p. 70).

This description of the state's role *vis-à-vis* the problems of urban America would read well in a political science or civics text describing the theory underlying our federal system of government. Time, however, may already have run out on efforts to create more viable relationships between the cities and the states. The problems are immediate and critical. Urban needs are now nationwide and supersede state boundaries. Only the national government may be in a position to compel compliance with policies that curb the competitive anarchy that has been so damaging to the development of urban America. Recent criteria for the funding of federal housing and community facilities programs require local government units to engage in regional planning processes. These requirements by federal agencies, such as the Department of Housing and Urban Development, may offer our best, and perhaps last, chance as a society to extricate ourselves from the urban morass we have permitted to develop. Such federal programs with fillips for regional approaches, however, have to accelerate at a much faster rate if the necessary progress is to be made. In conclusion, an urban nation must become more aware of the national nature of its "local" problems and initiate and quickly implement with the highest priority a coherent national urban policy.

NOTES

1. A standard metropolitan area is—with a few exceptions—defined by the U.S. Bureau of the Census as a single county containing a central city of at least fifty thousand, or "twin cities" with a combined population of fifty thousand, or a group of counties that have substantial urbanized areas contiguous to the central city.

2. For an account of efforts now under way to improve state leadership in education, see Morphet, Jesser, and Ludka (1972).

REFERENCES

Allen, James E., Jr. "Educational Priorities and the Handicap of Local Financing." In *Decentralization and Racial Integration,* edited by Carroll F. Johnson and Michael D. Usdan, pp. 69-81. New York: Teachers College Press, 1968.

Beckmen, Norman. "Metropolitan Education in Relation to State and Federal Government." In *Metropolitanism: Its Challenge to Education,* edited by Robert J. Havighurst, pp. 179-186. Chicago: National Society for the Study of Education, 1968.

Berke, Joel S.; Campbell, Alan K.; and Goetell, Robert J. *Financing Equal Educational Opportunity.* Berkeley, Ca.: McCutchan, 1971.

Campbell, Alan K., and Burkhead, Jesse. "Public Policy for Urban America." In *Issues in Urban Economics,* edited by Harvey S. Perloff and Lowdon Wingo, Jr. Baltimore: Johns Hopkins Press, 1968.

Committee for Economic Development. *Modernizing Local Government.* New York: 1966.

_____. *Modernizing State Government.* New York: 1967.

Fitzwater, C. O. *State School System Development: Patterns and Trends.* Denver: Education Commission of the States, 1968.

Flint, Jerry M. "Michigan Seeking State Take-Over of School Costs." *New York Times* 1 October 1969, p. 25.

Hamilton, Robert R., and Reutter, E. Edmund, Jr. *Legal Aspects of School Board Operation.* New York: Teachers College Press, 1958.

Herbers, John. "Panel Urges U.S. to Share Its Revenue with Local Areas to Meet Urban Crisis." *New York Times* 15 December 1968, p. 1.

Morphet, Edgar L.; Jesser, David L.; and Ludka, Arthur P. *Planning and Providing for Excellence in Education.* New York: Citation Press, 1972.

New York State Commission on Quality, Cost, and Financing Elementary and Secondary Education vol. 1. *Report.* New York: The Commission, 1972.

New York State Educational Conference Board. "We've Promises to Keep." 1973 Legislative Program. Albany, N.Y.: 1972.

Ranney, David C. "The Impact of Metropolitanism on Central City Education." *Educational Administration Quarterly* 5, no. 3 (Winter 1969): 24-36.

Rouse, James W. "Major Issues of Metropolitan Development." *Regional Plan News* 81 (February 1966): 7-8.

Serrano v. *Priest,* 5 C3d 584, 96 CR 601 (1971).

Wise, Arthur. *Rich Schools, Poor Schools: The Promise of Equal Educational Opportunity.* Chicago: University of Chicago Press, 1969.

6

Inside the Metropolis

Bernard C. Watson

A wide spectrum of groups and coalitions of groups is concerned with education: some of them see change as critically important; others reluctantly admit its inevitability; some oppose change of any sort. In many instances, in discussing the specific issues with which leadership must deal in running schools in big cities, I will be referring to my particular experience in Philadelphia, but, sure that the same forces are active in other cities, I will note cases from other settings. What will be clear, I hope, from this review is that the problems of the metropolis in general and of education in particular are exceedingly complex. Indeed, the Rand Corporation, hired by Mayor Lindsay of New York in 1968 to make systems analyses of five city departments, stated (1969) that the nation's defense problems were far simpler by comparison. "The complexity of the human element, the complexity of the fiscal and political element, the plain complexity of New York City, are something we haven't encountered before," said the information director of the New York office.

Business and Industrial Concerns

Let me begin by mentioning the business and industrial leaders of the community as a group whose stake in education is high. These are the people who sooner or later recognize that the public school system of a city plays a critical part in determining the image that the city has for prospective newcomers. Companies and individuals who are considering a move will certainly include the schools' reputations in their assessment of possible new locations. The quality of a new generation of civic leaders will also depend, in large measure, on the effectiveness of the schools, even though, as in Philadelphia, many will be expected to emerge from the traditional private academies. Perhaps most pressing, however, is the continuing dependence on the schools to produce future employees who are equipped with at least the basic skills that will allow them to function effectively and readily learn technical skills required by the job. The increasing concern about education on the part of the business community has been well documented. Even to list a sample of the variety of efforts that have been made, privately or through such organizations as the National Alliance of Businessmen, the National Association of Manufacturers, or the Urban Coalition, would take more space than I have. They range from the adoption of schools to the lending of key personnel as school administrators, from the sponsoring of storefront academies to the establishment of training programs jointly with school districts. Whether the commitment of funds and staff to these projects is motivated by newfound social concern or enlightened self-interest is far less important than is thoughtful consideration by both educators and business leaders of their joint concern for the public schools.

A Shift in Interest

In Philadelphia, the successful reform movement of the early 1950s, spearheaded by highly placed members of the business and professional establishment, soon shifted its focus from the political and civic arena to the educational one. Under the leadership of the Greater Philadelphia Movement, a group composed chiefly of bankers and lawyers, sporadic and ineffective criticism of the school system was welded into a political tool that forced legislative change, returned to the city control over school finances, and revised school board selection. Previously, school board members had been picked by judges of the Court of Common Pleas, themselves political appointees. This process resulted in boards composed mainly of businessmen who saw their chief responsibility as running the schools at minimal cost. The 1965 Educational Home Rule Charter specified that board members be chosen by the mayor from a list drawn up by a nominating panel consisting of the chief officers of a number of civic, labor, business, and education groups.

The subsequent history of education in Philadelphia might have been quite different—and no doubt less astonishing—had the new school board not acquired as its president a fiery patrician lawyer named Richardson Dilworth. Together with Joseph S. Clark, later a Senator from Pennsylvania, Dilworth had successfully crusaded against the entrenched Republican machine that had run Philadelphia since well before the turn of the century. Winning the post of treasurer in 1949, Dilworth moved on to become district attorney, succeeded Clark as mayor in 1955, and was reelected to that office in 1959.

Drawing on his experience in presiding over the renaissance at city hall, Dilworth called on professional leaders in such widely varying fields as finance, personnel, and engineering to review the school situation and recommend necessary changes. Almost all of what has been referred to as the "dramatic reform" and the ferment of change that swept over the School District of Philadelphia was the direct result of the intensive study and work of the task forces appointed in 1965. Although other groups have arisen to claim attention and exert influence in school affairs, the impact of this business expertise can hardly be overestimated.

The basic changes recommended by the task forces were made, but the continuing interest of the business community is expressed through its participation in the school district's Career Development programs and Urban Coalition projects. There are undoubtedly various degrees of business interest and cooperation that can be tapped for school improvement, ranging from general support and counsel to direct involvement in specific projects. A particularly interesting example of company activity on behalf of education is that provided by Illinois Bell Telephone, which sponsored newspaper advertisements detailing school needs and enclosed with all its Chicago bills flyers recommending support of the school bond issue.

Black Community Development

Another force with which urban education must reckon is that developed in the black community. The dramatic migration of black people to urban centers (blacks now constitute about 40 percent of the population of Philadelphia and 65 percent of the school enrollment) might not in itself account for the key role blacks are playing in bringing about educational change. But in Philadelphia, as in every other city, they inherited the oldest schools, the poorest teaching, the most meager supplies for their children. As one writer put it, "If the Philadelphia public schools were not fulfilling their promises to white children in the early '60's, they weren't even making promises to the black students (Roberts 1969, p. 88)." That this state of affairs was—and is—certainly not restricted to Philadelphia is well documented by Sexton (1961).

Recognizing that in education lay the key to improvement in other conditions of life, many black parents moved through the civil rights struggle, with its goal of integrated education, to the militancy of black power demands for good quality education under local black control. The pressure that has been building through years of dashed hopes and frustrated efforts for improvement can hardly be overestimated. The same explosive force, fueled by similar frustrations, exists in the Mexican-American communities of the Southwest and the Puerto Rican communities of the Northeast. Southern California, where there are two million Mexican-Americans, is perhaps more of a powder keg than any black ghetto.

The new school administration in Philadelphia, determined to redress at least some of the grievances of the past, made a number of notable attempts to meet the black challenge in such varied ways as appointing more black administrators and eliminating the worst of the firetrap schools in ghetto areas. A notable failure, however, was the plan to create a Model School District in North Philadelphia, which would place a large number of black schools under a semi-autonomous local board. Although in Chicago, the university and community residents successfully combined to establish the Woodlawn Experimental District despite initial school system opposition, Philadelphia's attempt foundered on the rocks of community suspicion and fear that the openness of the school administration simply veiled its intention of creating a "Bantu" district. Plans for educational improvement for the area, worked out through the Area Wide Council, a citizen group for the Model Cities program, bogged down almost completely in political and financial troubles because of differences in approach to the exercise of power by the Area Wide Council, the city administration, and a more conservative government in Washington. Some small-scale projects began functioning, such as the Mantua Mini-School, designed by the community as a model for a scattered-site middle school, and the Pickett Community Committee, organized to make citizens' participation (black and white) a reality in school planning. But it would be unrealistic in the extreme to think that pilot projects could, at this point, turn aside the powerful forces of anger, resentment, and need that threaten to plunge the school system and the city into unthinkable chaos. It is evident also that there is no model constellation of circumstances that will guarantee harmonious planning and successful implementation.

Student Dissatisfaction

Youth, of course, constitutes another increasingly vocal group pressing for change in the schools. This generation of young people, sophisticated beyond its years, yet alienated by adult failure to use technological competence to solve the problems of war, poverty, and racism, no longer believes that the school is always right and that teacher knows best and is battling for and occasionally winning the privilege of a voice in determining its own education. In many places, this force is almost indistinguishable from that of black—or Chicano or Puerto Rican—militancy, but it is developing with equal intensity among white, middle-class, college-bound youngsters.

A few years ago, several thousand youngsters, mostly black, flocked from black and integrated high schools to the Philadelphia school administration building to demonstrate their urgent desire for the inclusion of Afro-American history in school programs, the right to wear African dress, and more black principals. When the administration's response of discussion and negotiation was overwhelmed by police action in breaking up what was termed a "riot," trust and hope were all but destroyed. Mr. Dilworth, answering widespread criticism of the school board for "allowing" the students to congregate in the first place, put it bluntly when he said "You can't cap a volcano."

Schools in New York, Chicago, and Los Angeles have been closed by young people's making similar demands. In Chicago, for instance, twenty-five thousand black youngsters stayed out of school to dramatize their grievances over the lack of Afro-American studies —and were joined in their protest by a hundred professionals, including some principals. Whether, as in Chicago, school authorities refuse to deal with students while they are demonstrating without permission on the streets, or, as in Philadelphia, the superintendent and members of the board invite protesters in to negotiate, it is clear that there is no simple or easy solution to the growing pressure from students.

Another crowd, not quite as large and this time mostly white, later gathered at the beleaguered administration building to ask for changes in the school policy on draft counseling and on giving information to draft boards. Even more ominous were the storm clouds that gathered in one black high school when students boycotted the classes of a teacher they considered ineffective and irrelevant. Before any administrative action was taken, the teachers' union, sensing quite correctly the implications of this exercise of student judgment, polled its membership and received approval for a strike if the teacher in question were transferred. A most unfortunate development in this case was the injection into it of racial and religious overtones. Although students and their adult supporters were attempting to dramatize their right to effective instruction, the fact that the children were black and the teacher Jewish was carefully underlined by certain elements and cheerfully exploited by the media. That the school principal and many other supporters of the students' cause were white was often conveniently ignored.

Perhaps less threatening, but no less forceful, a display of student dissatisfaction with current educational programs is visible in the enthusiastic response to the Parkway Program in Philadelphia. Conceived by the school district's Director of Development to take advantage of the cultural and business resources of the city center, this freewheeling high school in which students investigate the whys and hows of institutions as well as the whats attracted ten thousand applications for six hundred places. That these came from well-heeled suburbs and local academic high schools is one indication that even our best traditional programs are missing the mark. Even when people do not know whether innovations like the Parkway Program will work or not, their dissatisfaction with what exists is making them willing to take chances in order to find relevance and humanity in the educational process.

Teachers and Administrators

I certainly cannot complete the list of forces pressing for change without including those teachers and administrators within the system whose concern and commitment, honed on the day-to-day experience with school problems, equal those of any other group. Though some of the best known exposés of educational horrors have been made by persons whose persistence in seeking solutions has apparently not matched the profundity of their shock, there are many other tales quietly told by those who continue doggedly to insist that children can learn and that schools must be made to serve them. New York had Elliott Shapiro and Seymour Gang, Philadelphia had Marcus Foster and Fred Holliday, Chicago had Joe Rosen, Margaret Lennen, and Barbara Sizemore—principals who came up through the system and who, in spite of it and frequently at the risk of being destroyed by it, turned schools around and rekindled the vision of learning as a vital and exciting thing.

Some of these people are involved with innovative programs of various sorts—teaching children how to use cameras, taking them out into the community, helping them run their own television shows, or introducing them to computers. Some are aides and volunteers who only recently discovered how good and how bad classroom life can be. Some are students studying urban affairs for a semester, or engaged in intern programs or practice teaching. All are, perhaps, part of a force that is not yet coalesced, but one that is gathering strength to demand, from the inside, that schools change and that the system change. If their commitment to humanizing education and making the schools responsive to the needs of children is focused and channeled, we will, I think, have on our hands a revolution in education.

But not all the metropolitan forces support change in education. Indeed, any planning done on the assumption that this is the case may survive academic arguments only to founder on the hard realities of urban life.

Community and Ethnic Provincialism

In contrast, for instance, to the business and professional leaders whose sense of responsibility is citywide in scope, there are many small businessmen whose loyalty and interest is strictly local. They are often members of neighborhood groups, who are closely knit through ties of kinship and common origin, and who are, quite naturally, concerned about preserving the gains they have made. Fearing change that might threaten their tenuous security, these groups are often violent in their opposition to any move that seems to encourage the rising aspirations of other groups and the breakdown of the status quo.

A clear example of the mobilization of this kind of force occurred in Philadelphia when room was needed for the expansion of one of the most overcrowded black high schools. Despite the fact that thousands of families, black and white, have routinely been required to move—to make way not only for schools but also for highways and other government projects—this case suddenly became the subject of citywide debate. Fourteen Polish families, still residents of a neighborhood that had long since become black, refused to sell their homes. The mayor expressed his shock that the school board would even consider forcing them to move, the city council president and several members took up cudgels on behalf of the homeowners, and newspapers reported the battle on their front pages. Only pressure from the school principal, staff, and students—and several tours of the school by the councilmen—persuaded the opponents of expansion that the school desperately needed more space.

A similar case of community antagonism to school construction occurred in a middle-class black community. Residents of a newer neighborhood, not far from the main north-south axis of Philadelphia, expressed considerable alarm about such issues as the adequacy of parking space for a high school being built nearby. Their questions, for some reason, did not become a public issue.

Another example of neighborhood hostility to a school developed in South Philadelphia, in an area populated largely by Italian-Americans. Bok is one of four vocational and technical high schools in the city, and its student body now happens to be predominantly black. Modern programs at the school instituted by a new principal were viewed with mixed emotions by local parents whose children attended school elsewhere. Resentment flared over minor street fights. Finally, at the height of the 1968 presidential campaign, neighborhood residents, egged on by rabid Wallace supporters, began defying the right of black students to pass through their neighborhood and accusing them of threatening residents and destroying property. The battle soon took on the proportions of a major confrontation in the streets, with city hall once more siding with the community against the school board. Despite the fact that there had been little difficulty within the school itself, the board of education was forced to provide bus transportation for the students to avoid almost certain conflagration.

Not all the forces opposing change are to be found in blue-collar ethnic communities. Middle-class parents, black and white alike, exert their influence on behalf of conservative values and traditional methods in school affairs. Unlike the many black parents who have too often seen the schools destroying rather than enhancing their children's chances of success, they tend to feel that what proved good enough for them is good enough for their youngsters. Storms of reaction break out when, for instance, a film that raises pointed questions about teaching and disciplinary methods in one of the "best" high schools in town is shown, or when a review of admission standards to an academic high school is perceived as a lowering of the school's quality.

Particularly heated was the controversy over the state Human Relations Commission's desegregation order to the Philadelphia school board. At a twelve-hour public hearing on the proposed plan, dozens of angry and emotional speakers decried even the mildest suggestion that white children be bused for occasional shared-time activities or classes with their black peers. At the evening session, hundreds of white parents, mostly female, nearly brought about an abrupt adjournment of the hearings when they began rapping on the

Board Room windows with their shoes. One police lieutenant, attempting to restore order, had his jacket and shirt literally torn off. But, as the board's vice-president remarked with heavy irony, the riot troops, who had been called into action the year before against students, were conspicuous by their absence. The intensity of the reaction forced the board to request an extension from the reluctant state commission.

Chicago has been the scene of similar disruptions. When the school administration decided to bus a few black students, from middle-class families, into schools on the southwest side, white parents banded together to threaten the Board of Education that they would block the buses and picket the school. Once again, the police had to be called to quell the disturbances. Parents elsewhere, like those in Philadelphia and Chicago, were displaying, it seems to me, not only bigotry and fear, but also their conscious recognition that black children have indeed been so damaged by typically inferior education that they are unable to compete in class with many white children. This intensity of parental protest is frightening, particularly when it is concentrated on protecting the children of one group at the expense of those of another. School systems today are feeling this force from both black and white communities.

Professional Conservatism

A major obstacle to educational change is increasingly proving to be the teachers'—and the even newer administrators'—unions. Few would question the justification for unionization and the benefits that it has bestowed on a group not long ago among the most scandalously underpaid in the nation. Teachers were all too often intimidated and even brutalized by powerful, paternalistic school administrations and boards of education; only when professional associations did not seem strong enough to withstand such pressures was unionization seen as necessary.

But teachers are now often proving to be an extremely conservative force, coming into direct confrontation with school boards and the community over not only financial matters but also questions of strategy and change. For instance, in Philadelphia, the Educational Home Rule Charter clearly specifies the superintendent's authority to "assign or reassign all professional employees of the District." Yet this legally constituted right to make transfers—to ensure fair distribution of experienced teachers as well as racially balanced faculties—was hotly debated during contract negotiations, and the board narrowly averted a strike by casting five votes to four in favor of a contract that included a clause leaving transfers on a voluntary basis.

A subsequent court decision, on a suit against the Board of Education for this action, upheld the superintendent's authority—but the probable political consequences of his exercising this right are such that extremely serious consideration would have to be given beforehand.

As I mentioned earlier, the union took a strike vote when students and parents at a Philadelphia high school requested the transfer of a history teacher; although the administration decided against the transfer, the union voted to "censure" the superintendent for his handling of the case. The president of the Board of Education, in a public statement, charged the union leadership with arrogance and "lack of interest in anything except sustaining all of its so-called privileges." He went on to cite the union's insistence on the maintenance of the seniority system and its fearful attitude toward even moderate decentralization recommendations as two examples of the union's opposition to "any change whatsoever in the status quo."

While financial settlements are at the heart of most disputes, there is little question that teachers, like those in Philadelphia and New York, are expressing organized opposition to administration thinking on matters such as community control, special education, discipline, and innovations in staffing and instruction. Even more recent is the emergence of principals' and other administrators' organizations as bargaining agents for personnel that in industry would be considered of managerial level and therefore ineligible for union membership.

Philadelphia administrators reacted to the elimination of some three hundred and eighty-one positions, necessitated by the board's severe financial straits but widely interpreted as a means of removing unnecessary jobs and less competent personnel, by forming an Administrator's Alliance and hiring legal counsel. And principals, after months of threatening to join the Teamsters' union, obtained bargaining rights for their association. Together with the other unions representing employees such as custodians, nurses, therapists, and aides, the teachers' and principals' organizations place enormous restraints on the freedom of the school administration. Only the most uninformed or naive of planners would design educational models today without thoroughly investigating the implications for the local unions.

Economic Constraints

Perhaps many of the problems facing school boards today would be eliminated or at least made easier to solve if more funds were available to run the schools. But all the battles with unions, and parents, and government agencies must be fought out against the ominous background of financial crisis. Inflation, pushing up costs for both materials and services, and competition for tax dollars from departments of police, welfare, and urban renewal, among others, place the school board in the ludicrous position of having to meet increasing demands with diminishing or at least static resources. The taxpayers—whether they are parents or not—are revolting and are expressing their anger by striking out at local bond issues and budgets. Pressure from those who do not have children or whose children are in parochial schools is particularly strong, stirring up confusing currents for politicians. The school systems, which were historically made separate from local government, now find that their autonomy has thrust them into a position of antagonist against or competitor with city hall for funds, public support, and prestige.

Other forces, too, are complicating the school systems' task. The national government's effort, limited as it is, to improve the urban situation through such programs as Model Cities and Neighborhood Services, inevitably requires school district cooperation in the local planning effort. The problems of coordination, to say nothing of the problems of steering a course between autocratic efficiency and democratic participation, require enormous time, patience, and energy from already beleaguered administrative staffs. Relations with universities and colleges, which supply the school systems with their teachers, is another heavy responsibility. One constellation of problems relates to the quality and relevance of training programs for urban teachers; another, to the articulation between the public school programs and students and the demands of institutions of higher education. Yet another pressure on school systems is being exerted by groups who have given up on the public schools and are attempting to set up alternative methods of education. Experiments, ranging from schools run by parents to storefront academies, from contractor-operated instruction to voucher systems featuring public payment of tuition at schools selected by parents, are being tried or talked about in many places. Whether successful or not, these ventures outside the traditional public school system serve to dramatize its failures and increase the strain on its resources.

Conclusion

That is what it is like for metropolitan school systems: powerful influences favoring change pressing in from the business community, the ghettos, the youth, and the new breed of teachers; other, equally powerful, forces resisting change being exerted by the conservative ethnic groups, the unions, the taxpayers, and many parents. Politicians tread a narrow line between the warring groups, aligning themselves with one side or the other, depending on where they sense their supporters to be and whether they are liberals such as Lindsay or conservatives such as Daley and Tate. In any case, the school board and the school administration are more and more frequently at the heart of the controversy.

Whatever one's perspective on the educational situation today, one is forced to admit, as did the Rand Corporation, that it is characterized above all by complexity. The crisis deepens: in Philadelphia alone, many blacks are dead as a result of gang rivalries fought outside the schools; in Washington, a vice-principal was shot to death; in East St. Louis, teachers are reportedly carrying guns to class. Current solutions are grim and inadequate, if not absurd, and congressional committees studying school violence, even though they produce concrete proposals, will encounter difficulties in persuading Congress to pay for them.

If statements such as mine seem alarming or exaggerated, perhaps the article in *Phi Delta Kappan,* written by Luvern Cunningham, Dean of the College of Education at Ohio State University (1969), will provide sufficient documentation. Mr. Cunningham took over a midwestern junior high school for a few days, and came away "haunted," to use his word, by the seemingly unanswerable problem of what could be done. "We have no experts in this sort of urban education anywhere. No one," he writes, "has *the* answer. Anyone who thinks he has is a fool. . . ."—and, I might add, a damned fool. Perhaps the problems he describes are a microcosm of the forces that intertwine to dictate what goes on in schools today.

The question is not whether we should change, but whether we can react and adapt fast enough and effectively enough to avert disaster. Will we be able to understand how radical our solutions must be and start arguing, and pleading, and pushing for change? Or will we continue, in Mr. Cunningham's words, to "stand impotent, frightened, disheveled in the face of such tragedy"?

REFERENCES

Cunningham, Luvern L. "Hey Man, You Our Principal? Urban Education as I Saw It." *Phi Delta Kappan* 41, no. 3 (November 1969): 123-28.
"Rand Corporation Finds Analysis of City More Challenging than Study of U.S. Defense Systems." *New York Times* 16 March 1969, p. 49.
Roberts, Wallace. "Can Urban Schools Be Reformed?" *Saturday Review,* 17 May 1969, p. 70.
Sexton, Patricia Cayo. *Education and Income.* New York: Viking Press, 1961.

part III

Operating Models for Metropolitan School Organization

Six currently operating models for the delivery of educational services are presented in this section. They represent cooperative systems that span school system boundaries and challenge the clash between demands for good quality education and equal educational opportunity. The models attempt to minimize the notion that good quality education is for those who can afford it, and maximize the notion of cooperative educational planning for purposeful educational change.

In chapter seven, Hooker and Mueller describe the cooperative federalism model operating in the Minneapolis and St. Paul metropolitan area. This examination of an educational research and development council elaborates on a cooperative effort to develop synergy among a group of school systems. They mention strengths and weaknesses of this council to focus attention on still unsolved problems.

In chapter eight, McKelvey and Harris outline the Board of Cooperative Educational Services model currently operating in New York State. This cooperative system provides broad educational services to member school systems that would not otherwise receive them and provides a state supported cooperative program that has a strong emphasis on manual skills that dignify necessary occupational roles.

In chapter nine, Caligiuri and Berg state the significance of the organization of education in the Catholic Diocese of Buffalo, New York, which they depict as essentially an informal organization, contrary to the common perception of a rigid authoritative system. This analysis of the metropolitan features of a Catholic school system elaborates on implications for and contributions to the study and development of metropolitan school systems.

Heller and Nystrand present, in chapter ten, a description and analysis of the merger of a large city school system and the county in which it resides. The historical development of the merger model focuses on the examples of Nashville and Davidson County in Tennessee, and Louisville and Jefferson County in Kentucky. Merger requires a long process of cooperative planning and political organization directed toward resolution of conflicting points of view by a vote of the people. The merger model challenges the belief that education necessarily must be totally autonomous and separate from other services in a metropolitan plan. It examines the conflict involved in planning the equalization of taxes, race, and power.

In chapter eleven, Rideout describes and analyzes Toronto's metropolitan school system. This unique structure of education came into being as a result of the inadequate tax base in the suburbs, contrary to most situations in the United States. The metropolitan board provides a regional tax base and becomes the arena for negotiated decision making. This nonpartisan education government structure is examined for the strengths and weaknesses that have been highlighted by several years of operation.

The Inner London Education Authority is virtually autonomous from other government units, but is directly attached to the political party in power and the loyal opposition. Griffiths points to the extraordinary features of the London Authority, one of which is the size of the education committee. American education has stressed relatively small governing boards because of a belief in the dysfunction of largeness. The partisan nature of the education committee challenges the efforts in the United States to keep education nonpartisan. Party representatives tend to overstate the issues, which leads to greater clarification. Such discussions seem to make the party in power responsible for good quality educational policy. The propositions that follow the description and elaboration offer suggestions for metropolitan system research and development.

Part three focuses on operating educational delivery systems and examines their development and function in the context of local and regional political, social, and economic conditions. The examination of such structures should add to our knowledge and motivate us to develop educational delivery systems to meet metropolitan educational needs.

7

The Cooperative Federalism Model

Clifford P. Hooker and Van D. Mueller

Educational reform, especially in the Standard Metropolitan Statistical Areas (SMSAs) of the nation is a national goal for the last half of the twentieth century. As Wise observed (1968, p. 3), "The concept of equality of educational opportunity, long a promise of American education, received renewed attention with the Supreme Court's decision in *Brown* v. *Board of Education* in 1954." This occasion gave impetus to the black revolution, saw the emergence of equality as a major guide to constitutional decision, and spawned the egalitarian revolution in judicial doctrine. The Brown decision also signaled the beginning of what Keppel (1966) has described as the second of three revolutions in American education. The first revolution pertained to quantity. Everyone, it was argued, should have a chance to attend a school of some sort. This argument received the sanction of law as all states eventually enacted compulsory attendance statutes. As education became available to all, all were compelled to avail themselves of it.

The second revolution in public education is that of equality of opportunity. This revolution is now under way. The notion that education is the privilege of the privileged and therefore subject to the inequalities of wealth and geography is being challenged in the courts of several states. Citizens are especially incensed over the conditions created by the combination of these two revolutions. It has become clear that children have been compelled to attend unequal schools.

According to Keppel, the third revolution emerging in public education is that of quality. Again, the conflict between earlier educational reforms and the emerging one is clear. Good quality education is often associated with liberty—the freedom of a community to purchase as much education for its youth as it can afford. Advocates of equality of educational opportunity counter with proposals that would place limitations on local options, insisting that everyone must urge good quality education for all. These polar positions on the issues of equal educational opportunity and quality education often separate the central city from the surrounding suburbs. Generally, the central city spokesmen support the egalitarian principles as enunciated recently by the United States Supreme Court. Tussman and tenBroek have provided further legal support to this position (1949): "The Constitution does not require that things different in fact be treated in law as though they were the same. But it does require in its concern for equality, that those who are similarly situated be similarly treated." Benson makes the same point:

> The one universally accepted criterion of a public activity is that it affords equal treatment to equals. With respect to schooling, this implies that any two children of the same abilities shall receive equivalent forms of assistance in developing those abilities, wherever they live in a given state and whatever their parental circumstances are (1965, p. 62).

The representatives of suburban schools, on the other hand, generally agree with the arguments of the early reformers who interpreted equality to mean liberty or the right to get ahead. Belief in this principle has encouraged socially and economically ambitious parents to search for conditions that insure good quality education for their children. An upper middle-class suburb is most conducive to this type of school. Having developed schools of their choice, suburban dwellers reject all proposals to reorganize education in metropolitan areas. The conflict between the revolutions for equality of opportunity and good quality education is brought clearly in focus. Any serious effort to make education equally accessible to all threatens alleged advantages of local control and many of the artifices that have been created to perpetuate the present system.

Most observers of the metropolitan scene would agree that an integration of the central city and suburban views is needed. Both must be accommodated within a new concept and structure for public education in a metropolitan area. While a new structure alone will not eradicate the philosophical conflict inherent in the two views, it will provide a mechanism to manage such conflict and channel its energizing forces to improve education. Certainly the present school district structure, which was created to serve a previous era, is not capable of this task.

COOPERATION + FEDERALISM = SYNERGISM

The redundancy in the term *cooperative federalism* is no thing of beauty and, therefore, in Keats's logic, will not be a joy forever. While the use of one word to describe another with virtually the same meaning may add something to the mix, in this instance it is not precision. The practice does, however, call attention to the need for a new term to provide the refinement that is needed. A search for the best term is now under way. In the meantime, both *cooperative* and *federalism* have been assigned special meanings.

In our contemporary metropolitan society, the term *cooperation* has taken on new dimensions far more encompassing than meanings traditionally ascribed to this concept, particularly in education. The interdependence of city and suburb, of local school districts, state departments of education, professional associations, colleges and university systems, and the federal educational agency, makes up the environment in which *cooperation* is an essential underlying element requisite to the solution of accelerating social and educational problems.

Interorganizational cooperation in education or any other major social activity entails the participation of public and private agencies at every level of government. The significant educational problems associated with the major metropolitan areas cannot be solved by organizational mechanisms of the past, by the independent efforts of hundreds of local school districts and other local political units. The problems of our interdependent urban society are likely to be too complex for the attention of local school districts even through their collective efforts. The Joint Center for Urban Studies has pointed out that

> many areas of concern require not only interlocal
> cooperation but joint action by higher levels of

government. Effective guidance of metropolitan development almost always depends on an intricate coordination of action by local and state governments, often involving federal agencies as well (1964, p. 7).

Until very recently the study of American federalism has emphasized the degree and complexity of arrangements of cooperation among governments and strongly inferred that the initiative in cooperation rested with the national government, not simply because of superior financial resources but also because national action more accurately reflected the realities of social and economic conditions as well as citizens' attitudes and needs (see Wildavsky 1967). Contemporary inquiries have cautioned that this emphasis may be creating a socialist state where only the legal fiction of federalism exists. However, exceedingly stubborn problems persist and defy solution, especially by state and local governments.

The Committee for Economic Development has stated that

fiscal realities have modified the legal concept that the states are the fountain source of all governmental powers. The states created the national government, assigning it certain functions and granting it essential powers. The powers of local units were also granted by the states. Realistically, however, capability of response to public desires and adequate resources take precedence over legal theory (1967, pp. 9-10).

A familiar theme interwoven throughout the current literature on federalism concerns an aspiration to rational decisions, made through rational forms and processes. In metropolitan areas, people do not live and work in compartments described by government boundaries; hence public decisions affecting them cannot be made rationally by local governments, but only by some mechanism reflecting the scope of the living and working pattern. Valerie Earle (1968, pp. 62-86) argues for the development of political community in the metropolitan areas of the country as a requisite to the development of sensible solutions to urban problems. Earle suggests that a larger meaning of American federalism is required, one supplied not by constitutional principle or confrontation, but by cooperation, a partnership between governments in which each is usually not so much concerned about legal rights and authority but rather about getting a job done.

The chaos of structure and functions in urban education can be resolved only through the development of a new awareness of the changing conditions of life in a complex, interdependent society. Hendrik Gideonse borrowed the concept of *synergy* from medical science:

> Synergy refers to the combined or correlated action of different elements of a system to make possible gains of coordinated action which exceeds the sum of the individual efforts. It is a way of achieving the critical mass which puts you over. It provides for a conception of systems in which the cooperating participants support one another in pursuit of a common objective. In short, synergy implies more than interrelation. It implies goal agreement and a continuing relationship. It implies a recognition of the complexity and mutual dependency of the many activities which comprise the human enterprise. Above all, as applied to human affairs, it implies mutual worth and respect (in Markus [1967], p. 33).

The search for an appropriate definition of cooperative federalism will no doubt continue. Meanwhile, the concepts embodied in *synergy* seem to provide an appropriate Rosetta stone.

GUIDELINES FOR COOPERATIVE ACTION

Nine general criteria for the development of cooperative federalism models were derived initially from the published remarks of speakers at a Kansas City conference (Markus 1967) and adapted by the Educational Research and Development Council of the Twin Cities Metropolitan Area, Incorporated in deciding new directions for major collaborative educational planning in the Twin Cities metropolitan area (Mueller 1968).

The guidelines that follow assume major points of convergence with the definition of cooperative federalism presented previously and, in particular, the concept of synergy. It is further assumed that these guidelines provided the primary rationale to support development of the Twin Cities cooperative model and required both acceptance and understanding by planners of this cooperative endeavor.

Guidelines

1. Meaningful cooperation requires commitment based upon the expectation of mutual advantage.

2. Cooperative endeavors are strengthened by involving all communitywide institutions, agencies, and services in implementing a systematic development plan.
3. Goals should be operationally defined, mutually acceptable, and capable of attainment.
4. Success in the attainment of initial goals enhances the likelihood of continued cooperative endeavors.
5. When personnel, resources, and funds are concentrated upon the attainment of a clearly perceived goal, both the impact of the endeavor and the likelihood of its success are strengthened.
6. Coordination among the various agencies is essential if a developing plan is to become the basis for decisions affecting a region.
7. In any cooperative undertaking, sound decisions are dependent upon ready access to a wide range of dependable information.
8. Cooperative endeavors should increase the power of each participant without sacrifice of autonomy.
9. Both the process and product of a cooperative endeavor are strengthened by recognizing that it must be a continuous, evolving activity.

Additional criteria, however, were necessary to guide the structural and functional development of the model. A more specific examination of the arrangements that provided the impetus toward cooperative development reveal the following organizational components:
1. Voluntary participation of school districts within the metropolitan area;
2. Inclusion of the numerous and varied noneducation governments and nonpublic agencies;
3. Securing and maintaining stable fiscal and legal bases; and the
4. Establishment of a governing structure providing equal partnership status for all participating agencies.

The organization of the cooperative federalism model in the Twin Cities was designed to accommodate the development of a variety of educational enterprises. The areas of common concern focused on educational program, finance, and consumer interests. The values associated with these interests seem to be compatible with Cunningham's suggestions (1968):

Education Program Values

These values would include:
Maximum diversity in response to educational needs;
The achievement of structural flexibility in order to realize any program advantages in economies of scale;

The ability of a school system continuously to alter and improve its programs;

The lodging of program decision making as nearly as possible to the affected constituency.

Financial Values

These values would include:

The efficient aggregation of resources;

The equalization of the revenue burden;

The perfection of mechanisms for the differential distribution of resources;

The development of mechanisms for decentralizing the responsibility of defining educational program needs and of effectively attending to the responsibility for budget construction;

The insurance of the best return on each dollar invested.

Consumer's (Citizen's) Values

These values would include:

The extension of citizen's opportunities for affecting educational policy;

The acknowledgement of and response to a wide variation in consumer demands for education.

It is recognized that the achievement of the goals for a cooperative federalism model for Twin Cities metropolitan education was not entirely a matter of conceptualization or of organizational structure. Much depended on the desires of the people, the quality of leadership provided, and the support resources that were available. The efficacy of the concept of synergy translated to organizational terms remains to be evaluated. Therefore, such values of structure and function as we describe provide only an opportunity for a productive and critical analysis of the present state of development of the cooperative federalism model in the Twin Cities metropolitan area.

COOPERATIVE FEDERALISM IN THE TWIN CITIES

If any concept of interorganizational cooperation, that is, cooperative federalism, is to become viable, it must be transformable into programs and activities that affect the course of events.

Background

Cooperative action is inherent in the term *council.* It describes a unified whole formulated of diverse parts; thus the council should contribute to common purposes of separate constituents. No council need operate unless these purposes can be met better in concert than solo. Since obviously these purposes vary among school districts, flexibility in organizational structure and programming is necessary.

Educational needs in the Twin Cities area are in transition, consequently, council functions have undergone frequent reassessment. The Educational Research and Development Council of the Twin Cities Metropolitan Area, Incorporated (ERDC) was created in 1963 by the central cities and suburban communities to promote cooperative school programs and to serve as a catalyst to bring about innovative ventures in the schools and other public and private agencies. Years of experience have by now demonstrated its capacity to use the resources of metropolitan agencies in coping with several types of educational problems. Examination of the early ERDC period provides evidence of the careful, painstaking development effort required to convince decision makers in independent school districts of the potential of cooperative endeavors. While substantial developmental problems still remain to be solved, there seems to be no disagreement about the need or advantage of cooperation. (See Hooker, Mueller, and Davis 1968.)

Historical and Legal Bases

The Council was organized specifically to avoid the weaknesses so typical of school study councils. The transition from a study-discussion orientation to an action-product orientation more closely aligned with Paul Mort's original conception was accomplished by establishing this Council as a legally incorporated entity rather than as a loose association. A legal requirement compelled the immediate establishment of purpose, stipulation of relationships with school and nonschool agencies, and establishment of policies to govern its functioning. Laws in Minnesota are neutral on the subject of inter-district cooperation. While there are no laws forbidding cooperative action, the legislature has studiously avoided compulsory legislation.

Organization and Structure

The ERDC is, in one sense, an expansion of a former agency; in another sense, it is an entirely new organization. It grew out of the

Minneapolis Area School Study Council, which was established in 1958. The newness stems from its incorporation in 1963 as a non-profit, tax-exempt corporation with new purposes and functions and from a strengthened partnership among the school districts of the entire metropolitan area, the University of Minnesota, the State Department of Education, and other organizations and institutions dedicated to educational improvement.

While membership in the previous council extended to two counties of the metropolitan area, the evolution in 1963 saw the membership expand to include school districts from all seven counties included in the metropolitan area (SMSA). Membership as of October 1972 included forty-five of the forty-eight eligible public school districts and also encompassed the private schools of the Archdiocese of Minneapolis and St. Paul.

While membership of the Council is limited to the formal school organizations in the metropolitan area, one of the Council's primary goals is to become familiar with the activities of cultural, educational, and government agencies in order to avoid duplication and to maximize all contributions to the improvement of education. Coordination has been established with such agencies as the Metropolitan Council, Minnesota League of Municipalities, State Planning Agency, Citizens' League, State Department of Public Welfare, Minnesota Symphony, and Minnesota Theatre Company.

The membership of the Council is divided into two categories: active membership, which is open only to public school systems in the seven-county Twin Cities metropolitan area, and associate membership, which is available to other institutions, agencies, and individuals. The Council's financial support is based on a percentage of local school district operating budgets.

The governing body of the Council is a board of directors elected by the superintendents of active member districts. The board of directors, consisting of eight superintendents, meets monthly.

The major research and development efforts of the Council are carried out through a commission structure designed to provide optimum local district participation. As of October 1969, the board of directors had established four commissions and one committee. The members of each unit include at least one representative of each active member school system. The Commission on Administration identifies research and development priorities relating to the organization and operation of schools and school systems. The Commission on Curriculum and Instruction coordinates research, evaluation and in-service activities of instructional programs. The Commission on Exceptional Children coordinates activities and studies designed to strengthen the curriculums for exceptional children. The Audio-Visual Committee assists with, consults, and designs audiovisual programs and materials in cooperation with the commissions and member districts. The newest functional unit, the Commission on Teacher Education, provides a forum for school district adminis-trators and teachers, as well as teacher educators, to design, test, and evaluate new cooperative approaches to the preparation and con-tinuing education of teachers.

Objectives and Purposes

One of Parkinson's laws holds that, once an organization is formed for a good reason, the organization tends to perpetuate itself after that reason has been fulfilled. An organization can justify its continued existence by pursuing new objectives. The stated purpose of the Council at its inception was

> the conduct of responsible research relating to the conditions of learning for children and classroom practice, and the cooperative development of school system personnel and instructional programs through curriculum studies and in-service professional devel-opment programs (Mueller 1968, p. 2).

The keynote was the concept of sharing: sharing problems, ideas, information, and solutions among the school districts of the Twin Cities metropolitan area.

In 1968 new directions for the Council were adopted. The new purpose is

> to promote purposeful educational change through systematic cooperative planning. The terms included in the purpose were assumed to have the following meanings: (a) *cooperative educational planning*—the cooperative development, dissemination, and applica-tion of tools, techniques and relevant data for effect-ing purposeful and continuous educational change; and (b) *purposeful educational change*—those changes which are built upon basic research or theory, tested through pilot or demonstration projects in a represent-ative educational setting, and adopted in a school setting where learner behavior changes can be and are measured. The new objectives of the Council relate to five primary areas of activity: planning, research, as-sessment, development, and dissemination (ibid., p. 9).

Program and Activities

The traditional activities and programs of the Council have included research and development programs related to reaching stated goals. With the adoption of a new focus for Council direction, those traditional activities and programs that have not significantly contributed to planning are being phased out to allow consideration of new, more appropriate activities and programs. A description and review of some of the Council's diversified activities, undertaken and nurtured through cooperation between schools and other agencies follows. The central focus of all ERDC programs has been the concept of sharing.

1. The studies of specific problems common to all school districts in the area have included normative analyses of school district revenue and expenditure patterns, salaries and fringe benefit surveys, and such school finance topics as equalization and municipal overburden. Annual studies have also focused on questions about the numbers of professionals and types of skills required for good quality learning programs. The scope and quality of curricula have also attracted the attention of Council schools. Some studies have been limited to specific cognitive areas, such as sex education, vocational education, and social studies, while others have focused on the effectiveness of instructional models and on mechanisms for curriculum improvements, such as the examination of team teaching practices, elementary school admission policies, and the role of department chairmen in ERDC schools.

2. Dissemination of information on new and emerging educational practice has been coordinated with a broad-scale professional development program for school personnel. The Council has accepted major responsibility for in-service education programs. Workshops, seminars, and clinics have provided teachers, administrators, and school board members with new insights into problems such as decision making, metropolitan planning, educational information processing, instructional technology, organization of instruction in elementary schools, evaluation of personnel, salary policy development, collective bargaining, and program-planning-budgeting systems. Since the Council is associated with the University of Minnesota's College of Education, access to the tremendous intellectual resources of the entire university are made available to the school districts. Also, access to libraries, research laboratories, and computing facilities is accomplished through the Council.

3. The Council has provided access to such metropolitan and state-wide agencies as the Metropolitan Council, Citizens' League, Minnesota Symphony Orchestra, Minnesota Theatre Company, State Planning Agency, and the League of Minnesota Municipalities. The Council thus has provided the structure for dealing with educational problems on a metropolitan basis through the involvement of personnel from school districts and other community agencies and institutions.

4. Council programs have encouraged innovation and experimentation in member school districts through assistance in cooperative planning and through the establishment of pilot or demonstration programs involving several member districts. An example of such a demonstration program with a metropolitan approach is the Cooperative School Rehabilitation Center sponsored by the Council. This experimental research and demonstration project is aimed at establishing a cooperative school rehabilitation program for the less able retarded adolescent who is not served adequately in existing school programs. Major initial support of a five-year program beginning in 1965 was provided by a grant from the Vocational Rehabilitation Administration. These funds have been used to plan and provide a day school program of relatively long-term prevocational and personal adjustment training for mentally retarded adolescents. Through the cooperative efforts of Council school districts, the University of Minnesota, and the state Departments of Education and Public Welfare, the Center provides intensive evaluation counseling, social casework, and placement and follow-up services to over 260 clients from over 40 metropolitan area school districts. Innovation in curriculum and instructional methods developed cooperatively also includes the production of films and video tapes created through the cooperative efforts of the Council, St. Paul and Minnesota Theatre Companies, KTCA (an educational television channel), and other metropolitan artistic and cultural agencies.

Other evidence of cooperative effort is noted in the activities associated with educational information processing services. Through cooperation with local, state, and federal agencies, the Council planned and developed a total information systems consortium. Presently twenty-nine school districts representing over two hundred and fifty thousand students are receiving management, pupil and professional personnel, and computer-assisted instruction. The planning was expressly designed to involve all potential users of a cooperative service center. After completion of the initial planning and development, the operation of this cooperative program was turned over to a separate legal entity, the Minnesota School Districts Data Processing Joint Board, and direct ERDC involvement with the program ceased in 1967.

5. It has been the policy of the Council to encourage research relevant to the cause of education in the Twin Cities metropolitan area. This encouragement has included the identification and publication of reports of research or annotated lists of research projects, the initiation and sponsorship of research projects, the consideration of support for research projects initiated outside the Council, and the support and conduct of personnel and curriculum improvement activities within the schools of the Council. In essence, the Council determines the research that will give insight into the problem under consideration, conducts such enumerative surveys as are necessary to define the scope and dimensions of the problem, designs and conducts basic research to develop needed knowledge, identifies the possible solutions, evaluates these solutions in terms of their adequacy for solving the problem, and communicates the desired solution through publications, workshops, and clinics. This general procedure applies equally to school organization and administration, curriculum and teaching methods, to the identification of educational needs within the metropolitan area, and to the determination of the adequacy of current efforts to meet these needs.

The structural procedure required to accomplish this mission is titled *The Research Clearing House.* A board of review including in its members administrators, teachers, and university research specialists monitors the process and recommends actions to the Council's Board of Directors. Research needs of the schools are shared with graduate students and university researchers so that their efforts may be directed to priority needs of the schools. Although the Council is just emerging from its organizational phase, research priorities have been established and several dozen basic and applied research studies have been completed. The school districts are supporting research on a scale that few, if any, independent school districts could implement.

Voluntary associations have been credited with reinforcing our democratic political system in three ways. The Carnegie Corporation suggests (1967, pp. 8-9) that they distribute power widely in the society and permit the individual a share of it; enable the ordinary citizen to understand better the processes of democracy through his own participation in them, and provide a mechanism for the continual promotion of social change. This concept of involvement of individuals seems to be analagous to the Council's structure and intention of involving school districts and other metropolitan agencies in a mutual effort to solve urban educational problems.

Council programs and activities have generally resulted from the efforts of member districts to answer the question, "What unique functions can be carried out by a coalition of school districts, other government and private agencies, and a major university?" It could well be that only a fraction of the strength inherent in this relationship has been discovered, or else that the solution to metropolitan educational ills depends upon different conceptual, structural, and functional responses.

THE MODEL'S STRENGTHS AND WEAKNESSES

The Educational Research and Development Council of the Twin Cities has demonstrated the advantages of interdistrict cooperation in school improvement. Tangible evidence of achievement abounds in published research studies, monographs, and conference reports. (For an extensive review of the activities of the Educational Research and Development Council of the Twin Cities metropolitan area, Incorporated, see Hooker, Mueller, and Davis [1968], pp. 328-51.) Moreover, the general level of acceptance of the Council, with no district's failing to continue its membership after joining, suggests that its work is valued. However, of greatest significance is the number of innovations and experiments in the Twin Cities area schools that can be traced directly to the Council's activities.

As a model of cooperative federalism, the Council has been most effective in hastening the coming of the quality revolution in education, within individual school districts. The loose organization of the Council, with voluntary membership and local option on participation in any activity, readily adjusts to the varied interests and needs of the constituent districts. In this fashion, the Council pools the resources of small groups of districts or the total membership to work on projects. The central thrust of such activity is generally improvement within individual districts. Exceptions to this analysis seem to be present in only those circumstances in which programs and activities have focused on cooperative planning. Even then, such programs as the Cooperative School Rehabilitation Center and the Cooperative Information Services were removed from the Council's jurisdiction when they began actual operation.

The principal limitations of the cooperative federalism model reside in the philosophical conflict between quality and equality in education. While the Council can promote improvement in the quality of education within districts, it is less effective in achieving equality of educational opportunity for the entire metropolitan area. As a general pattern over past years of operation, the major recipients of Council services tend to be the "haves" rather than the "have nots." The continuing problem of orienting services to meet the needs of the two largest members—Minneapolis and St. Paul—should also be noted. The disparity between the best and the worst has not been a major concern of the Council. The representatives of the districts are inclined to view equality as freedom to get ahead, and they seek to utilize the Council to achieve that end. This is not to be critical of the administrators or board members for, indeed, such progress as has been achieved in recognizing the problems of others could undoubtedly be ascribed to the communcation opportunities provided by the Council's activities and programs. However, it remains that unequal distribution of wealth and educational needs combined with a large measure of local control of education simply make it difficult for Twin Cities school people to be educational statesmen and also serve the special interests of their constituents. Thus, it appears that the cooperative federalism model suffers the same limitations as its constituent school districts and, therefore, cannot respond to the current revolution of equality of educational opportunity except within individual districts.

The cooperative federalism model in the Twin Cities adds to the capacity of educators and interested laymen to discuss the problems besetting education and to engage in cooperative planning at an elementary level where organizational overlap and conflict are not present. Cooperative planning efforts have been most successful in filling gaps in programs and services, rather than in providing general improvement. However, the inability to execute plans makes problem solving near impossible. If the Council is to justify the definition of a cooperative federation, it must be legitimized by statute and given sufficient management and regulatory power to accomplish its purposes. Moreover, in creating a stronger federalism, order must replace chaos in the local school district structure. No council can establish a true partnership between districts that have been gerrymandered to create tax islands, ghettos, and cellophane sanctuaries. A major restructuring of local school units in not only the Twin Cities area but also in metropolitan areas is a prerequisite to the creation of a truly cooperative federalism. This problem was revealed in studies conducted in St. Louis and Kansas City (Hooker and Mueller 1969). The multitude of tiny school districts surrounding those cities and the enormous bureaucracies in the cities have spawned virtually every educational problem that can be imagined. There is simply no solution to these problems short of major surgery on existing structures. Such a need also exists in the Minneapolis-St. Paul area.

The principal alternatives Hooker and Mueller offered were the Supra System Model or a Cooperative Federalism Model. The Supra System was rejected mainly because of the large bureaucracy that would be needed to govern school districts with more than three hundred thousand pupils. While some progress has been made in decentralizing authority within such systems, the center continues to exert the strong gravitational pull in decision making. As Polley has observed:

> When authority is decentralized, the person granted local power remains responsible to the same group of officials that delegated the authority. Because local officials are responsible to higher authority, rather than to those they serve, their clients have no direct means of influencing policy or action, even more important, perhaps, the official loses the freedom of action which true responsibility could confer on him. What now exists ... in most large cities is authority without responsibility (1962, pp. 122-123).

Effective decentralization requires that responsibility commensurate with delegated authority be exercised at the level at which decisions are made and action taken. Accomplishing this objective in urban school systems requires organizational patterns that produce an immediate interaction between school personnel and people at the local level.

This persuasion dictated a cooperative federalism model for St. Louis and Kansas City. The first step was to recommend a restructuring of local school units. Application of selected criteria to the conditions in the two major metropolitan areas in Missouri resulted in a recommendation for nine and sixteen districts in the metropolitan areas of Kansas City and St. Louis respectively, each having approximately thirty thousand students. In each instance, the plan recommended abolishing the central city districts as they now exist. Portions of the cities were to be joined with the suburbs to form local school units.

The plan also envisaged a regional board of education with limited responsibilities and local boards of education to perform most of the traditional functions of a school board. The regional board would levy a uniform tax for education throughout the region and distribute such tax money to local boards of education. The regional board would also construct all school buildings, operate vocational education and compensatory education programs, and provide long-range planning for education. The boards in the local school units would select and assign teachers and administrators, determine the quality and scope of the education program, levy local taxes within prescribed limits, and direct all pupil personnel services.

This example of a cooperative federalism could be the synergetic force to deal with contemporary problems in metropolitan areas. It circumvents the limitations present in the existing Twin Cities cooperative endeavor and, on paper at least, better meets the guidelines discussed for such action. While it places serious limitations on the freedom of citizens in homogeneous communities to improve schools without helping others in a process, it recognizes the interdependence of cities and suburbs and possibly provides a last opportunity for the suburban dweller to have some control over education in the central city. Failure to obtain and exercise such control may result in central city schools that are counterproductive, not only to values of city dwellers but also to the values possessed by those who use the city but reside outside its boundaries. The politics of metropolitan educational change require a new, specialized structure, flexible enough to allow concerted efforts to be focused on all related parts of the problem—synergetic in conception and implementation.

REFERENCES

Benson, Charles S. *The Cheerful Prospect: A Statement on the Future of Public Education.* Boston: Houghton Mifflin, 1965.

Carnegie Corporation. *The Quasi Nongovernmental Organization.* Annual Report, 1967. New York: The Carnegie Corporation, 1968.

Committee for Economic Development. *Modernizing Local Government.* New York: The Committee, 1966.

Cunningham, Luvern L. "Organization of Education in Metropolitan Areas." In *Metropolitanism: Its Challenge to Education* (Sixty-seventh Yearbook of the National Society for the Study of Education part 2), edited by Robert J. Havighurst, pp. 91-122. Chicago: University of Chicago Press, 1968.

Earle, Valerie. *Federalism: Infinite Variety in Theory and Practice.* Itaska, Ill.: Peacock, 1968.

Hooker, Clifford P., and Mueller, Van D. *Equal Treatment to Equals—A New Structure for Public Schools in the Kansas City and St. Louis Metropolitan Areas.* A report to the Missouri School District Reorganization Commission, June 1969. Jefferson City, Mo.: Missouri School District Reorganization Commission, 1969.

Hooker, Clifford P.; Mueller, Van D.; and Davis, Donald. "Cooperation Among School Districts in a Metropolitan Area: A Case Study." In *Metropolitanism: Its Challenge to Education* (Sixty-seventh Yearbook of the National Society for the Study of Education), edited by Robert J. Havighurst, pp. 328-351. Chicago: University of Chicago Press, 1968.

Joint Center for Urban Studies of the Massachusetts Institute of Technology and Harvard University, in cooperation with the Subcommittee on Intergovernmental Relations of the Committee on Governmental Relations of the United States Senate. *The Effectiveness of Metropolitan Planning.* Washington, D.C.: U.S. Government Printing Office, 1964.

Keppel, Francis. *The Necessary Revolution in American Education.* New York: Harper and Row, 1966.

Markus, Frank W., ed. *Partners for Educational Progress (PEP): An Analysis of Cooperation: Importance, Status, Principles, Examples and Action Programs.* Kansas City, Mo.: University of Missouri, School of Education, The Metropolitan School Study Group, 1967.

Mueller, Van D., ed. "The Educational Research and Development Council of the Future." Mimeographed. Minneapolis, Minn.: The Educational Research and Development Council, 1968.

Polley, John W. "Decentralization with Urban School Systems." In *Education In Urban Society*, edited by B. J. Chandler, Lindley L. Stiles, and John I. Kitsuse, pp. 117-28. New York: Dodd, Mead, 1962.

Tussman, Joseph, and tenBroek, Jacobus. "Equal Protection of the Laws." *California Law Review* 37 (September 1949): 341-81.

Wise, Arthur E. *Rich Schools, Poor Schools.* Chicago: University of Chicago Press, 1968.

8

The Board of Cooperative Educational Services Model

Troy V. McKelvey and William B. Harris

and William B. Harris

This chapter is concerned with the Board of Cooperative Educational Services (BOCES), an educational organization servicing most of the suburban and rural areas surrounding the city of Buffalo, New York. The data were collected through a series of personal interviews with administrative staff members of BOCES (the superintendent, the assistant superintendent, directors, and supervisors), a sample of superintendents of school districts that belong to and share BOCES' services, and a review of official documents. The material presented represents the perceptions of the writers and confirmation that the representation is reasonable was received from the BOCES organization.

In 1948 the New York State legislature (New York Education Law, article 40, sections 1958, 1959 as amended) authorized local school districts to form Boards of Cooperative Educational Services (BOCES). These corporate bodies are extensions of the local schools, subject to their control. The legislation underscores the BOCES as a step toward the ultimate organization of an intermediate district.

Previously, the supervisory district organization, with a professional staff of only the District Superintendent (in all but a few instances), attempted to provide a general supervisory service to the school districts under his jurisdiction. A forerunner of BOCES was an earlier board known as the Vocational Extension Board that legalized joint efforts by two or more school districts and offered shared programs. However, it seems to have declined partly because of the inception and growth of the BOCES movement. By comparison, BOCES is a more flexible, comprehensive, and responsive organization in which the participating schools share equally in control and influence.

Purposes of BOCES

The purposes of a BOCES are:

1. To appoint a district superintendent of schools.
2. To operate the supervisory district educational program and to prepare a budget to finance that program.
3. To make available on request cooperative part-time educational services to school districts too small to employ full-time teachers in certain subjects.
4. To make available on request, under certain conditions, cooperative part-time educational services supplemental to local staff to provide adequate staffing and services.
5. To coordinate and administer surveys and research projects to determine the need for cooperative services and the manner of improvement of educational opportunities in supervisory districts.
6. To introduce new cooperative service to meet the needs determined from surveys and studies.
7. To develop and operate area programs in vocational and technical education.
8. To assist in the development, coordination, and operation of area programs for the physically handicapped and mentally retarded.
9. To provide means of communication between and among teachers, administrators, and boards of education to improve educational practices.
10. To provide administrative and supervisory service on an areawide basis as a responsibility of the supervisory district program to improve the quality of education in the district's schools (The University of the State of New York 1962, p. 1).

General Criteria for BOCES

The general criteria for operating a BOCES are:

1. Service must be on a truly shared basis. A service rendered to a single district alone will not be considered shared. Service must be provided to two or more districts to be considered a shared service. Services shared between boards of cooperative educational services must originate with one board and be made available to the other board by contract.
2. Applications for service to be established in place of services presently provided on a sound basis by individual districts will not be approved.
3. Applications for services that could or should be rendered effectively by individual local districts will not be approved.
4. Services provided must meet recognized standards to justify expenditure of state money.
5. Arrangements that provide a single district with more than 3/5 (60 percent) of a full-time position will not be approved. A district may not expect to use most of a person's time in token sharing with one or two other districts.
6. Where shared services are proposed for school districts that are outlined for reorganization, evidence must be presented to indicate that such services will not retard reorganization. Where it appears evident that shared services are retarding reorganization, it may be necessary to limit or discontinue shared services to schools so affected.
7. Approval of a shared service application is for one year only. The Assistant Commissioners will review annually the services offered and will determine which may be continued and which should be terminated.
8. Boards of cooperative educational services may provide cooperative services for which no state aid is claimed. Applications for such services must be approved by the Commissioner of Education before the board can offer such shared services without state aid.
9. Sparsity of population, distance, and other pertinent factors will be given due consideration with respect to criteria for specific services.

10. Physical facilities essential to the effective render-
    ing of a service must be available and must meet
    department standards.
11. Combinations of classroom teaching or special
    service areas that reasonably may be considered
    full-time local positions will not be approved on a
    cooperative basis; e.g., agriculture-industrial arts,
    nurse teacher-attendance teacher, industrial arts-
    driver education.
12. Teachers and other professional employees of
    boards of cooperative educational services shall be
    subject to the same certification requirements as
    though they were employed by local school dis-
    tricts.
13. A person may not be an employee of the coopera-
    tive board providing service to a school district
    and at the same time be an employee of the local
    school district in a similar or different in-
    structional area (ibid., pp. 7-8).

Membership in BOCES

School districts of a Supervisory District may, by a majority
vote of their Boards of Education and School Trustees and with the
approval of the State Commissioner of Education, establish a
BOCES. An independent school district, which is not a member of
the Supervisory District but which lies within the territorial jurisdiction of the Supervisory District, may become a member of the
BOCES upon the resolution of the Board of Education and the
BOCES organization. These resolutions are subject to the approval of
the Commissioner of Education. Once this resolution is approved,
the school district may not withdraw from membership and, regardless of whether it utilizes BOCES services or not, would still have to
participate in the *administrative costs* of operating the BOCES.

In 1963 an amendment to the original New York education law
extended BOCES membership to city and village school districts.
However, this extension is limited to cities with a student enrollment
of less than one hundred and twenty-five thousand. This present
restriction affects the five cities of New York, Yonkers, Syracuse,
Rochester, and Buffalo.

Financing of BOCES

BOCES is supported by two sources of revenue: local and
state.

Local Support

The BOCES budget is in two parts: administrative costs, which are charged to all member school districts, and service costs, which are charged to those member school districts that participate in specific cooperative services.

A = Administrative Costs (mandatory for all members):

$$\frac{\text{District Weighted Average Daily Attendance (WADA)}}{\text{Total BOCES WADA}}$$

= % of total WADA

B = Service Costs (only for services used):

Cost of services x % of use

= District share

A = Administrative Costs + B = Service Costs

= The total assessment for each member school system

State Support

Requests for services from BOCES are approved by the state before the beginning of each fiscal year. The state supports the costs of all services that are approved. State aid is returned to BOCES the following year, with the exception of Rental or Building Aid, which is paid in the current year. This aid to BOCES is separate and distinct from regular state aid for education and is not subject to the $860 per pupil state-aid ceiling that applies to regular school districts in the state. Formulas for state aid are:

Service and Administrative Aid (paid the following year):

District Service and Administrative Costs
– Salary excess over $8,500

= Approved Costs

Approved Costs x District Aid Ratio (or Save-Harmless on previous year's BOCES aid)

= BOCES Aid

If the BOCES aid ratio is greater than the District Aid Ratio, the following formula is used to compute state aid for Administrative and Service Costs:

$$\frac{\text{Approved Expenditures x 6 mills}}{\text{True Value Tax Rate}}$$

= BOCES percentage True Value Tax Rate

Building Aid (paid on the current year):

District share of rents and/or building costs
x District Aid Ratio

= District share of Building Aid

Total BOCES state aid:

Service and Administrative Aid + Building Aid

= Total aid

Cooperative Board Membership

The Cooperative Board consists of between five and nine members who are elected by a majority vote of School Board members of component member school districts at an annual meeting held each April. They serve for five years, and the elections are staggered so that terms are not completed all in the same year. Except for employees of a school district within the BOCES area, any eligible voter can be a candidate for the Cooperative Board. School districts that have more than five Board of Education members are limited to five votes on any matters relating to the Cooperative Board of BOCES.

The Board of Cooperative Educational Services is a separate entity from the school district Boards of Education but, in effect, is a legal extension of the local school districts into an area organization (see figure 8:1).

The District Superintendent of Schools

One of the chief powers of the Cooperative Board is to appoint a District Superintendent of Schools and then, upon the recommendation of the District Superintendent, to employ administrative assistants, teachers, supervisors, clerical help, and other personnel to

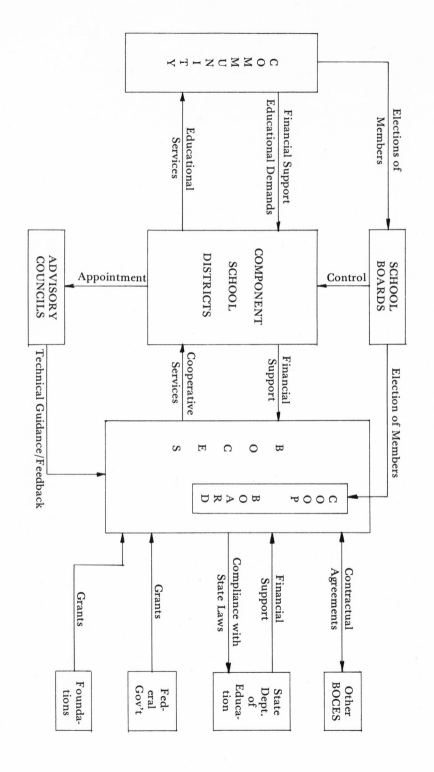

FIGURE 8:1. THE BOCES SYSTEM

carry out the administration and services of BOCES. The District Superintendent of Schools becomes the chief executive officer of BOCES and the Superintendent of schools serving his supervisory district. As a result of his two distinct and separate responsibilities, the superintendent has two administrative functions (see figure 8:2). His salary as a member of the staff of the State Commissioner of Education is supplemented by a supervisory district, and his appointment runs for five years.

Ownership of Property

As a legal corporate body, BOCES owns all property in the district vested in it when it is established, transferred to it, or constructed by it later.

Advisory Boards

BOCES operates primarily in a service and advisory capacity for component member school districts. Each member school district is directly involved in planning cooperative service programs by way of the Chief School Administrators Council, an advisory council made up of the administrative heads of each of the member school districts, which initiates new services when needed, and when member school districts are sufficiently interested. Other advisory councils in the organization include the advisory councils for occupational education (required by law), curriculum, communications, special education, the Data Processing School Users Committee, and the Learning Disorders Screening Council.

ERIE DISTRICT # 1

The BOCES of the First Supervisory District, Erie County (Erie District #1) as it is today is the result of a consolidation of two existing BOCES, Erie districts #1 and #2 in 1963, which brought together eighteen school systems. Since then, four other school systems (Sloan, Kenmore, Hopevale, and the City of Tonawanda) joined, and one small district merged with a larger district so that the total number of member districts in 1972 was twenty-one. BOCES Erie District # 1 now covers approximately 800 square miles of Erie County, surrounding the city of Buffalo. The combined school enrollment is approximately one hundred and twenty thousand pupils. From a first year budget in 1963 of approximately

FIGURE 8:2. DISTRICT SUPERINTENDENT—BOCES

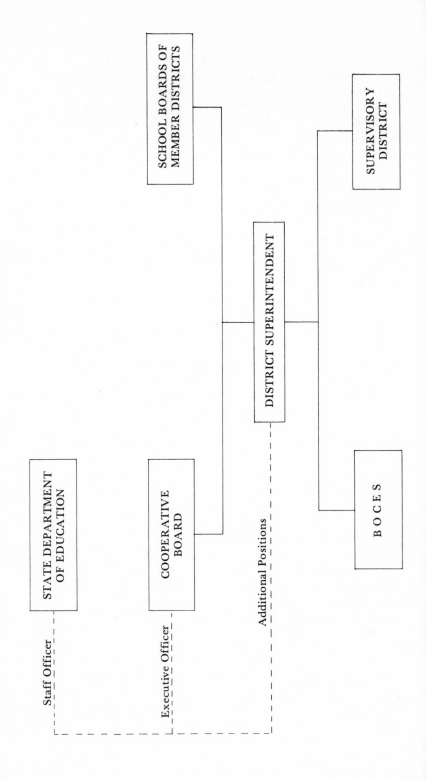

TABLE 8:1. COMPONENT MEMBER SCHOOL SYSTEMS,
ERIE DISTRICT #1

School system	Enrollment	Area (sq. miles)
Akron Central	2,044	120
Alden Central	3,075	144
Amherst Central	2,848	
Amherst District #13	1,096	5
Amherst District #18	1,325	
Cheektowaga Central	3,789	11
City of Tonawanda	5,206	20
Clarence Central	4,606	55
Cleveland Hill	2,631	6
Depew	3,949	13
Frontier Central	6,981	24
Grand Island Central	4,299	35
Hamburg Central	6,002	31
Hopevale	30	1
Kenmore	19,726	50
Lancaster Central	6,863	34
Maryvale	7,375	6
Sweet Home Central	7,470	12
Sloan	2,952	5
West Seneca Central	14,744	24
Williamsville Central	11,840	40

$1,800,000, BOCES Erie District #1 has grown to a budget of approximately $11,000,000 for 1972/73. Services are provided in occupational and special education, and computer, instructional, shared, and administrative services. This BOCES serves as the administrative unit for regional planning services to the six western New York counties (see figure 8:3).

The district superintendent of BOCES Erie #1 also administers a supervisory district consisting of six school systems headed by supervisory principals: Amherst Central, Amherst District #13, Amherst District #18, Akron Central, Cleveland Hill, and Hopevale (see table 8:2 for financial data).

Occupational Education

BOCES Erie District #1 has four occupational centers, which serve 3,200 students (see figure 8:4). Two occupational centers were established in 1961—Harkness and Potter Road. For the two previous years technical and trade training was conducted in rented facilities.

FIGURE 8:3. BOCES ADMINISTRATIVE ORGANIZATION

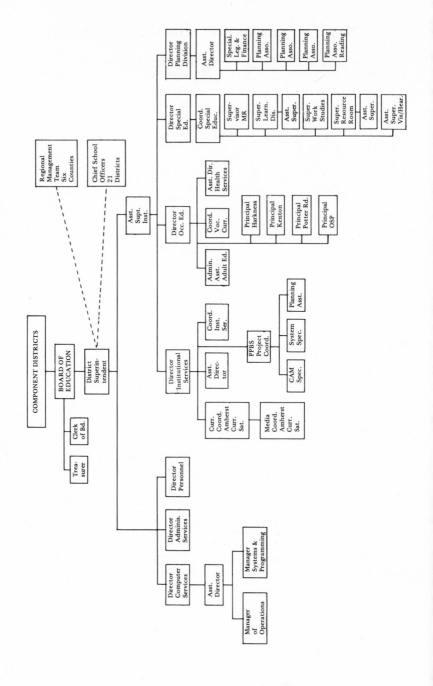

FIGURE 8:4. ADMINISTRATIVE ORGANIZATION—OCCUPATIONAL EDUCATION

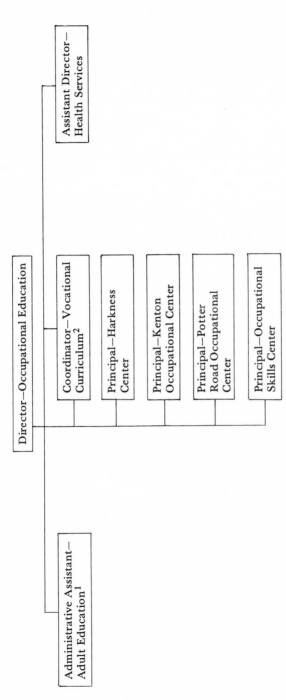

Note: All personnel are supported through district requests for service, with the exceptions noted below.
1. Fifty percent of salary and expenses are provided by federal grant.
2. One hundred percent of salary and expenses provided by federal grant.

TABLE 8:2. BOCES #1

	Spec. Ed. Services	Tuition & Home Teaching	Occupa- tional	Shared Services	Computer Services	Instruc. Services
Amherst # 1	90,888	11,910	93,110	24,654	33,413	116,432
Amherst #13	122,617	1,200	—	24,305	8,553	37,845
Amherst #18	153,398	400	—	24,305	8,996	37,889
Grand Is.	104,522	20,394	50,785	—	16,436	18,456
Akron	65,900	650	83,130	17,374	11,297	18,881
Alden	98,198	18,402	59,324	11,093	15,072	24,966
Cheekt. #1	169,115	38,506	64,215	11,094	26,202	48,324
Maryvale	194,369	34,000	73,350	—	34,144	40,475
Cleve. Hill	125,430	23,310	61,125	8,874	8,283	23,945
Frontier	295,273	26,334	333,582	—	14,062	49,933
Clarence	134,393	14,006	62,755	—	38,225	29,788
Depew	113,573	26,165	57,050	13,313	825	15,429
Lancaster	283,454	13,220	81,500	—	44,220	30,891
Hamburg	227,554	13,443	133,907	20,500	37,510	70,463
Williamsv.	349,131	33,531	115,725	25,140	92,108	87,264
Sloan	107,874	13,680	167,890	—	985	25,933
Sweet Home	488,060	22,670	73,350	—	34,070	24,372
West Seneca	322,315	48,961	305,625	—	62,356	102,805
Tonawanda	77,821	12,451	253,670	—	17,325	42,307
Kenmore	234,268	155,000	606,975	—	140,000	38,500
BOCES Other			61,940			
Hopevale			22,005			
Sub Total	3,758,153	528,233	2,761,013	180,652	644,082	884,898
Others	4,587		13,336		598,086	34,626
CFK Ltd.						3,000
Title II						50,000
Title III						
Publications						
NYS Ed. Conf. Bd.						
Escrow						
TOTAL	3,762,740	528,233	2,774,349	180,652	1,242,168	972,524

BUDGET SUMMARY 1972/73

Planning	Transportation	Rental	Administration	Gross Total	Est. State Aid & Bal. (Credit)	Bal. Due 72-73 Net Total
2,347	20,100	16,932	8,611	418,397	250,560	167,837
772	7,000	5,148	2,618	210,058	110,517	99,541
1,000	5,000	6,006	3,054	240,048	133,527	106,521
1,714	—	20,021	10,182	242,510	160,602	81,908
2,115	—	9,896	5,033	214,276	140,371	73,905
—	250	14,415	7,331	249,051	138,874	110,177
2,036	10,982	17,961	9,134	397,569	172,643	224,926
5,400	1,800	36,266	18,443	438,247	253,318	184,929
3,855	2,475	13,957	7,098	278,352	138,726	139,626
2,765	—	33,692	17,134	772,775	449,628	323,147
2,205	385	24,025	12,218	318,000	190,365	127,635
—	19,882	16,360	8,320	270,917	162,921	107,996
3,100	5,870	32,777	16,669	511,701	288,254	223,447
8,447	29,850	28,544	14,516	584,734	309,399	275,335
—	750	53,827	27,374	784,850	440,050	344,800
—	10,000	15,273	7,767	349,402	165,450	183,952
—	37,510	33,692	17,134	730,858	386,938	343,920
3,800	2,589	63,894	32,494	944,839	532,603	412,236
2,250	20,988	25,798	13,120	465,730	313,392	152,338
7,800	—	103,536	52,650	1,338,729	598,318	740,411
3,234				65,174		65,174
						22,005
52,840	175,431	572,020	290,900	9,826,217	5,336,456	4,511,766
85,923				736,558		736,558
				3,000		3,000
				50,000		50,000
133,641				133,641		133,641
3,000				3,000		3,000
17,000				17,000		17,000
1,800				1,800		1,800
294,204	175,431	572,020	290,900	10,771,216	5,336,456	5,456,765

In 1971, a third center was established in the northern area of the county—the Kenton Center.

The Harkness Center has 36 teachers and 1,135 students; the Potter Road Center has 34 teachers and 1,147 students; the Kenton Center has 21 teachers and 745 students. A fourth center, and the most recently established, the Occupational Skills Center, is designed for problem adolescents and school dropouts and has 180 students and 8 full-time and 4 part-time teachers. The students spend alternate weeks at the center, learning communications skills and receiving occupational training. The intervening weeks are spent in their own schools. All students are bused from their schools to the various centers where they attend classes on a half-day basis, except for the students at the Occupational Skills Center, as mentioned previously.

The occupational education division also cooperates with local industries and hospitals in work-study and nursing training programs, and provides occupational training for adults in its shops and laboratories during the evening. The courses for adults are approved for apprenticeship training and veterans benefits.

The basic training programs offered are:

Trade—auto body repair, auto diesel, auto mechanics, building maintenance, commercial art, cosmetology, dental office assisting, data processing, electronics maintenance, food preparation and service, heating and air conditioning, home and institutional health services, household appliance repair, machine shop practice, mechanical design and construction;

Multi-occupational orientation for students with special needs—assembly and bench work, building and grounds maintenance, food service, gas station operation, mail room operation, practical nursing, welding;

Technical—electronics;

Work-Study—part-time sales and related work, Vocational Industrial Cooperative Program (for multi-district work-study coordinators);

Adult education program—Occupational Extension Courses: auto body repair, auto mechanics, electronics, computer circuitry, fundamentals of refrigeration, machine shop practice, numerical computer programming; Practical nursing;

Driver Training.

In addition to the twenty-two occupational courses, students are offered placement guidance services.

The curriculum development coordinator conducts research and consults with occupational teachers, administrators, school district personnel, teacher training institutions, and post-secondary schools.

BOCES Erie District #1 also contracts with the city of Buffalo to provide occupational training for approximately 130 additional students of component member systems. Tuition and transportation are handled by BOCES and later charged to the school system. (See Table 8:2, BOCES District #1 Budget Summary for 1972/73.) These students need occupational training that is not available in the four occupational centers, but can be provided by the Buffalo school system.

Special Education

The Special Education Department provides services for children who are emotionally handicapped because of physical, mental, or emotional problems. Its facilities are leased whenever possible within the member districts. The department coordinates and supervises the programs and provides the teachers (see figure 8:5).

The department is currently operating twelve classes for trainable retarded children, fifty for educable retarded children, and

FIGURE 8:5. ADMINISTRATIVE ORGANIZATION—SPECIAL EDUCATION

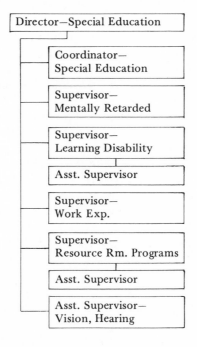

Note: All personnel are supported through district requests for service.

fifty-six for children who have special learning difficulties. It also provides special resource rooms staffed by fifty-five teachers for children with learning disorders and five for children with impaired hearing. The services of itinerant teachers for the blind, the partially sighted, and those whose hearing is impaired, speech therapists, psychologists, and social workers are shared among the member school systems.

The department provides for: children with seeing and hearing difficulties, and those who are mentally retarded; in-service teacher training and child evaluation; and separate summer programs for the mentally retarded, for preschool children and those with learning difficulties, and, again, in-service teacher training.

Physically handicapped students attend other school systems or community agencies within the city of Buffalo, and the Special Education department coordinates placement and tuition payments and contracts for the necessary transportation (see table 8:2).

Computer Services

The Computer Services Center is equipped with a 370-145 computer and provides fifty-five member school systems with a number of services and programs (see table 8:2 and figure 8:6):
Integrated School Information Services:
> *Students*—census, scoring of standardized tests, transcription generation, scheduling, grade reporting, attendance reporting, transportation scheduling;
> *Finance*—payroll, accounts payable, budget analysis and preparation, cafeteria accounting, bid list generation, bus maintenance control, plant and facilities inventory;
> *Staff*—professional and nonprofessional, skills inventory;
> *Instructional use of the computer*—Computer Based Resource Units (CBRU), computer science, computer math, Computer Assisted Instruction via terminal (CAI), in-service training for computer use.

Currently fifty-five school districts in seven western New York counties use the services of the center for pupil and financial records. Additional administrative charges are added to the service costs for those school systems that are not members of BOCES Erie District #1.

Instructional Services

The Instructional Services department (see figure 8:7) operates a Learning Resource Center, film library, and materials production

FIGURE 8:6. ADMINISTRATIVE ORGANIZATION—COMPUTER SERVICES

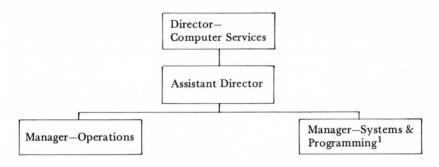

Note: All personnel are supported through district requests for service, with the exception noted below.
1. Seventy-five percent of salary and expenses provided by state and federal funds; the remainder by requests for service.

and instructional television services, and provides in-service training and consultative services. The department also researches, tests, designs, and constructs new curriculum programs. The programs include:

Learning Resources Center
Teacher Training Program—modern mathematics, systems training, biology, geography, chemistry, instructional TV utilization, metallurgy, developing the middle school, and economics;
Materials production and design, film library, instructional television, videotape library, communications planning, duplication of audio- and videotapes, consulting on bids and purchases, and in-service training;
TV repair and maintenance;
Performing arts.

Regional Planning Services

The BOCES regional planning services (see figure 8:8) conducts a variety of comprehensive activities to assist participating districts to improve planning skills; it runs workshops for specialized school personnel and acts as a consultant on single or multidistrict planning problems. It publishes comparative studies of salaries, analyses of school district financial policy, and bulletins on legislative developments affecting education. The division also represents education

FIGURE 8:7. ADMINISTRATIVE ORGANIZATION–INSTRUCTIONAL SERVICES

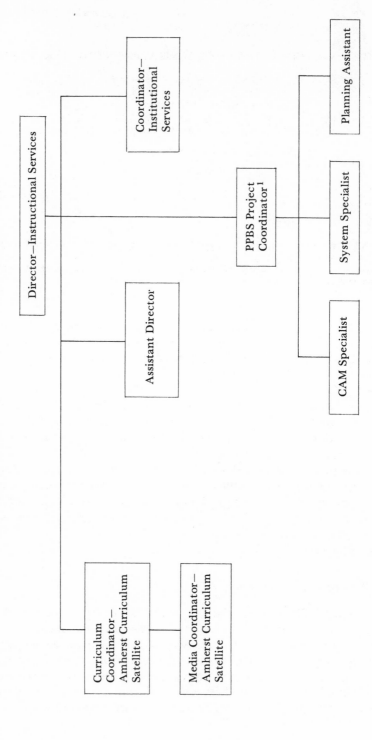

Note: All personnel are supported through district requests for service, with the exception noted below.
1. Partially supported by state, federal, and local funds.

FIGURE 8:8. ADMINISTRATIVE ORGANIZATION—REGIONAL PLANNING

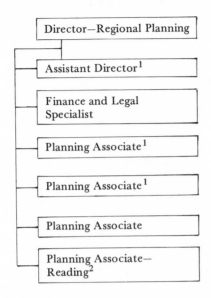

Note: All personnel are supported by district requests for service, with the exceptions noted
below.
1. One hundred percent of salary and expenses are provided by federal funds.
2. Partially supported by state, federal, and local funds.

interests, when they come under the jurisdiction of other regional
planning agencies, and coordinates the participation of western New
York school districts in Project Redesign, a statewide project of the
New York State Department of Education to effect change in education (Board of Cooperative Educational Services 1972). Examples of
the department's activities would include: the development of financial profiles to give boards of education an idea of financial policy
and its relationship to other school districts of the region; budget
simulations to assist boards of education to project their budgets for
the next year, anticipate state aid, predict tax rates, and develop
alternatives before budgets are determined; five-year plans for developing philosophy and broad goals, making objectives operational,
and providing a comprehensive accountability system; goal-setting at
the district and school level for assessing educational needs, project-
ing possible future occurrences and conditions, and identifying activities for accomplishing goals and objectives.

Workshops in the evaluation of pupils and teachers, curriculum design, decision making, and school board policy are offered, as are planning activities with classified personnel and training in the teaching of management by objective (Lamitie 1972).

Shared Specialists

BOCES provides the administration and offers the services of professional specialists to member school systems (see table 8:2), home teaching, and a psychological internship program. Consultative psychiatric assistance, when needed, is contracted for and coordinated by BOCES.

Shared specialists are provided to schools needing less than full-time assistance. Presently there are five psychologists, two social workers, and seven speech therapists on the staff of the Coordinator of Special Education.

Contractual Agreements

When practicable and logical, BOCES provides and contracts for some services with other BOCES, as well as with other agencies to prevent unnecessary duplication of effort, excessive travel time, and inefficiency. For example, BOCES Erie District #1 contracts to receive, for its member school systems, programs for the physically handicapped that are provided by various school systems and agencies in Buffalo. The district itself provides data processing services for school systems of the eight-county western New York region. Some services, such as occupational education and special education, fall under its own programs but, because of the location of the pupils to be served, another BOCES can provide the services more efficiently, and so, for those pupils, services are contracted out by BOCES Erie District #1.

Special Projects and Grants

The BOCES units throughout New York State participate fully in both state and federally supported programs. Table 8:3 shows the programs funded by the Elementary and Secondary Education Act and the Vocational Education Act in which BOCES Erie District #1 is participating.

There are forty-seven Boards of Cooperative Educational Services in New York State, which had a $160 million budget for school year 1971/72. Fifty-five percent of this amount was provided from

TABLE 8:3. SPECIAL PROJECTS AND GRANTS

Project #	Description	Date Begun	Date Ended	Appropriation
ESEA Title III F030	SEIMC Film Strips	1971	1972	$ 50,000
VEA 73-1-85 F085	Dental Laboratory Technician	7/1/72	6/30/73	60,181
VEA 73-1-87 F087	Commercial Art (Harkness)	7/1/72	6/30/73	22,745
VEA 73-1-88 F088	Trade Electronics (Kenton)	7/1/72	6/30/73	18,250
VEA 73-1-89 F089	Auto Electronics (Potter)	7/1/72	6/30/73	10,386
VEA 73-8e-90 F090	Curriculum Co-ordinator	7/1/72	6/30/73	27,388
VEA 73-8d-307 F307	Career Education	7/1/72	6/30/73	98,837
VEA 73-3-318 F381	Adult Education (Potter)	7/1/72	6/30/73	36,617
ESEA Title III F546	Research and Evaluation	7/1/72	6/30/73	459,816
VEA 72-C-779 F779	Motivation Success	3/6/72	9/30/72	3,000
VEA 72-6-902 F902	Placement Co-ordinator	7/1/72	6/30/73	25,914
VEA 72-G-903 F930	Cooperative Education Coor-dinator	9/1/72	8/31/73	18,464
VEA 72-3-913 F913	Adult Education (Kenton)	9/1/72	6/30/73	5,802
VEA 72-3-942 F942	Adult Education (Harkness)	9/1/72	6/30/73	13,128
VEA 72-3-996 F996	Adult Education Coordinator	7/1/72	6/30/73	6,994

state funds, 6.7 percent by the federal government, and 48.3 percent was contributed by local school districts. This cooperative system was originally intended as temporary, pending the development of intermediate school districts. The BOCES flourished to the extent that the intermediate units have yet to emerge.

Strengths of BOCES

1. BOCES operates under a voluntary system that allows the pooling of resources to accomplish an educational objective.

2. The BOCES design is especially helpful to rural school systems.
3. The occupational emphasis of BOCES programs meets a specific need.
4. BOCES represents a mechanism for increased state matching funds.
5. The dependency of BOCES on local school districts motivates local school district initiative.
6. BOCES programs offer students an educational opportunity not offered by local school systems.
7. BOCES membership programs offer school districts the opportunity to fill the unexpected needs of students.
8. BOCES offers the opportunity for school districts to cooperate and share ideas, programs, and personnel.
9. BOCES offers the opportunity for the state to support adult education programs.
10. BOCES functions as a coordinator of training programs that involve industry, business, unions, and lay citizens.

Weaknesses of BOCES

1. BOCES programs have been most extensively developed among suburban school districts.
2. BOCES programs have not developed evenly throughout the state.
3. Cities with populations of more than one hundred and twenty-five thousand are excluded from BOCES.
4. Wealthy school districts gain more financial benefit from BOCES than poor school districts.
5. The administrative heads of BOCES have a conflict of interest in acting as state supervisors of local school districts while serving on a local BOCES board.
6. Student placement in a BOCES program is sometimes based on what the local school district can afford rather than on what the student needs.
7. Too many students who should be enrolled in a BOCES program are assigned to lower track programs at the local school district.
8. Poor school districts, which might need a BOCES program, can refuse to participate.
9. Many BOCES have limited resources for long range planning and forecasting educational needs.
10. There is considerable overlapping of program services among BOCES, school districts, and community colleges.

The strengths and weaknesses have been substantiated by several research studies on regional education in New York State (Egnar, Lowe, and Stutz 1970; New York State Commission on the Quality, Cost, and Financing of Elementary and Secondary Education 1972; Joint Legislative Committee on Metropolitan and Regional Areas 1972).

Most agree that the success of the BOCES unit has established its value in providing support and supplementary services to local school districts. There seems to be no doubt that the provision for BOCES will continue however modified by the state legislature. All indications are that recommendations are being made to eliminate the present weaknesses and promote the strengths of the BOCES unit.

CONCLUSION

There is a belief in this country that better education leads to a better life for the individual and enriches the entire society. Today school districts, with rising costs and increased demands, have joined together to provide needed services. The BOCES organization may be a viable structure for further study in the economic and efficient delivery of educational service in metropolitan areas.

REFERENCES

Board of Cooperative Educational Services. "A Better Future Can Begin with BOCES." (Pamphlet) Cheektowaga, N.Y.: Board of Cooperative Educational Services #1, Erie County, 1972.

Egnar, J. R.; Lowe, W. T.; and Stutz, F. H. *Regional Educational Development in New York State.* Albany, N.Y.: New York State Department of Education, 1970.

Lamitie, Robert. "Memorandum: Planning for 1972/73." Mimeographed. Cheektowaga, N.Y.: Board of Cooperative Educational Services #1, Western Regional Planning Office, 1972.

Joint Legislative Committee on Metropolitan and Regional Areas Study. *Regionalism: Helping Schools Meet Children's Needs.* Albany, N.Y.: The Committee, 1972.

New York State Commission on the Quality, Cost, and Financing of Elementary and Secondary Education, vol. 3. Albany, N.Y.: The Commission, 1972.

University of the State of New York, and New York State Education Department, Office of School Services. *Handbook of Boards of Cooperative Educational Services.* Albany, N.Y.: New York State Department of Education, 1962.

9

Metropolitanism and the Parochial School System

Joseph A. Caligiuri and S. Theodore Berg

The United States is going through a profound change as a result of population shifts and growth. Urbanization is a fact; our urban areas have accounted for over 80 percent of population growth for the past two decades. Population predictions indicate that, in the next fifteen years, growth in metropolitan areas will equal half of our total urban population in 1950 (Department of Commerce 1971, pp. 6-12). Such an increasing rate of growth has implications for education that are in need of rigorous analysis.

In recent years the concept of metropolitanism, and especially its implications for education, has been receiving increasing consideration and study by professional educators, sociologists, and political scientists. Part I of the 1968 yearbook of the National Society for the Study of Education reflects this concern about metropolitanism and education by presenting the research and opinions of members of several disciplines under the general title of *Metropolitanism: Its Challenge to Education.*

In 1960, the United States Bureau of the Census listed 212 Standard Metropolitan Statistical Areas (SMSAs) in this country; in 1970, 243. (An SMSA is defined as a city of fifty thousand or more with its surrounding county and all contiguous counties that are functionally bound to the central city [Department of Commerce

1972, pp. 1-2].) In 1960, 63 percent of the total population lived in the 212 SMSAs; today, 68.6 percent live in 243 SMSAs (ibid., p. 16). Clearly we are a metropolitan people, if not in our thinking, attitudes, and actions, at least by our physical location. This nationwide trend toward creating new and expanding metropolitan areas has brought with it numerous social, economic, cultural, political, and educational problems.

THE SIGNIFICANCE OF METROPOLITAN CATHOLIC SCHOOLS

Whatever one's attitude toward the private school and its role or lack of role in American society, parochial schools do exist and educate a significant portion of our country's youth. Greeley and Rossi (1966, p. 231) point out that ". . . being for or against a school system with over five million students is like being for or against the Rocky Mountains; it is great fun, but it does not notably alter the reality." The very existence of the parochial school gives it the right and the obligation to contribute its energies and resources toward the solution of the problems facing our increasingly metropolitan population. Several authors view metropolitanism in education as desirable and, once achieved, providing a better chance to solve many of the problems facing education in an increasingly urbanized society.

The Catholic schools of the United States enroll approximately 3.82 million elementary and secondary school children (National Catholic Education Association 1972). The Catholic school systems are organized along the same geographic boundaries as the larger systems of which they are subsystems, the 154 Roman Catholic archdioceses and dioceses of the United States (*The Official Catholic Directory 1968,* 1968). The geographic territory of the diocese and therefore the diocesan school system may be small, the Diocese of Brooklyn covers 179 square miles, or extremely large, the Diocese of Reno embraces the entire state of Nevada. The size and density of the Catholic population in a particular region determines the geographic size of the diocese. Most dioceses are organized along similar lines with the same kinds of basic subsystems, one of which is the diocesan school department. Most diocesan school systems are organized similarly. Therefore, in discussing the school system of the Diocese of Buffalo, which is structurally representative of almost any Catholic school system in this country, we assume that what is true of the social control mechanism of one Catholic school system can be generalized to others. Different Catholic school systems may and do function differently. The memberships may differ greatly in ethnicity, culture, and socioeconomic status. Members of the same system differ among themselves. Nevertheless, all the Catholic school systems embrace the same overarching ideology, which, theoretically, governs the values of the structural and functional relationships of all the systems.

In terms of numbers, support, and influence the parochial schools are strongest in metropolitan areas. Erickson and Greeley report statistics for 1960 gathered by the Bureau of the Census:

> In ten (4.6 percent) of the nation's 212 Standard Metropolitan Statistical Areas (SMSA's) more than one elementary pupil out of every three is enrolled in a non-public school. In 39 SMSA's (18 percent) more than one pupil in every four is so enrolled. In 56 SMSA's (26 percent) the figure is better than one pupil in every five; in 71 SMSA's (33 percent), more than one in six; in 91 SMSA's (43 percent) more than one in seven; in 104 SMSA's (49 percent) more than one in eight; in 119 SMSA's (59 percent), at least one in nine; and in 131 SMSA's (61 percent) at least one in ten (1968, p. 287).

According to the same 1960 census figures, 29.9 percent of all elementary school pupils in the Buffalo SMSA were enrolled in private schools. In 1970, of the 139,419,000 school children in the 243 SMSAs of the United States, 58,766,000 were enrolled in private schools—by then the enrollment had dropped substantially. Between 1966 and 1970 enrollment of elementary school children decreased by 663,000 because of schools closing, the lower birthrate, and increased costs, which encouraged parents to send their children to public schools (Department of Commerce 1972, p. 105).

We cite these statistics to reinforce a belief that, in those metropolitan areas where there are significant numbers of parochial school pupils, attempts to deal with the problems of metropolitan development, especially educational problems, without taking into consideration the status and resources of the local private schools will prove to be less effective for the omission.

THE DIOCESE OF BUFFALO'S SCHOOLS

The Roman Catholic Diocese of Buffalo and its school system embraces the eight counties of western New York: Erie, Niagara, Cattaraugus, Chautauqua, Allegany, Genesee, Orleans, and Wyoming.

The 1972/73 combined elementary and secondary school enrollment in the Catholic schools of the diocese was 65,535, making it one of the largest school systems, public or private, in western New York. Of this total enrollment, some 59,760 or 91 percent are enrolled in schools in Erie and Niagara counties, which, with Buffalo and Niagara Falls as the core cities, constitute the twenty-fourth largest SMSA in the nation (Diocese of Buffalo 1972). Enrollment and staff statistics are shown in table 9:1.

TABLE 9:1. ENROLLMENT AND STAFF STATISTICS—1972/73

	Erie County	Niagara County	Totals
Number of Schools	153	19	172
Pupil Enrollment	54,448	5,312	59,760
Teaching Staff	2,610	272	2,882
Teacher-Pupil Ratio	1:21	1:19	1:20

Source: Data to be used in the annual report of the Diocese of Buffalo, Department of Education, 1972/73.

METROPOLITANISM IN A CATHOLIC SCHOOL SYSTEM

Geographic Comprehension

The first and most obvious metropolitan feature of the Catholic school system is its geographic comprehension. Instead of a multiplicity of Catholic school systems to serve the many legally constituted local governments of the metropolitan region, there is only one school system, which disregards local government boundaries and embraces the entire metropolitan area. The Catholic school system in Erie and Niagara counties might be compared, in physical makeup, to the pattern of metropolitan educational government exemplified in Minneapolis and St. Paul, which consist of more than one core city, their suburban fringes, and the county. The parallel, however, is not exact since each of the two core cities of Buffalo and Niagara Falls is in a different county and the two counties are embraced by the same Catholic school system.

Administrative Network

Since the entire metropolitan region is embraced by the one school system, all the Catholic schools in the region fall under the same central office administration, and there is one superintendent. A central office is one of the focal points for what Kaplan describes in Parsonian terms (1967, p. 15) as the "normative integration of the system." The impression that this normative integration is absolute would not be correct, but it is sufficient to give the system a satisfactory degree of equilibrium. The degree of normative integration varies with the type of school. There are four types of Catholic schools: parish elementary (166 schools), diocesan secondary (16 schools), private elementary (8 schools), and private secondary (14 schools). The superintendent is finally and directly responsible for the entire educational program of the diocesan secondary schools; he shares responsibility for the parish elementary schools with pastors and the religious communities staffing the schools; he serves in an advisory capacity to the private schools, both elementary and secondary. The superintendent and his staff issue identical policies, regulations, and guidelines for all the schools of a type. There is a resulting metropolitan network of information communication from the central office to the schools, from the schools to the central office, and among the schools of the metropolitan region.

Supervision

(The comments made in this section pertain only to the parish elementary schools.) Along with the administration of the Catholic school system on a metropolitan basis goes the supervision of the schools. Most Catholic school systems draw their religious personnel from a number of different religious communities, mostly of women. Each community normally assumes responsibility for the staffing and administration of several schools within a particular diocese. To effect some degree of unity and cohesion in its schools, each religious community appoints a community supervisor who visits the schools regularly to assess and upgrade all the facets of the educational program being offered.

In the Diocese of Buffalo the supervisors of the various communities meet once a month with the superintendent to discuss common concerns, aid one another, and relate the performance of the schools in their charge to the goals of the larger system, the diocesan school system. Since the schools staffed by a religious community are normally scattered throughout the diocese, the community supervisor's tasks take her across the boundaries of many local government units, and gives her function in the Catholic school system a metropolitan flavor.

Personnel and Staffing

Religious personnel normally live in a residence close to the school and may be assigned to any school in the diocese staffed by their community. This can and does take religious personnel to a variety of local government units in a metropolitan area. The same is true, but to a lesser degree, of lay personnel hired by the Catholic school system. However, since they must commute between school and home and, since account must be taken of time and distance, lay teachers are allowed to state their preferences for assignment and, if feasible, their preferences are honored. This method of operation takes some lay personnel also to many different civic communities of the metropolitan area while they remain in the employ of one school system.

While the salary scale for lay personnel is necessarily higher than that for religious personnel (woefully low, in elementary schools, when compared with public school salaries), within each group the same minimal scale applies to all members of the group. In other words, all religious personnel in the employ of a particular diocesan school system have the same salary scale, and all lay teachers on a particular level, elementary or secondary, in the system have the same salary scale.

Most religious communities look after the professional preparation and certification of their own members by sending them to public or private institutions of higher learning. Some religious communities staff and operate their own colleges or junior colleges and use these for the professional training of the members of the community. The central office, therefore, does not oversee the training and certification of religious personnel. However, it does for all the elementary lay teachers in the Catholic schools of Erie and Niagara counties. The central office has traditionally required lay teachers to enroll in a certain number of specified courses leading to diocesan certification. These courses have been organized and the staff for them secured by the central office. Since these courses were not part of any approved college program of teacher preparation, those lay teachers successfully completing the courses were awarded "diocesan credits."

In September 1968, however, the central office discontinued its diocesan certification program and required that all elementary lay teachers work for state certification by enrolling in an approved college program of teacher preparation. This new policy, as with the old certification program, applies to all the lay teachers in the metropolitan Catholic elementary schools. Lay teachers at secondary schools meet certification requirements before they are employed. Any in-service programs offered by the central office are made available to all the teachers, religious and lay, in the metropolitan schools.

Education Program

Over and above the requirements of the State syllabi, the curriculum of the metropolitan schools is generally the same and based on diocesan courses of study. Where local conditions or circumstances dictate, adaptation of the curriculum is possible, as are opportunities for innovation and textbook selection. The textbooks selected by the central office will be used by all the schools in the metropolitan area. Apart from state mandated tests, the standardized testing program of the Catholic school system is metropolitan, and the same standardized tests are used. Until a few years ago, all content testing was done by diocesan examinations and was therefore metropolitan oriented. Today some content testing is done by diocesan exams and some by tests the teachers compile.

THE USES OF METROPOLITANISM

Several other features, for example, the school calendar, extracurricular programs, coordination of federal and state aid programs, of the Catholic school system could be discussed here but they can be logically inferred from one or other of the major considerations already mentioned.

Equality of Educational Opportunity

Probably no other topic is as widely discussed and written about in educational circles than that of equality of educational opportunity. For example, the Winter 1968 issue of the *Harvard Educational Review* is devoted entirely to this subject. The phrase "equality of educational opportunity" has many dimensions but the dimension most frequently associated with it is that of equal opportunity for the black minority. The plight of the black has been placed in relief mainly as a result of the efforts of the civil rights movement. We are beginning to realize, in detail, just how ineffective our schools have been in making education profitable and productive for most of the black people in this country. One frequently suggested means for helping to erase the inequalities in educational opportunity for this minority is integration. David Cohen, in speaking of the relative merits of compensatory and integrated education, concludes that

> when everything else is said, then, and all the educational and fiscal evidence is in, the most compelling reason for a policy of improved and integrated schools is that only this policy will make it politically feasible for the destinies of America's two separate nations to become bound up together. A policy of segregated compensation cannot provide that binding tie and, therefore, can promise only the continuance of a segregated, closed, and inferior system of education for Negro Americans (1968, p. 137).

There is still a fair amount of debate going on in professional educational circles about whether or not integration is the answer, or at least part of it, to the educational problems of black and other minority groups. Rather than argue the merits of integration, we would point out how, assuming that it is a worthwhile goal of the educational system, the parochial school system might help effect integration. Many factors have traditionally militated against metropolitan public school districts' working cooperatively to effect racial integration in the local schools. Kenneth B. Clark, speaking of barriers to the attainment of efficient public education, mentions "those obstacles which reflect historical premises and dogmas about education, administrative realities, and psychological assumptions and prejudices (1968, p. 102)." While Clark is not speaking specifically about metropolitan education, what he says applies. He speaks of such obstacles as the inviolability of the neighborhood school concept, parents' and taxpayers' groups opposing integration, control of boards of education by whites who resist change, and school officials who have not provided leadership and who have tended to go along with the level of community readiness and the "political realities." He also classifies the black power movement and its demands for racial separatism as an obstacle to integration.

What has all this to do with the parochial school system? Simply this: the parochial school system, its supporters, and its administration have been just as guilty as the society at large in placing the obstacles of which Clark speaks in the way of equality of educational opportunity. It appears, however, that the parochial school system is in a better position than the public school system, structurally and functionally, to overcome at least some of the barriers. Harold Howe II, formerly a Commissioner of Education, expressed the reasons well in his address to the 1968 National Catholic Education Association Convention in San Francisco. He mentioned the ability of the parochial school system to operate outside the political system that sometimes prevents public school superintendents from doing what they know to be the wisest thing for education, and the fact that the political boundaries of the parochial school system embrace both cities and suburbs, permitting a metropolitan approach to educational problems.

These characteristics of the parochial school system certainly give it a greater freedom to attempt a program of integration than the public school systems possess. There would be no retaliation at the ballot box (though, as Howe warned, it might be encountered in the collection basket). Most Catholic school systems in metropolitan areas enroll a sufficient number of Negro children to make such a program possible (approximately 2,400 in the Buffalo diocesan school system, most of whom are not Catholic). It would constitute an exercise in educational leadership on the part of the parochial school system and provide some more common ground for working with public school authorities. (As an aside, the Regents of the University of the State of New York recommend "a continuing emphasis upon racially comprehensive enrollment policies in non-public schools and an active effort on the part of public school authorities to bring non-public schools into the total community efforts to eliminate racial segregation in education [State Education Department 1968, p. 13].")

The ideology of the parochial school system can and must be used to support a metropolitan approach to racial integration and to other problems as well. The Catholic church, and therefore the Catholic school system, is founded on the basic Christian message: love God; love your neighbor. Ideally then, the Catholic school system has an added advantage in this spiritual and moral dimension that should enable it to implement a program such as school integration, or integration in housing and employment, with less difficulty than social systems that do not possess this foundation.

Kaplan (1967) mentions several indices used to gauge the degree of normative integration in a system. Normative integration embraces roughly the same concept as does a system ideology, that is, a belief and value system espoused and supported by the members of a system. One of the indices is "a growing consensus on goals, a lessening degree of overt conflict, and a willingness to smother conflict in order to preserve the system (p. 25)." On this index, one would have to conclude that the parochial school system is in no better a position, ideologically, to attempt a program of school integration than is any other system. We see in the Catholic church today, and therefore in the Catholic school system, a lessening consensus on goals, a growing degree of overt conflict, and an unwillingness to smother conflict to preserve the system. Yet, if one views these phenomena positively, one finds that they point, not to the normative disintegration of the system but, paradoxically, are the results of new insights into and a new understanding of the same system ideology, and lead to a renewed commitment to that basic ideology. (One can possibly oversimplify the issue by not considering the adaptive as well as the integrative functions of a system as Kaplan does.) This dynamic process, with all of the conflicts it brings, is far from complete and has really just begun. The point in this digression is that there still exists a basically stable ideological foundation, as reinterpreted by the Second Vatican Council in the light of today's social needs, that can and must be used by the parochial school system in its attempts to improve the educational opportunities of the citizens of the metropolis.

Financing Education

How else might the parochial school system use its metropolitan orientation to improve education and exercise leadership? One fertile possibility would seem to be in the allocation of financial resources. Alkin says that "research findings have clearly demonstrated that the social, economic, and political characteristics of communities determine the amount of locally raised funds that will be available for the operation of the schools and thus, to a considerable extent, the quality of the schools in the communities (1968, p. 128)." The Catholic school system embraces all types of socially, economically, and politically different metropolitan communities. The Catholics in these different communities voluntarily give varying amounts of money to support their parochial schools. Financial support for the parochial schools is stronger in the suburbs than it is in the central city, especially the inner city, because suburban Catholics are more numerous and affluent. Accepting Alkin's assertion, we might assume that the quality of education is better in the suburban parochial schools than it is in the city parochial schools. This need not be so.

Presently each parish is responsible for financing its parochial school. The wealthier Catholics of the suburbs do little to help educate poorer families of the city. The structure, however, is present for eliminating this inequity. Since the school system stretches across the metropolitan area to include city and suburb, it is possible to establish some form of centralized financing so that all funds for parochial schools flow into a central coffer for redistribution in accord with the relative needs of each school. This is not to say that this centralization would be easy: parochial school parents are just as fervent about "local control" as are public school parents. It does however say that such a step is well within the realm of possibility and might set a precedent for public schools to evaluate and, if successful, imitate. Here again, the system ideology plays an important role. Christ says, "If you do it to one of these, the least of my brethren, you have done it to Me." It would be interesting to discover how readily such a practice would be accepted.

Innovation

In its experimental and innovative programs the parochial school system might exercise educational leadership in the metropolis. Such programs can be mounted in the parochial school system in a variety of socially, economically, and culturally different settings without the slow process of formal public approval. Operating experimental programs simultaneously under a variety of conditions would give greater validity to the testing of hypotheses by taking into account more of the possible conditions under which the variables operate. The Catholic school system could use this opportunity, with a daring that may be denied to public education officials, to do much needed educational research that would benefit the children in the schools. It could also provide both public and private school teachers and administrators with opportunities to visit and observe innovative programs in operation.

Nor need experimentation and innovation be limited to the classroom. The parochial school system has the freedom and opportunity to test hypotheses generated by various theories of administration. Much attention is paid today to the issue of centralization or decentralization in the administration of city schools. We have the Bundy Report, which recommended that the New York City public school system be broken down into between thirty and sixty almost autonomous units, each governed by a Community School Board (Mayor's Advisory Panel on the Decentralization of the New York City Schools 1967). The Passow Report (1967) recommended the decentralization of the Washington, D.C. school system into eight subsystems of equal size. The events in New York City's Ocean

Hill-Brownsville District received almost daily newspaper coverage for several weeks.

The parochial school system presently operates through a mixture of centralization and decentralization. The central office oversees the general operation of the schools within a broad framework of administrative policy and regulation. Yet, a good deal of authority for the administration of each school is left in the hands of the local parish unit and the principal of the school. Etzioni cites evidence to support his "intuition that centralized organizations allow for less local experimentation and grant less unit-flexibility, although they are more likely to be able to provide facilities that independent units could not afford, and to enforce 'labor relations' standards such as tenure, more efficiently (1964, p. 29)." We intend, not to defend the existing structure for sharing administrative authority in the parochial school system, but to highlight the opportunity for the parochial school system to experiment with and evaluate differing mixes of centralization and decentralization in the administration of its schools in an attempt to approach the best method.

Metropolitan Federation of School Systems

We have witnessed in recent years a growing involvement of parochial schools with public schools. This involvement should and will continue to grow. This contact has in part been forced upon both systems by federal aid programs, such as those provided by the Elementary and Secondary Education Act, and by state aid programs, such as the New York State Textbook Loan Law and aid for transportation. Forced or not, this contact has been most beneficial to both systems. Each system has for too long acted as if the other did not exist. Should not two systems work together at least toward the accomplishment of those goals (and there are many) that are common to each? Each system ought to get to know and understand the other better.

Robin H. Farquhar, reporting the results of his research in "A Public School Administrator Views the Catholic School—Or Does He?" states that "public school administrators tend to be neither familiar with nor interested in Catholic schools (1968, p. 2)." Catholic school administrators, too, have been less familiar with and interested in public schools than is desirable. Here then, is an opportunity for the Catholic school system, because of its metropolitan orientation, to communicate and cooperate with the public schools. The one parochial school system should initiate communication with the numerous public school districts in the metropolitan area rather than wait for each of the several public school districts to communicate with it. Communication thus initiated would provide greater coordination of joint efforts between the public and parochial school systems to solve common educational problems.

One problem the public schools face increasingly is that of adequate financing. It appears that more and more public school budgets get voted down each year. The parochial school system can help (even though the financial crisis of the parochial schools is much more acute than that of the public schools). One frequently hears the charge made against parents with children in parochial schools that they reduce the funds available for public education. Erickson and Greeley cite several research studies done to determine the truth or falsity of the allegation and conclude that "according to the limited evidence, then, proponents of Catholic education have opposed liberal support of public schools in some areas and encouraged it in others. This discrepancy should come as no surprise (1968, pp. 300-301)." Whatever the case in a particular community, the parochial school system may be able to use its offices to impress upon its supporters, who are spread throughout the metropolitan area and reside in a number of different public school districts, the importance of strong support for the public school system and their obligation to provide it.

Public school officials in turn might aid the parochial school system in its financial crisis by attempting to understand the problems faced, conveying their understanding to their communities, and aiding in the search for solutions to the problems within the framework of constitutional law. However, before either system can help the other, the communication between them must increase; the parochial school system is in an advantageous position to exercise its initiative.

Catholic schools have long been successful with a metropolitan educational organization, and so Catholic school administrators do not hesitate to encourage a metropolitan federation of school systems. The effectiveness of such a federation is a function of the extent to which all school systems in the metropolitan area become members. Obviously, the cooperating members of the federation would include the Catholic school system of the area as well as any other private school systems.

PROBLEMS FACING CATHOLIC SCHOOLS

In order to give an honest appraisal of the possibility that the Catholic school system of the future will play the metropolitan role thus far outlined, it is necessary to give some indication of the problems and difficulties currently facing Catholic education throughout the nation and especially in New York State. Catholic schools in large cities are old; they were initially established at the beginning of the present century. Buildings are deteriorating because of age. Personnel are present, interest and desire are present, but the facilities are fast approaching a substandard level. Financial resources are not available in the inner city to repair, replace, or renew these buildings.

Another difficulty was mentioned by Monsignor Thomas J. Costello to the Board of Regents of the University of the State of New York (1968, p. 3): "As an example of our dilemma, we are advised that state funds for the correction of racial imbalance are totally restricted to public schools. They may not even be employed for transportation to a non-public school." Monsignor Costello went on to point out that legal strictures of the New York State constitution presently prevent any significant expenditure of public monies for the education of children in private schools. Unless such strictures are removed, the very life of the Catholic school system is endangered, and any possible contributary role that may be exercised by the Catholic school system in the solution of metropolitan educational problems diminished.

Monsignor Costello suggested that, if the constitutional strictures were removed: cooperative efforts in meeting the needs of urban children; mutual concern for school desegregation and subsequent integration; sharing by all children in state funds for correcting racial imbalance; participation through dual enrollment of all children who can benefit from occupational and vocational education; expansion at state expense of the specific services offered under Section 912 of the Education Law; provision from state funds of shared services, similar to those provided by the Elementary and Secondary Education Act; and meaningful partnerships in preschool programming might all be accomplished.

CONCLUSION

The major conclusion to be drawn is that the parochial school system is in an advantageous position, *vis-à-vis* metropolitan development, to exercise real educational leadership and service to the community. One should not be naïve enough to think that the possibilities projected for the parochial school system would be easily translated into reality. When people are against a change in the status quo, be they Protestant, Catholic, Jewish, or atheist, they tend to react against that change in fairly similar ways. Nevertheless, the parochial school system could begin to effect change, and how it uses this advantage will have a great deal to say about the future state of education in metropolitan areas.

REFERENCES

Alkin, Marvin C. "Revenues for Education in Metropolitan Areas." In *Metropolitanism: Its Challenge to Education* (Sixty-seventh Yearbook of the National Society for the Study of Education), edited by Robert J. Havighurst, pp. 123-47. Chicago: University of Chicago Press, 1968.

Clark, Kenneth B. "Alternative Public School Systems." *Harvard Educational Review* 38, no. 1 (Winter 1968): 100-113.

Cohen, David K. "Policy for the Public Schools: Compensation and Integration." *Harvard Educational Review* 38, no. 1 (Winter 1968): 114-37.

Costello, Thomas J. "Statement of Rev. Thomas J. Costello, presented before the Board of Regents of the University of the State of New York." Mimeographed. Albany, N.Y.: The New York State Council of Catholic School Superintendents, 1968.

Department of Commerce, Bureau of the Census. *Statistical Abstracts of the United States, 1971.* Washington, D.C.: Government Printing Office, 1971.

_____ . *Statistical Abstracts of the United States, 1972.* Washington, D.C.: Government Printing Office, 1972.

Diocese of Buffalo, Department of Education. Annual Report, 1972.

Erickson, Donald A., and Greeley, Andrew M. "Non-Public Schools and Metropolitanism." In *Metropolitanism: Its Challenge to Education* (Sixty-seventh Yearbook of the National Society for the Study of Education), edited by Robert J. Havighurst, pp. 287-316. Chicago: University of Chicago Press, 1968.

Etzioni, Amitai. *Modern Organizations.* Englewood Cliffs, N.J.: Prentice-Hall, 1964.

Farquhar, Robin H. "The Public School Administrator Views the Catholic School—Or Does He?" *Educational Administration Quarterly* 4, no. 3 (Autumn 1968): 2-15.

Greeley, Andrew M., and Rossi, Peter H. *The Education of Catholic Americans.* Chicago: Aldine, 1966.

Kaplan, Harold. *Urban Political Systems: A Functional Analysis of Metro Toronto.* New York: Columbia University Press, 1967.

Mayor's Advisory Panel on the Decentralization of the New York City Schools. *Reconnection for Learning. A Community School System for New York City.* New York: The Advisory Panel, 1967.

National Catholic Education Association. Data Bank Bulletin #37. Mimeographed. Washington, D.C.: National Catholic Education Association, 1972.

New York State Education Department. *Integration and the Schools.* Position Paper no. 3. Albany, N.Y.: New York State Education Department, 1968.

The Official Catholic Directory, 1968. New York: P.J. Kenedy, 1968.

Passow, A. H. "Summary of a Report on the Washington, D.C. Public Schools." Mimeographed. New York: Columbia University, Teachers College, 1967.

10

The Metropolitan Merger Model

Robert W. Heller and Raphael O. Nystrand

Metropolitan school reorganization has been recommended by scholars and study groups in countless instances, but little implementation has occurred. This chapter will attempt a partial explanation of this circumstance by comparing events in two areas where reorganization was attempted. In one of these areas, Louisville-Jefferson County, in Kentucky, champions of reform have been persistent but unsuccessful. In the other, Nashville-Davidson County, in Tennessee, a form of reorganization was achieved and has been widely acclaimed.[1]

In addition to being situated in border states, the two areas we discuss share at least one other important characteristic. In both instances, the proposed reorganization involved bringing only two units of school government, a city and a county district, into a new relationship with each other. Hence, we use the term *merger model* to refer to the joining of two previously independent jurisdictions. Merger models differ from rural reorganizations because they are not mandated by state requirements and from urban annexations in that both existing jurisdictions give way to a single new one.

THE LOUISVILLE-JEFFERSON COUNTY EXPERIENCE

Interest in merging the Louisville City and Jefferson County school districts dates back to the late 1940s and early 1950s. At that time, the city was essentially white and middle class and its schools, backed by a relatively strong tax base, were considered good ones. The county, although largely rural, was on the verge of becoming suburban and its tax base and level of public services were low in contrast with those of the city.

The past two decades have been a period of great change in the Louisville metropolitan area. The trends of suburban growth and urban decline have been marked here as elsewhere. Industry and middle-class residents have sought locations in the suburbs and the fiscal problems of the city have become severe. Growth in the county school system has been great; enrollments have increased by approximately four thousand students a year for fifteen years. At present, there are approximately eighty-one thousand pupils in the county, which does not have a kindergarten program, and fifty-one thousand pupils in the city, including three thousand kindergarten students. Forty-five percent of the city school enrollment is black.

Attitudes Toward Merger

As the city and county populations have changed, so have the attitudes toward merger in the respective locales. When interest in merging the two districts first emerged in the late 1940s and early 1950s, most of this sentiment was expressed by county residents. City officials showed little interest in merger because of its questionable benefits to city dwellers. More recently, these positions have shifted. Although some support for the most recent merger proposal was found in both city and county, the most important opposition came from the county.

No fewer than six efforts have been made to merge the two systems during the past twenty years. In 1951, pressure from suburban residents, the League of Women Voters, which issued a report on the subject, and the city newspapers led the city board of education to announce support for merger in principle without taking action. However, the board soon reassessed this position, citing cost factors as its rationale. Opposition to merger at this time was made known by the Chamber of Commerce, city political leaders, and city teachers. The latter were probably influenced by the fact that their salaries were considerably higher than those paid county teachers.

When the boards of both districts acknowledged severe financial problems two years later, they agreed to merge but reportedly tied this proposal to a request for an $8 million dollar tax package. The city mayor reportedly opposed this proposal so vigorously that some observers credit his action with defeating the plan. Public opinion leaned to the view that merger was being proposed to increase taxes, and opposition developed around this point. Sensing the lack of public support, the two boards retreated from their proposal and announced their intention to remain independent.

In 1954, the education committee of the city Chamber of Commerce conducted a study of merger possibilities and issued a report in favor of such action. Faced with opposition by the city board of education, the Chamber recommended that an outside organization study the entire question. This recommendation was accepted immediately by the county school board, which also endorsed the subsequent report in favor of merger. The city board of education waited some time before agreeing to the study and ultimately denounced the report as incomplete and the recommendation of merger as unacceptable.

Just one year later, the city schools were so pressed for funds that they dropped kindergarten from their program. Financial problems also continued to plague the county schools. Once again, an internal study called for merger. Officials of both systems agreed to support the necessary enabling legislation. However, this agreement reportedly broke down when consensus could not be reached on a procedure for electing members to the new board of education.

Following this set of events, interest in merger appeared to slacken although concern about the financial condition of the two districts continued. Because neither had been successful in passing a major tax package, the two districts agreed to still another internal study of the merger possibility in 1961 and 1962. Again no action resulted.

In 1964, a new citizens' organization called Help Educate Louisville for Progress (HELP) was formed. Comprising both city and county residents, the group's major objective was to win increased tax support for education. While they had support from the press, received fifty-five thousand dollars in donations, and recruited fifteen thousand workers, their tax issue was defeated at the polls. At this point, the organization called upon the governor to convene a special session of the legislature in 1965. During this session, an occupation tax of 1/2 percent was enacted and resulted in revenue beyond the level sought by HELP in the defeated referendum. Persons associated with HELP became increasingly committed to the merger as the key to educational change as they studied the prevailing state of education.

The Beginnings of Cooperation

In the meanwhile the two districts had learned to cooperate in several ways. Cunningham et al. (1966) noted that, by 1966, cooperative action had produced comparable salary schedules in the two districts and the settlement of bothersome questions associated with attendance areas. In addition, school calendars were coordinated, some joint bidding and purchasing of supplies occurred, and there were examples of cooperation in developing some programs. However, the Cunningham team also reported that strong opposition to merger was present among leaders in both systems when they interviewed them in 1966.

During the 1966 state legislative session, two assemblymen submitted a bill calling for the forced merger of the two school systems. Although the bill passed in the lower house, it was stalled in the senate. Officials from both the city and county school districts reportedly worked hard to prevent its passage. A *quid pro quo* was reached whereby the bill was not passed and representatives of both school boards agreed to abide by the recommendations of still another study by an outside team. This action on the part of the school boards was partially precipitated by a speech given before the Louisville Rotary Club late in 1965 in which was outlined a proposal to develop a charter commission of twenty-one members with the authority to implement any plan of merger thus giving the charter commission authority, once and for all time, to resolve the problem. This proposal appeared to gain wide community support.

The new study team was headed by Luvern L. Cunningham. He and his colleagues prepared a report calling for a metropolitan educational district with smaller, semi-independent community school districts, each having its own school board and limited taxing powers. The metropolitan district would be responsible for raising and allocating resources for operating and capital purposes, school construction, research and planning, some special education programs, and certain administrative services (for example, purchasing, transportation, educational television). General policy would be developed by a metropolitan education commission and implemented through an executive director.

The Charter Committee

A critical recommendation of the Cunningham report called for the formation of a fifteen-member charter committee of city and county leaders. This committee was to be appointed by the respective boards of education and given the responsibility to work out details within guidelines set forth by the report and to shepherd their implementation. A committee was appointed in August 1966 when the two boards voted unanimously to establish a metropolitan education district through the charter process.

The charter committee, composed of over 100 prominent citizens who were experts in data processing, management, purchasing, and so on, worked hard itself and commissioned several task forces to refine particular aspects of the plan. Most community groups expressed support for the work of the group. However, significant opposition came from the county teachers' association. The opposition of the teachers reportedly had three facets: concern that merger would work to their disadvantage in terms of salaries, uncertainty about the continuing power of the association in a structure that provided for subdistricts under the metropolitan umbrella, and effort to build organization strength by taking a strong position.

As the charter committee continued its work, opposition began to crystallize in various quarters. Two members of the county board spoke against the proposal, the county teachers continued their opposition, and some county administrators spoke against the plan. When the charter committee presented a first draft of their report to the boards of education in September 1968, disagreements were apparent. The boards had not actively been involved in the deliberations of the committee and some members felt that the charter committee was usurping responsibilities of the board. For example, the charter committee recommendation that the first metropolitan education director not be an educator provoked considerable disagreement.

It is clear that the merger plan prompted anxieties associated with race. In particular, the boundaries for the semi-independent districts were never announced. Noting that the Cunningham report called for "continued progress toward effective integration of the schools," persons developed fears that district boundaries would be designed for this purpose and labeled the merger proposal as a busing plan. This was particularly true in the county where the population is predominantly white.

In retrospect, public opposition to the merger plan appeared to be related to four issues. The first was the general apathy toward and lack of public confidence in the schools. The second issue, not unrelated to the first, was the continuing financial plight of the schools. The merger offered little in the way of immediate financial salvation and stimulated concern that higher taxes would inevitably result. The third issue dealt with public participation. The implementation procedure developed by the charter committee did not allow for public referendum on the merger. Instead, the new structure was to be created by act of the state legislature. Also important, but difficult to measure, was the degree of vested interest on the part of those to be directly affected by merger and the role they played in opposing the plan. The fourth issue, although the least discussed, might well have been the most pervasive. Without a doubt the plan for merger prompted anxieties associated with race. The plan stressed the necessity for continued progress toward an integrated school system. Proposals associated with integration were in most cases associated with busing and feared by the white populace.

The recommendations of the charter committee died, at least for the time being, in the education committee of the Kentucky senate after being passed by the lower house. Two of the three local senators opposed the bill. Supporters and opponents of the measure both lobbied strongly for their positions. In retrospect, it appears that the lack of local senate support was perhaps decisive. Legislators from other parts of the state viewed the measure as area legislation and were inclined not to support it over opposition by local legislators.

THE NASHVILLE-DAVIDSON COUNTY EXPERIENCE

Discussion of the consolidation of government agencies in Nashville-Davidson County, Tennessee, began in the late 1940s. Talks focused on such services as fire protection, police, sewers, water authorities, and so on, which were not uniformly available to citizens and frequently only available through private, not public, agencies.

By 1950, with the population exodus from the cities to the suburbs, the problem of services to the residents of Davidson County became acute. Urban living under the rural county government presented many problems. However, Tennessee constitutional limitations at that time made it difficult to consolidate government units.

The city of Nashville was experiencing serious difficulties at this time also. It was providing many services to residents that the county lacked, but its taxing limitations were being reached. Approximately 40 percent of the land in the city was tax exempt, including fourteen universities and colleges and much church and government property. Industries and businesses felt that they were paying too high a proportion of the taxes and not receiving appropriate services in return and, in some instances, were threatening to move.

Merger Efforts Begin

In 1951, the General Assembly of Tennessee created a fifteen-member Community Services Commission to study the problems associated with rural urbanization. In 1952, the commission published a comprehensive report entitled, *A Future for Nashville.* Recommendations in the report called for the transfer of services such as health, welfare, hospitals, and schools to the county. The only tangible result of the study was the development of a county-wide health service unit that serviced both the city and county. This came about simply because the city abandoned its own department and left the provision of health services up to the county.

Because of the constitutional restrictions on consolidation, the report also contained recommendations for the large-scale annexation of suburban Nashville. The report was received and apparently "filed away" by both the county and city governments who, at the time, perceived each other as political foes.

The state Constitution was amended in 1953 to allow the General Assembly to consolidate municipal corporations and the counties in which such municipal corporations were located. However, it was some time before any formal action was taken to bring together the government units of the city of Nashville and Davidson County.

The Executive Officer for the county called for a study to look at means for consolidating the two existing government units into one. The concept of "one government" received the backing of many groups within the community including the Chamber of Commerce, service clubs, and a local newspaper. Shortly thereafter a Joint Planning Division was organized by the Nashville City Planning Commission and the Davidson County Planning Commission. The division, funded equally by the city and the county, and receiving some federal monies, produced about fifty studies that improved the credibility of some form of metropolitan government unit. In 1956, a report entitled *Plan of Metropolitan Government for Nashville and Davidson County* (Nashville City Planning Commission and Davidson County Planning Commission 1956) was released. The report became the foundation for additional enabling legislation, a Charter Commission, and the birth of a movement that culminated in the adoption by popular vote of a metropolitan government. The report presented step by step alternatives and anticipated many of the possible issues that could arise from consolidation. It suggested the creation of a metropolitan government to replace the existing city and county governments. It proposed a tax structure, eventually accepted, that provided services financed by two taxes, from an urban service district and a general service district. This report was the first formal document to address itself to the consolidation of the area's two governments.

The division report stressed the need for additional enabling legislation. A general bill was drafted cutting across the many lines of jurisdiction within the state. The bill limited the combined government units to populations of two hundred thousand and thus excluded all but four counties of Tennessee. Thus legislators from outside the Nashville-Davidson County area had an opportunity to vote for the bill without being grossly affected by it. It provided that no charter commission could be created without the affirmative vote of the involved city council and the county governing body. This legislation, passed by both houses of the Tennessee legislature in 1957, implemented the consolidation amendment to the Tennessee Constitution.

The Charter Commission

Following this legislation, a ten-member Charter Commission was authorized by companion resolutions of the Nashville City Council and the Quarterly County Court of Davidson County. The city mayor and county judge each selected five members of the Charter Commission. The Charter Commission plan was submitted to referendum in June 1958 and the proposed Charter was defeated by 24,043 votes to 21,591. Voters in the city of Nashville had approved the Charter by a 7,797 to 4,808 vote, but the defeat came in the county where 19,235 voted against and 13,794 voted in support of the proposed Charter (Nashville Area Chamber of Commerce 1963).

An analysis of the voting patterns revealed that the lower the income of the voters, the more opposed they were to the Charter. The financial power base of the community along with most of the leaders in education, politics, and businesses supported the metropolitan plan. The black vote in the city of Nashville was only moderately negative, 55 percent against, to 45 percent for. The major opposition appeared to come from conservative, grass root voters most of whom lived in the county.

When the Charter Commission developed the proposed Charter, it did not include a master plan for education. Educators appeared not to be convinced that consolidation was the answer to their problems and consequently gave little organizational support to the proposed Charter. In general, school administrators from both districts favored the plan but only teachers from the city lent their support. The county teachers' groups opposed the merger.

The Annexation Issue

Almost one month to the day after the defeat of the Charter, the Nashville City Council annexed 6.91 square miles of the county —a small industrial area with a population of about forty-six hundred people. The annexation was needed to increase the city's tax revenue and was a "finger" annexation, that is, the developed areas on both sides of major arteries leading to and from the city were annexed. Residents living in this area did not raise any objections until they discovered that they were being taxed, but were not receiving the additional services that other city residents were enjoying. Annexation became a touchy issue and the city mayor pledged not to annex any land without first getting approval of the voters. Despite this pledge, the Nashville City Council went ahead and annexed 42.46 square miles of county property with a total population of 82,512 people. This was over the veto of the mayor, but nevertheless, many citizens continued to hold him responsible. For this he was criticized, and the annexation became a factor in the growing opposition to the mayor.

In 1961, the state legislature again amended its enabling act to permit a Charter Commission to be created by a Private Act of the Tennessee General Assembly. Before this Private Act could be drafted, the general assembly amended a section of the Tennessee Code on annexation procedures to provide that any annexation of more than 1/4 of a square mile or over five hundred persons must include an adopted plan of service and a projected timetable for extending the service. This action by the legislators provides some indication of the furor that the city's policy on annexation had created.

The Second Charter Commission

In 1961, a second ten-member Metropolitan Government Charter Commission was approved by the voters and organized. Eight of the members had served on the 1958 Commission. The second Charter Commission had a subcommittee on education. While many educational issues were reviewed and discussed, two particularly important topics were the autonomy of the existing school districts and an elected school board for the metropolitan educational district. Both of these issues were resolved similarly: they were defeated. It was agreed that the educational organization would be placed within the framework of the total metropolitan plan. This accomplished, the five-member subcommittee on education concerned itself with developing a plan for an interim period of two years between the adoption of the metropolitan charter and the actual consolidation of the two school systems. Provisions were also made for an interim board of education and for a series of surveys and studies to be conducted as necessary groundwork for the consolidation.

With education now a major constituent in the proposed Charter, the educators organized themselves to support the plan. As previously pointed out, during the 1958 Charter movement, the educators did not organize to support the merger. However, during 1959 the four teachers' associations, white city and county, and black city and county, had merged in an education council. They hired an executive secretary and gave strong support in helping draft the second metropolitan Charter and in campaigning for its passage.

On 28 June 1962, the citizens again went to the polls and this time approved the metropolitan Charter. In the city of Nashville 21,064 voted for approval; 15,599 voted against. In Davidson County it was approved by 15,914 votes to 12,512. The total vote for the second Metropolitan Government Charter was 36,978 in favor and 28,113 opposed (ibid.). The number of voters was exceeded in recent years only by presidential elections and statewide general elections. The Charter of the Metropolitan Government of Nashville and Davidson County became effective on 1 April 1963. A mayor serves as the executive officer with a Metropolitan Council as the legislative body. Forty members serve on the council, thirty-five elected from council districts and five elected at large.

The Metropolitan School District

It was not until 1 July 1964 that the metropolitan school district went into effect. (For a detailed account of the Nashville-Davidson County Metropolitan Charter Plan, see Harris, Hemberger, and Goodnight [1968].) The period between the successful Charter vote and the consolidation of the two school districts was set aside for planning the new metropolitan school district. During this period provisions were made for the establishment of a transitional school board and administrative organization. The transitional school board had nine members, three representing the previous county school board, three from the previous city school board, and three appointed by the mayor, one of whom was designated chairman. The term of the transitional board expired on 30 June 1964, at which time the metropolitan school district officially came into being.

During the tenure of the transitional school board a comprehensive study of both school systems was undertaken and recommendations for the new metropolitan school system were made (Cornell 1963). Both school districts continued to operate during this interim period as two separate school systems with one board of education. Both of the school district superintendents continued serving during the interim period and retired when the first Director of Schools for the Metropolitan School District assumed office.

The present metropolitan school district is organized into three area districts each headed by an Area Superintendent. Each of these areas is so structured as to include a portion of the inner city, with the result that a wide range of needs and variations in the community has been achieved. Each area has a Director of Elementary and Secondary Education, and each of these directors has available two consultant teachers and a representative for each of the major disciplines, usually five in number.

The Area Superintendents are responsible directly to the Director of Schools who in turn serves as the Executive Officer of the Metropolitan Board of Education. The three Area Superintendents work closely in coordinating their activities under the framework of the metropolitan school district. There is also a Director of Curriculum to coordinate and influence the curricular decisions for the entire metropolitan district.

The metropolitan school district is presently semi-independent fiscally. The Metropolitan School Board must develop a budget, which is then sent to the mayor through the Metropolitan Director of Finance. The proposed budget is reviewed by the Education Committee of the Metropolitan Council which then offers its recommendations to the council. The school board can, under the provisions of the Charter, go directly to the people, via referendum, for additional monies if the operational budget approved by the Council is declared inadequate by a two-third majority of the school board. The procedures for this process are carefully spelled out in the Charter.

The Metropolitan School Board has adopted a 6-3-3 grade organizational plan: grades one through six, elementary; seven through nine, junior high; and ten through twelve, senior high school. There are, however, still some schools that offer grades one through twelve. The enrollments of the schools range from two hundred to nine hundred at the elementary level and from approximately seven hundred to fifteen hundred at the secondary level. Small elementary schools are being phased out, as are teaching principalships. Several new school buildings have been constructed to replace the smaller and older facilities. New schools are constructed to handle approximately six hundred to six hundred and fifty children.

There is still a great deal of effort being exerted in developing the needed and necessary cooperation between the activities of the central Metropolitan School District administration and that of the three Area Superintendents. They are working together in formulating policy suggestions for the Metropolitan School Board to consider. The equalization of services throughout the district still presents some problems.

The development of the metropolitan government and the metropolitan school system, as they are presently structured in the Nashville-Davidson County area, has generally improved and upgraded the educational system. A unified salary schedule has been adopted, bringing about a substantial increase in the salary base for professionals. There has been an improvement in the physical facilities, and a systematic master plan for educational planning has been incorporated into the operation of the metropolitan government planning units. The curriculum has been greatly expanded and improved. The need for innovative approaches to education appears to have become an integral part of the school district thinking and planning. The metropolitan school system is perceived by many as being "on the move."

CONCLUSION

The most fundamental difference between the two reorganization plans was that the Louisville efforts focused entirely upon schools while, in Nashville, school reorganization was only one part of proposals for total government reform. This alone obviously was not the reason that reform succeeded in Nashville because an almost identical plan was defeated before success was achieved. Moreover, we would expect from the folkthought regarding school government that proposals to consider reorganization of schools and general government together would have little popular appeal. The view that schools are special purpose institutions, which should be protected from partisanship and the general polity, has been widely shared. The Nashville model challenges this belief.

The experiences of the two cities suggest that the model of school reform as part of general reform has much to recommend it. The ideology of school independence notwithstanding, it seems clear in these two cities, at least, that residents perceived substantial interrelations between school and general-purpose government. In Nashville, this perception stemmed from appointment procedures for school board members and a variety of tax questions. In Louisville, the links appeared to be concern over taxes and downtown redevelopment. Adding to this awareness of the issues were the vigorous speeches about the issues made by the mayors and other political leaders in both cities. We are attracted to the generalization that Nashville citizens who considered and defeated the first proposal and Louisville citizens who followed all proposals were bothered by ambiguity about intergovernmental relationships. Explicitness on this point and on the related matter of tax obligations seemingly has merit.

A related point is that reorganization proposals cannot escape association with other issues. In Nashville, these issues were taxation, challenges to contemporary political leaders and, to a lesser extent, race. Taxation and, more recently, race have been prominent variables in Louisville. That race appeared to be a more important force in the latest Louisville efforts probably reflects both changing demography in the area and the general temperament of the nation. If central cities continue to become increasingly black and suburbs are preserved as white sanctuaries, questions associated with race will continue to be relevant to proposals for reorganization. Although racial issues are probably a deterrent to reorganization at present in both black and white neighborhoods, they may not continue to have this effect. Even if polarization continues, it is possible in the long run, for example, that central city blacks will be attracted to metropolitan reform as a means of expanding the revenue base for schools in their neighborhoods, and that suburban whites will see such reorganizations as means of protecting central cities from total black control (Nystrand and Cunningham 1970). (The idea was prompted by a discussion, by Anthony Downs, Jr. [1968], of incentives for desegregating cities.)

Finally, the cases make it clear that metropolitan plans can be designed by the most competent experts and have the support of many powerful groups without being enacted. For example, the support of the media, business leaders, top politicians, and blue ribbon citizens' groups has not been enough to secure passage in Louisville. While the support of such groups is undoubtedly important, the nature of existing jurisdictions suggests that the most important support must come from school personnel, state legislators, and the general public. The positions of these groups appear interdependent in some respects.

Citizens traditionally respect the views of educators about school matters. Consequently, it seems important that the administrators' and teachers' organizations in both systems support merger if it is to be accomplished. This occurred in Nashville but not Louisville where the open opposition of county teachers and limited support of county administrators helped create public doubt about the issue. Interesting in this regard was the finding of Zimmer and Hawley (1968, p. 304) that the suburban school officials were less likely than the citizens to support metropolitan reorganization.

The support of local state legislators is critical as various legislative measures are required to introduce metropolitan government. Legislators in both states were subjected to extensive lobbying by partisans on both sides of the issue. Tennessee legislators followed the lead of their Nashville members in supporting the necessary legislation. In Kentucky, however, legislative approval was denied when senators, noticing that two of their three Louisville members opposed the measure, declined to vote in opposition to their wishes.

In the final analysis, the extent to which local citizens favor reorganization is probably the most important determinant of success. This was clearly the case in Nashville where a public referendum was required for passage. In Louisville, where such a referendum was not required, legislators appeared reluctant to act without guarantee of widespread public support. It is the importance of grass roots citizen support that, more than anything else, suggests that the short-range prospects for metropolitan school government are bleak. In a survey of citizens in six metropolitan areas, Zimmer and Hawley (1969, p. 309) found that the greatest obstacle to reorganization is the opposition of suburbanites except for those who reside in relatively small metropolitan areas. The Nashville and Louisville experiences support this finding. They also support the conclusion of these authors that efforts to achieve reorganization should concentrate upon winning popular support for the plan among suburban residents (ibid.).

NOTES

1. The data for this paper were gathered by Robert W. Heller and Troy V. McKelvey on visits to Louisville and Nashville. Expanded versions of these cases appear in "A Comparative Analysis of the Planning Process and Development of Metropolitan School Organization," currently being written by Robert W. Heller and Troy V. McKelvey.

2. This point is consistent with the observation of Masters, Salisbury, and

Eliot (1964) that Missouri legislators followed the lead of the big city members when considering city legislation.

REFERENCES

Community Services Commission. *A Future for Nashville.* Nashville, Tenn.: Community Services Commission, 1952.

Cornell, Francis G. "A Comprehensive Survey of the Metropolitan School System: Nashville and Davidson County, Tennessee." White Plains, N.Y.: Educational Research Services, 1963.

Cunningham, Luvern L.; Dykes, Archie; Kincheloe, James; and Ostrum, Vincent. "Report on the Merger Issues to the Louisville Public School System and the Jefferson County Public School System." Mimeographed. Louisville, Ky.: Louisville and Jefferson County Boards of Education, 1966.

Downs, Anthony, Jr. "Alternative Futures for the American Ghetto." *Daedalus* 97 (Fall 1968): 1331-78.

Harris, John H.; Hemberger, Robert C.; and Goodnight, Frederick H. "School Reorganization in a Metropolitan Area: The Nashville Experience." In *Metropolitanism: Its Challenge to Education* (Sixty-seventh Yearbook of the National Society for the Study of Education, part 1), edited by Robert J. Havighurst, pp. 352-83. Chicago: University of Chicago Press, 1968.

Masters, Nicholas A.; Salisbury, Robert H.; and Eliot, Thomas H. *State Politics in the Public Schools.* New York: Knopf, 1964.

Nashville Area Chamber of Commerce, Division of Civic Affairs and Governmental Relations. "Metropolitan Government for Nashville and Davidson County." Mimeographed. Nashville, Tenn.: Nashville Area Chamber of Commerce, 1956.

Nashville City Planning Commission, and Davidson County Planning Commission. "Plan of Metropolitan Government for Nashville and Davidson County." Mimeographed. Nashville, Tenn.: Metropolitan Planning Commission, 1963.

Nystrand, Raphael O., and Cunningham, Luvern L. "Federated Urban School Systems: Compromising the Centralization-Decentralization Issue." In *Toward Improved Urban Education,* edited by Frank W. Lutz, pp. 95-111. Worthington, Ohio: Charles A. Jones, 1970.

Zimmer, Basil G., and Hawley, Amos H. *Metropolitan Area Schools: Resistance to District Reorganization.* Beverly Hills, Ca.: Sage Publications, 1968.

11

The Supra-System Model: The Toronto Experience

E. Brock Rideout

The municipality of metropolitan Toronto is the capital of the province of Ontario and the site of the first experiment in metropolitan government in North America. The municipality, with a population of over 2,000,000 and an area of 241 square miles, stretches some 12 miles north from the north shore of Lake Ontario and extends along 26 miles of the lakefront. When the municipality was created in 1953, the area consisted of the city of Toronto and the twelve southernmost municipalities of York County. (In Ontario, cities are administratively completely separated from the counties in which they lie.) These thirteen municipalities varied greatly in area, population, school enrollment, and municipal status as may be seen in table 11:1.

It will be seen that the city of Toronto contained 56 percent of the total population but only 45 percent of the public school enrollment. Toronto had ceased its policy of annexation in the early thirties and, by 1953, was surrounded, as may be seen from figure 11:1, by an inner ring of urban townships (York and East York), towns (Leaside, Weston, Mimico, and New Toronto), and villages (Forest Hill, Swansea, and Long Branch), and an outer ring of three

TABLE 11:1. METROPOLITAN TORONTO (1953-1954)

Municipality	Status	Area (sq. mi.)	Population (1953)	Public School Enrollment (1954)	Number of Schools (1954)	Number of Teachers (1954)
Toronto	city	35.1	665,502	83,159	107	2,888
North York	township	68.1	101,311	23,972	50	850
Scarborough	township	70.0	78,803	17,749	34	450
Etobicoke	township	44.8	70,209	15,038	23	494
York	township	8.0	100,463	16,154	23	532
East York	township	5.9	65,736	10,017	17	320
Forest Hill	village	1.5	17,719	3,121	5	123
Leaside	town	2.4	15,910	3,083	4	118
Mimico	town	1.0	12,301	5,117[a]	9	192
New Toronto	town	1.2	9,744			
Long Branch	village	.9	9,140			
Weston	town	1.0	8,374	2,663[b]	4	97
Swansea	village	1.1	8,344	784[c]	1	30
Metropolitan Toronto		241.0	1,172,556	180,857	277	6,094

a. The Lakeshore Board of Education served the three municipalities of Mimico, New Toronto, and Long Branch.
b. The Weston Secondary School drew more than half of its pupils from outside the town.
c. Swansea operated no high school, sending its high school pupils to Toronto.

Source: Goldenberg, Report of the Royal Commission on Metropolitan Toronto (1965), pp. 1, 11, 121, 123, 124.

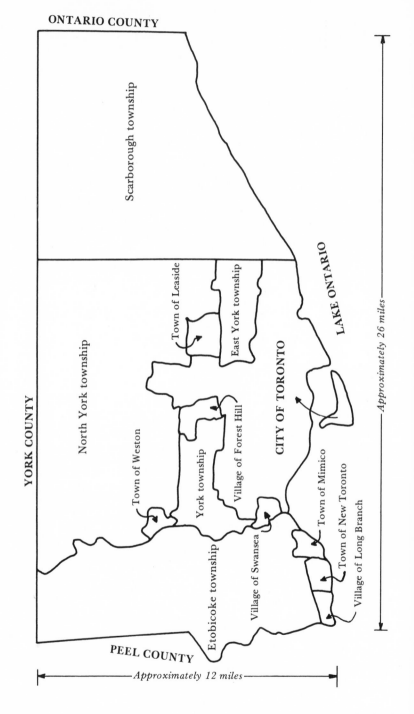

FIGURE 11:1. THE MUNICIPALITY OF METROPOLITAN TORONTO 1954-1966

ONTARIO COUNTY

Scarborough township

LAKE ONTARIO

Town of Leaside

East York township

YORK COUNTY

North York township

CITY OF TORONTO

Town of Weston

York township

Village of Forest Hill

Town of Mimico

Town of New Toronto

Village of Long Branch

Etobicoke township

Village of Swansea

PEEL COUNTY

Approximately 26 miles

Approximately 12 miles

semirural but rapidly urbanizing townships (Etobicoke, North York, and Scarborough).

Educationally the area was administered by twenty-five school boards (excluding Roman Catholic separate-school boards). The three lakeshore municipalities of Long Branch, New Toronto, and Mimico had already united for school purposes under the Lakeshore Board of Education; there was one board each for Toronto, York Township, East York Township, Leaside, Weston, Forest Hill, and Swansea; Etobicoke had two boards, North York, four; and Scarborough, eleven.

As of 1 January 1954, the thirteen municipalities were federated by an act of the provincial legislature into the Municipality of Metropolitan Toronto—a two-tier system of local government. At the same time provision was made for ten of the municipalities to be administered by one board of education each. The Lakeshore Board continued. Thus the twenty-five previous boards were replaced by eleven plus the Metropolitan School Board.

THE POLITICAL SETTING

So that this Canadian development may be better assessed by those concerned with metropolitan problems in the United States, a look at the political setting in which metropolitan Toronto was created is warranted. In many ways, municipal and school government in Canada parallels that in the United States. Education is a provincial matter in Canada as it is a state matter in the United States. Municipalities and school boards are creatures of the provinces as they are of the states. Education is administered locally by elected school boards and financed by a combination of taxes on real property and grants-in-aid from the provinces (states) in both countries. But there are differences. All Canadian provinces operate with a unicameral legislature. A more important difference than this, however, is that there are no provincial constitutions as there are state constitutions in the United States. Canadian provinces follow the British pattern whereby the "constitution" at any given moment consists of all the laws on the statute books. All that is required then, to change the "constitution" provincially, is to pass a new act or amend an existing one. This admittedly has its drawbacks, but it does have the advantage of making it comparatively easy to pass needed legislation in emergencies without recourse to long-drawn-out proceedings to amend restrictive constitutional provisions inherited from a different past.

A third difference that makes reorganization of municipal and school government easier in Canada than in the United States is that the Canadian movement toward grass roots democracy in the nineteenth century did not go as far as it did in the United States. Although recognized in most matters, it is not permitted to hamstring the efforts of the provincial legislature to make those changes that while not favored by the citizens of a particular community, are seen by the representatives of the total provincial community to be in the best interests of the larger community. This makes it easier for the province to exercise its overriding responsibility for municipal and school government.

A fourth difference is the greater relative strength of provincial governments vis-à-vis the federal government than is typical in the United States. The provincial departments of education and municipal affairs are (if I read the literature on the topic correctly) much stronger than the state departments of education and municipal affairs.

In Ontario there are two additional factors that helped facilitate the formation of metropolitan Toronto. First, a strong political party, the Progressive-Conservatives, has been in power continuously since 1944. This party, with a relatively weak opposition, and with the strong party discipline characteristic of the Canadian parliamentary system, has been able to push through what it considered to be desirable legislation, without fear of being ousted at the next provincial election. Second is the existence of a powerful semijudicial body, created after the depression-induced bankruptcies of many municipalities: the Ontario Municipal Board, which has wide powers with respect to the creating of municipalities, their change of status, amalgamation, and powers of annexation. In addition, this body, known by its acronym, the OMB, must approve all capital borrowing by municipalities and school boards. Coupled with all this was the realization, even in 1953 when the legislature was rurally dominated, of the centrality of the metropolitan Toronto area to the total provincial well-being.

THE FISCAL SETTING

In 1953 the central city of Toronto was in much the same fiscal situation as large United States cities were before World War II. School expenditure per pupil was substantially higher than in most suburbs; the assessed values of property per capita and per student were much higher than in the rest of the metropolitan area (except in some of the small villages); over 60 percent of the taxable assessment was commercial and industrial.

The school boards in Ontario were fiscally independent to a greater degree than in any other jurisdiction in North America. Municipal councils were required by law to levy and collect the requisitions submitted to them by school boards for operating expenditure. There was no statutory limitation on mill rates for education; no vote of the electors was required to approve the school operating budget; and even in the matter of capital borrowing, school boards could bypass the necessity for a vote of the ratepayers on a bond issue if they could get the approval of the municipal council, which approval was granted at least 95 percent of the time. The city benefited too by the system of provincial school grants-in-aid, which had a flat-grant component with respect to both current and capital financing.

The Problem

In the light of all these factors, the questions might well be asked "What then was the problem? Why the urgency to establish a metropolitan form of government?" The major problems were in the suburbs—chiefly in the three outer ring townships, which after 1945, rapidly became dormitory municipalities for the industrialized city and inner suburbs. There was mass migration from the city, and the former city dwellers were replaced largely by new immigrants from Europe, most of whom did not speak English. There was not the corresponding flight of major industry, although there was a rapid increase in subsidiary industry in the outer ring municipalities, but not enough to provide the tax revenue to supply municipal and school services for the large numbers of families with young children moving to the suburbs. It soon became apparent that the tax base in the three townships was not sufficient to provide their massive needs for sewers, water supply, and schools. It became increasingly difficult to float new bond issues for schools; water taps often ran dry in summer, and septic tank sewage disposal became the rule. Several attempts to provide cooperative solutions failed; applications were made to the OMB by three municipalities for various forms of amalgamation or annexation. But, in spite of their problems, the suburbs wanted to be aided rather than swallowed by the city.

It will thus be seen that the problem in the Toronto area was just the reverse of that which faces the large metropolitan areas in the United States.

The Solution

The OMB turned down Toronto's application for the amalgamation of the thirteen municipalities into one large city of Toronto and suggested instead a federal system patterned on the existing county system in the province, but with greater powers granted to the intermediate tier than was typical in the county structure. In April 1953, the provincial legislature passed Bill 80: "An Act to Provide for the Federation of Municipalities in the Toronto Metropolitan Area for Certain Financial and other Purposes." Not all of the OMB's suggestions were embodied in the act, but the main ones were. A two-tier system was set up, with thirteen first-tier municipalities and one second-tier metropolitan municipality headed by a Metropolitan Council. The act also provided for eleven boards of education and a Metropolitan School Board. After this system had been in operation for ten years, the government appointed a Royal Commission to investigate the problems of metropolitan Toronto. The Royal Commission made its report in 1965, and the legislation was amended to provide for a somewhat expanded city of Toronto (including the former villages of Forest Hill and Swansea) and five boroughs: Etobicoke (including the former lakeshore municipalities of Long Branch, New Toronto, and Mimico); East York (including the former town of Leaside); York (including the former town of Weston); North York; and Scarborough. Figure 11:2 shows the municipal structure of metropolitan Toronto in 1973. At the same time provision was made for one board of education each for the city and the five boroughs and for the Metropolitan School Board to continue, but with increased powers. The new legislation went into effect on 1 January 1967.

Division of municipal powers

For municipal purposes, the federation works as a federation is usually thought to work: through a division of powers with each level responsible for the administration and financing of its own areas of responsibility. Thus, the Metropolitan Council has complete responsibility for some services: assessment of property (although, since January 1970, property assessment has become a provincial, rather than a municipal, function), capital financing, police protection, public assistance, public transportation, and traffic lights. The area municipalities have complete responsibility for fire protection, garbage collection and disposal, public health, street lighting, parking

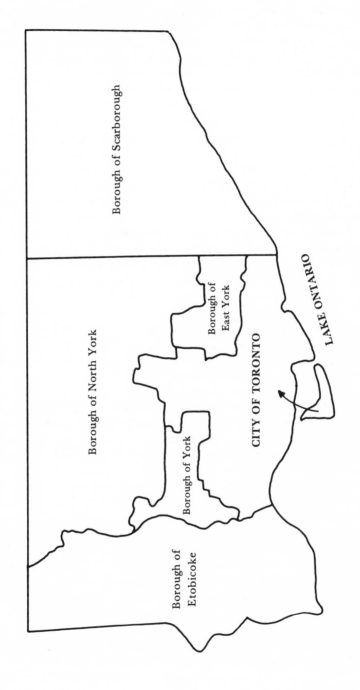

FIGURE 11:2. THE MUNICIPALITY OF METROPOLITAN TORONTO 1967-1973

Borough of Scarborough

Borough of North York

Borough of East York

Borough of York

Borough of Etobicoke

CITY OF TORONTO

LAKE ONTARIO

lots, sidewalks, and the levy and collection of taxes, both local and metropolitan. In all other areas of municipal government the responsibility is shared, with the metropolitan council being responsible for those aspects of a service that are of concern to the entire metropolis, while the local councils are responsible for purely local matters. For example the metropolitan council is responsible for arterial streets and roads, and for expressways, while the city and boroughs take care of local streets and roads; the metropolitan council builds and maintains major trunk sewers and sewage disposal plants, while the local municipalities look after feeder sewer lines and local sewage disposal. Other services that are similarly operated on a shared basis are water supply, public libraries, parks and recreation areas, licensing, public housing, and traffic control. Thus, while many of the major services of the area are financed by a common levy over the whole metropolitan area, both the type and the cost of the services left to the local municipalities vary, and these variations, together with variations in the taxable assessment of the local municipalities, result in varying mill rates for purely local services.

School Organization

For school purposes, however, even in 1954, metropolitan Toronto was not a true federation. There was no clear-cut division of power between the Metropolitan School Board and the eleven area boards. The plan's major features were:

1. The Metropolitan School Board, through the Metropolitan Corporation, assumed all school debenture liabilities of the area municipalities outstanding on 1 January 1954. (In Ontario the issuing of debentures for school purposes was a function of the municipal, rather than of the school, authorities and this is still so in metropolitan Toronto. However, the costs of debt repayment and interest are still charged by the municipal authority to the particular school authority.)

2. Subsequent debt created for the erection of new schools and the acquisition of school sites was apportioned between metropolitan Toronto and the area municipalities, with the former assuming the local share of school debt that was recognized by the province for grant purposes. In 1964, this policy was changed and for the next two years metropolitan Toronto assumed the municipal share of standard school construction costs under a ceiling cost formula established by the Metropolitan School Board, with the area boards continuing to be responsible for all costs in excess of the

ceiling. The provincial grants on debt service charges were paid to the Metropolitan School Board.

3. The metropolitan board made to each area board maintenance assistance payments of the same dollar amount per pupil to each board but varying with type of pupil. The metropolitan board financed these maintenance assistance payments and the annual debt charges on debentures assumed by metropolitan Toronto, together with the expenses of the metropolitan board itself, from two sources: the provincial grants earned by the area boards (except for a few special grants), which were paid by the province to the metropolitan board, and the proceeds of a metropoliswide levy at a common mill rate to make up the difference. These maintenance assistance payments at no time exceeded 60 percent of the actual operating costs of the area boards and tended not to rise proportionately with annual increases in costs. (These three programs did, however, result in some equalization since it soon became evident that some municipalities were paying more into the metropolitan "pot" than they were receiving from it. It was probably this realization on the part of metropolitan board members, a majority of whom represented net-paying boards, that prevented the board from raising the payments to a more equitable level.)

THE PRESENT ORGANIZATION

Since 1 January 1967, the Metropolitan School Board has had greatly enhanced powers. Although there is still no division of power as in the municipal field, the metropolitan board has almost complete control of both current and capital financing, and this is the ultimate control in decision making. At first glance, then, one might assume that education decision making in metropolitan Toronto is highly centralized. This would indeed be true if the Metropolitan School Board were an independently elected body; but it is not. It is composed of fifteen members of the six area boards: the chairman of each of the six boards, five additional members of the Toronto board, two of the North York board, and one each of the Scarborough and Etobicoke boards. The Metropolitan Separate School Board appoints three persons to the Metropolitan School Board to represent the interests of separate-school supporters in matters not exclusively affecting the public elementary schools. (Separate schools operate only to the end of grade ten and their pupils then attend either parochial high schools or the public high schools; separate-school supporters thus pay taxes to support the public high schools but they do not pay taxes to support public elementary schools.) The existence of publicly supported separate schools for Roman Catholics is one of the reasons that over 95 percent of the school children living in metropolitan Toronto attend publicly supported schools there—a figure much higher than in most large United States cities.

Education in metropolitan Toronto is administered by six boards of education, each elected by the ratepayers (including tenants) of the city or borough. Separate-school supporters elect two of the members of each of the six boards to represent separate-school supporters' interests in secondary education.

Each of these six boards of education is responsible for the programs for kindergarten through grade thirteen. Each has a chief education officer, called a Director of Education, who is also officially the secretary-treasurer or chief executive officer of the board. He has a large staff of superintendents, assistant superintendents, area superintendents (sometimes called inspectors), school business officials, consultants, special subject supervisors, and so on. Principals and teachers and all other staff are hired, paid, assigned duties, and so on by these boards. Buildings are built, operated, and maintained, and transportation provided by the boards. Each board prepares a current budget and a capital budget annually for presentation to the Metropolitan School Board. Thus all the major functions of a school board are performed by the six local boards. In some respects their relationship to the Metropolitan School Board is like that of a fiscally dependent school board to its municipal council in the United States. The difference is that the body on which they are dependent is not a noneducational body, nor is it an independently elected school authority. It is, in a sense, a place where the six boards' representatives come together to rationalize their proposed expenditure programs so that equality of educational opportunity may be achieved, through differing programs, but can be financed by a uniform metropolitan mill rate. Figure 11:3 illustrates the relationships among the electors, the area boards, the Metropolitan School Board, and the Metropolitan Separate School Board.

The Metropolitan School Board does not have a large staff. Until 1969 it operated no schools. (In 1969, for the first time, schools for the trainable mentally retarded have come under the jurisdiction of school boards in Ontario, and in metropolitan Toronto it was decided that these schools be operated directly by the metropolitan board.) The metropolitan board has a Director of Education who is also secretary-treasurer and who has three chief assistants:

FIGURE 11:3. THE EDUCATION STRUCTURE OF METROPOLITAN TORONTO

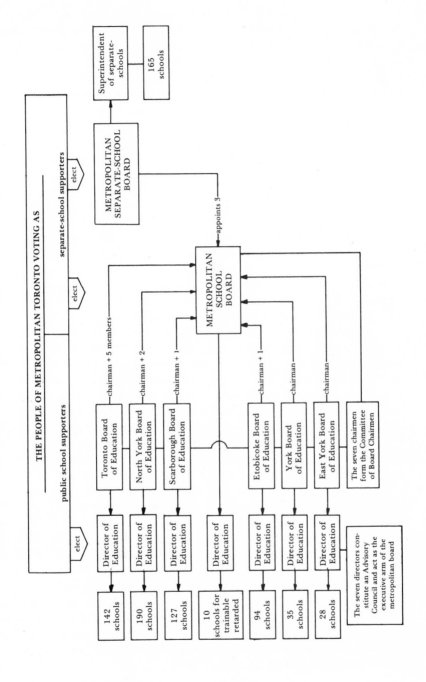

A *coordinator of academic programs* who works with the Academic Committee of the Board in devising and assessing the academic standards on which decisions will be made in coordinating the budgets of the six area boards. This official chairs a number of committees of key personnel from each of the six area boards. These committees are concerned with summer schools, night schools, class size, pupil-teacher ratios, inner-city schools, audiovisual aids and educational television, special education, junior kindergartens, psychological services, and research;

A *comptroller of finance* who works with the board's standing Committee on Finance and who is responsible for coordinating on a year-round basis the current budgets of the six area boards and for regulating the flow of funds from the metropolitan board to the area boards;

A *director of planning and research* who works with the board's standing Committee on Buildings and Sites and who is responsible, in consultation with local officials, for planning the sites of new schools and for school building and renovation; he is also responsible for the capital budget finally submitted by the metropolitan board to the Metropolitan Council for approval.

The metropolitan Director of Education and the six directors of the area boards of education constitute the Advisory Council of Directors. This council, which meets weekly, acts as the executive arm of the metropolitan board. All major problems and decisions, first discussed and ironed out here, form the basis for metropolitan board action and influence the decisions of the area boards.

The metropolitan board chairman and the chairmen of the six area boards constitute the Committee of Board Chairmen, originally convened for salary negotiations with the various locals of the Ontario Teachers' Federation and its constituent bodies, but increasingly to consider other matters of broad policy. The organization of the Metropolitan School Board is shown in figure 11:4.

It will thus be seen that the metropolitan system of education has some of the features of cooperative federalism in that it works efficiently and with a minimum of friction only when there is mutual trust and respect among the area boards and between them and the metropolitan board. This cooperative effort has come about chiefly through such nonstatutory devices as the Advisory Council of Directors and the Committee of Board Chairman; it has been helped by the practice of the metropolitan board—the local boards "writ large"—in limiting itself to a small coordinating staff that operates in close consultation with area board staff.

FIGURE 11:4. STAFF AND FUNCTIONS OF THE METROPOLITAN SCHOOL BOARD

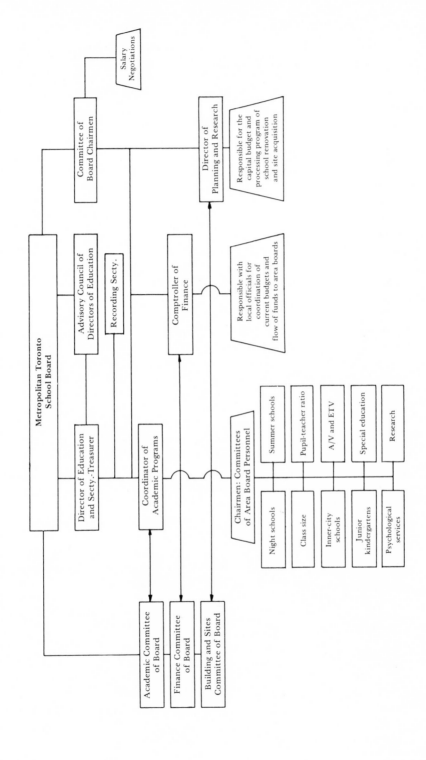

Comparison with Large-City Decentralization

The metropolitan Toronto system might also be compared with the systems developing in some large United States cities in which community school districts are being formed for some functions. The emphasis is different, however. In Toronto it is the local boards that have the large administrative staffs, that have most of the powers and duties laid on school boards by provincial statute and regulation and, finally, that control the Metropolitan School Board. Then too, most of the area boards are too large to be realistically termed *community school districts* in the usual sense of the word. Table 11:2 shows the area, population, public school enrollment, number of schools, and number of teachers in the six area municipalities, as of September 1972.

It will be seen that at least four of the area municipalities are as big as major cities, each with a population of more than a quarter of a million, and public school enrollment of more than sixty thousand pupils. Each of these municipalities is diverse in its ethnic, socio-economic, and religious composition; each represents a rather plural-ist society in terms of values, goals, and expectations. At present the only direct participation by parents and ratepayers in education is through the election of the six area boards of education and the Metropolitan Separate School Board, and elections take place only every two years at the time of the biennial municipal elections. There are no provisions for a vote of the electorate on either the current or the capital budgets. It is my personal opinion that mechanisms should be devised to permit a greater involvement of smaller com-munities within each of the area municipalities in educational mat-ters. Suggestions have been made for the formation of councils of parents and other ratepayers to work with the principal of each school or with the administration of each high school and its feeder elementary schools. Such councils could deal with such matters as the use of the school for community purposes, adaptations of the curriculum to local needs, the use of the resources of laymen in school programs, the relation of the school to the world of work and leisure, and the emerging problems of drug abuse, student alienation, and school discipline.

The Royal Commission on Metropolitan Toronto, which re-ported in 1965, recommended that metropolitan Toronto be divided into eleven school districts, disregarding municipal boundaries, dis-tricts that would, by 1980, be of approximately equal population and whose boundaries would be determined chiefly by such

TABLE 11:2. THE AREA MUNICIPALITIES OF METROPOLITAN TORONTO (1972-1973)

Name	Status	Area (sq. mi.)	Population (1971)	Public School Enrollment	Number of Schools September 1971	Number of Teachers
Toronto	city	37.7	680,319	108,228	142	5,379
North York	borough	68.1	514,817	106,610	190	5,060
Scarborough	borough	70.0	325,331	87,757	127	4,146
Etobicoke	borough	47.9	280,722	61,158	94	2,982
York	borough	9.0	142,296	24,755	35	1,170
East York	borough	8.3	101,965	14,218	28	652
Metropolitan Toronto		241.0	2,045,450	402,726[a]	616	19,389

a. In addition there are 82,261 pupils enrolled in the 165 schools under the jurisdiction of the publicly supported Metropolitan Toronto Separate-School Board, and 1,239 trainable mentally retarded pupils enrolled in 10 schools under the direct jurisdiction of the Metropolitan School Board.

Sources: *Area*—Goldenberg (1965), table 1, p. 1.
    Population—Ontario Department of Municipal Affairs, *1972 Municipal Directory*, 1972.
    Enrollment, Numbers of Schools and Teachers—Ministry of Education, *Directory of Schools 1972/73*, 1972.

geographical factors as ravines, expressways, major railway lines, and arterial highways. The act passed by the legislature in 1966 rejected this suggestion, which indeed had been coupled with a recommendation for a stronger Metropolitan School Board and local boards with decreased powers. For the operation of the metropolitan Toronto school system, this was probably a fortunate decision, since it would have been much more difficult, if not impossible, for the Advisory Council of Directors of Education to function effectively if it were composed of twelve members rather than seven. It is probably easier to get agreement or consensus among a smaller than a larger number of boards and board executives, and the metropolitan Toronto system stands or falls on its ability to achieve such agreement.

Financing Education in Metropolitan Toronto

The most startling aspects of the metropolitan Toronto educational system since it was reorganized in January 1967 are that over 98 percent of the total local share of school board expenditures is raised by a uniform mill rate over the whole of the metropolitan area, and that this has been achieved, so far, without the creation of identical services in each area municipality. What is being sought is equality of educational opportunity rather than uniformity of educational provisions.

In 1963, as a result of widely differing assessment per pupil (which, in 1964 (expressed in Canadian dollars), per elementary school pupil, averaged $18,000 in metropolitan Toronto, but varied from a low of $9,700 in Scarborough to a high of $45,700 in Leaside, with the city being $25,800), and because the Metropolitan School Board had failed, during the previous nine years, to keep its maintenance assistance payments at equitable levels, current expenditure per elementary pupil varied from a low of $378 in Scarborough to a high of $611 in Leaside, with the central city spending $523; at the same time, current expenditures per academic high school pupil varied from $796 in Forest Hill to $562 in Weston, with the average at $684, while those for technical high school pupils ranged from $1,212 in Toronto to $797 in Weston, with the average at $1,111. These differences could be attributed to many factors besides the obvious one of greater property assessment per pupil: the rapidly growing municipalities tended to have a higher percentage of newly qualified and hence less highly paid teachers; pupil-teacher ratios showed considerable variation; building maintenance and operation costs tended to be higher in municipalities with more older schools. Some boards had a full range of services for atypical children, while others did not and, in the outer ring townships, transportation costs were considerable while in the city and inner suburbs they were nil. Debt service charges per pupil were much higher in the outer suburbs than in the completely built-up areas.

Mill rate variations

Naturally these differences in program, coupled with differences in assessment per pupil, resulted in rather wide variations in mill rates for school purposes. In 1964, as reported by the Royal Commission on Metropolitan Toronto, school mill rates varied from 31.61 mills in Scarborough to 24.19 mills in Weston. (These mill rates are based on a property and business assessment equalized at approximately 32 percent of sale value.) It was true, however, that mill rates did not vary as much as did assessment per pupil, a fact that reflects the equalizing effect of the metropolitan board's assistance, in which was included the provincial grants-in-aid. It did often mean, however, that some local boards were not able to offer the full range of services they desired because of a relatively low tax base.

Financing local programs under a uniform levy

With the advent of the uniform school levy for programs approved by the metropolitan board, starting in January 1967, many of the former handicaps were removed. There is, of course, a tendency for boards that had been forced by circumstance to curtail their spending in certain areas (school supplies, free periods for teachers, secretarial help for principals, and special classes for atypical pupils, and so on) to begin to spend more money in these areas. But, so long as a board can convince the other five boards, through the metropolitan structure, that it is not putting in unnecessary services, in relation to what other boards are doing, its full program is usually recognized as a part of the metropolitan budget. Different boards have different growing points, different emphases in the field of innovation. The metropolitan board then becomes a place for trade offs, for political decision making. The Coordinator of Academic Services and his ten committees of area board personnel are beginning to set up criteria to help guide local boards in their decision making. One of the greatest boons to the three rapidly growing boroughs has been the assumption by metropolitan Toronto of all school debenture liabilities outstanding on 1 January 1967 and its assumption of all debt service charges in the future. What the area boards give up under this arrangement is the right to provide school accommodation beyond the levels approved by the metropolitan board, that is, beyond levels deemed adequate by representatives of all the boards.

Teachers' Salaries

Since teachers are employed by area boards and not by the metropolitan board they would like to negotiate with their own boards for salaries and fringe benefits. But, under a system using a uniform tax levy, it seems unjustifiable to have different salary scales in different parts of metropolitan Toronto. For the past several years the Committee of Board Chairmen has been the medium through which joint negotiations have been carried on with the teachers, with difficulty, but successfully.

Budget items not approved

When budget items of an area board are not approved by the Metropolitan School Board, the area board has three alternatives: it can live within its approved budget; it can appeal the decision of the metropolitan board to the Ontario Municipal Board (OMB), a provincial body with wide powers in matters concerning local government, for an order reinstating the disallowed items; it can requisition the additional sums required from its own city or borough council, which is required to raise such moneys to the extent that they can be raised with a levy not in excess of 2.5 mills. So far no board has appealed to the OMB and very little use has been made of the third alternative. This is a pretty good indication that the essential needs of the area boards are being met under the approval system set up by the metropolitan board.

Capital Financing

The procedures by which the eventual capital budget for metropolitan Toronto schools is drawn up, assessed, submitted, and resubmitted to the various boards and committees has been well described by McCordic (1969). Essentially they consist of a series of staff consultations, metropolitan and local board and committee hearings, and negotiations between the metropolitan board and the local boards. They result in a composite capital budget in which each of the proposed projects is placed in one of five categories of priority. These priorities form the basis on which projects are deleted by the metropolitan board before submission of the composite budget to the Metropolitan Council for approval. The council enters the picture because all capital borrowing in metropolitan Toronto is a function of the Metropolitan Council, which each year, in consultation with the OMB, sets an overall limit on new capital borrowing for *all* metropolitan purposes. By mutual agreement there is usually a prior earmarking of the total sum among the capital requirements of the Metropolitan Council, the local councils, and the Metropolitan School Board. If and when the Metropolitan Council fails to approve the composite capital budget as presented by the Metropolitan School Board, projects in the lowest priority categories are cut out until the Council's approval limit is reached. (Usually, however, the Metropolitan School Board has prior knowledge of what the ceiling on the school capital budget will be, so that the final submission to Metropolitan Council becomes a formality, with the cutting having been done by the metropolitan board beforehand.)

Provincial Grants-in-Aid

Provincial grants-in-aid on behalf of the area boards have been paid to the metropolitan board since 1954 but, since 1969, the grants have been calculated using the enrollment and financial data for the whole of the metropolitan municipality, which is considered as a single board for grant purposes. This became necessary when the entire eligible program was being financed by a single mill rate. This is not the place to describe the grant plan in detail. Suffice it to say that the Ontario plan is a variable percentage plan somewhat similar to that used in New York state. It differs from the New York plan in that the aid ratio applies only to what are termed "ordinary operating expenditures"; approved "extraordinary expenditures"—debt charges, capital expenditure from current revenue, and expenditure on transportation—are eligible for grant at a higher percentage than that represented by the aid ratio and this percentage increases as the unit cost of such extraordinary expenditures increases beyond certain fixed points. It also differs in that weighted average daily membership rather than average daily attendance is used and in the fact that high school pupils are weighted by a factor of about 1.8 (instead of the 1.25 in the New York plan).

In addition, the Ontario provincial-aid plan utilizes a number of weighting factors, among which are factors recognizing the special needs of large conurbations. The hope is that a formula of this type will prevent the educational deterioration to be found in large cities. That metropolitan Toronto is well above the provincial average in assessment per weighted pupil was evident in the early years of the new aid plan when, even after the weights were applied, the Metropolitan School Board received its grant under a "save-harmless" provision in the plan.

Since 1970, the Ontario government has been setting ceilings on operating expenditure per weighted pupil. This is beginning to pose problems for the Metropolitan School Board, since, in its case, the ceiling is on the total metropolitan expenditure per weighted pupil. This means that any significant increase in the expenditure per weighted pupil by the lower spending boroughs must be achieved by decreases in the expenditure per weighted pupil by the city and by the higher spending boroughs.

STRENGTHS AND WEAKNESSES
OF THE METROPOLITAN TORONTO PLAN

Strengths

1. The municipal structure of metropolitan Toronto has been reorganized so that six municipalities exist, each capable of operating a full range of municipal and school services.
2. The taxable assessment of the whole metropolitan municipality stands behind the current and capital requirements for the education of each public elementary and secondary pupil in the area.
3. The determination and administration of educational programs is left with elected boards of laymen in each local municipality. Thus each board has the freedom to fix educational goals that reflect the needs and aspirations of the community and to modify its program and make innovations to meet its special needs.
4. The relative dominance of local boards is ensured by having the upper-tier authority composed of members of the area boards, including their chairmen, and by ensuring that local board staff have a role to play in the staff functions of the metropolitan board.
5. The existence of a central coordinating board to ensure that new and renovated school accommodation is provided on a priority basis over the whole metropolitan area, and to ensure that, while local programs may differ, no one board may advance on many fronts while others are forced to mark time. In other words, the two-tier system means coordinated central planning of the area's total educational needs.
6. The metropolitan board has a stronger voice with the provincial government than would any one of the area boards. This is important in pressing for increased financial aid.
7. And finally, the metropolitan school system was fortunate to have had a knowledgeable, far-sighted, and dedicated professional educator, W. J. McCordic, as its chief executive officer for its first eighteen years of existence.

Weaknesses

1. The metropolitan plan as it applies to education does not yet have adequate mechanisms for the participation of parents and other laymen in the education process. This is more a *de facto* than an inherent weakness of the plan.
2. The plan might not function as well as it does if party politics became a major factor in the election of school board members, particularly if different local boards were controlled by different political parties.
3. Since each school board member's first responsibility is to his own local board, it takes time for metropolitan board members to develop a metropolitan outlook. The original three-year term of office on local boards was of some help, but this has been reduced to two years. There are changes in membership on the metropolitan board even between elections, and some new members tend, as McCordic has said, to start off on a "local autonomy kick" before becoming socialized to the metropolitan concept.
4. A major weakness, from the standpoint of the taxpayer, is that there is little incentive for an area board to curtail unnecessary services or refrain from instituting a higher level of services. If one board is extravagant, its extravagances are borne by all taxpayers in metropolitan Toronto and, if it tightens its belt, its ratepayers reap only a small proportion of the savings effected. This has been a strength during the first few years under the new plan since it enabled boards that were previously "have-nots" to catch up; but political decision making being what it is, there is always the danger that the former "haves" will use their bargaining power to trade off the expenditures for catching up to increase levels of service in their schools. Even this may not be an absolute weakness since it ensures the continuance of the growing edge of school change and provides something for the other boards to catch up with.

REFERENCES

Goldenberg, H. Carl. *Report of the Royal Commission on Metropolitan Toronto.* Toronto: 1965.

McCordic, William J. "Urban Education: An Experiment in Two-Tiered Administration." In *Politics and Government of Urban Canada*, edited by Lionel D. Feldman and Michael D. Goldrick, pp. 108-120. Toronto: Methuen, 1969.

Ministry of Education. *Directory of Schools 1972/73.* Toronto: Ministry of Education, 1972.

Ontario Department of Municipal Affairs. *1972 Municipal Directory.* Toronto: The Department, 1972.

12

The Inner London Education Authority

Daniel E. Griffiths

While most people look for models in the common, the general, and the most frequent practices, some look to the unique. The Inner London Education Authority (ILEA) stands alone in a country whose approach to governing education is itself unique. A study of the ILEA, which is organizationally and governmentally so different from anything that exists in the United States, opens up a wide range of drastically opposing alternatives to the traditional American approach to big city school governance. While there is no question that the ILEA grew out of a particular social, political, cultural, and historical environment that does not exist in the United States, it is entirely possible that certain aspects of the ILEA can be adapted to big city education in America.

The purpose of my study was to investigate the governance and organization of several European cities (London, Edinburgh, Glasgow, Berlin, and Madrid) to determine if there are viable alternatives to American practice. These alternatives would then be stated in a form to generate discussion that might give rise to new forms of governance and organization in this country. Although five cities were studied, this chapter deals with only one: London. The need for brevity is not the most compelling reason for this choice, rather the ILEA was found to offer the widest range of observable differences.

OVERVIEW OF THE ILEA

The ILEA is responsible for the education service in London's twelve inner boroughs and the City of London. The other boroughs administer education separately, so that education in the Greater London area falls under two types of control: that of the ILEA on one hand, and that of twenty different local authorities on the other. (An excellent discussion of the rationale for the two types of organization is to be found in Reller 1968.) The map of Greater London (figure 12:1) shows the two types of organization. The ILEA is a special committee of the Greater London Council (GLC), a body responsible for virtually all municipal services. "It is special in the sense that, once constituted, it is virtually autonomous (Inner London Education Authority 1968, p. 5)." It seems, however, that the GLC and the ILEA work very closely together. Indeed, it would be difficult to conceive otherwise since forty of the fifty-three members of the ILEA are also members of the GLC. The other thirteen consist of one representative from each of the twelve inner-London borough councils and one from the Common Council of the City of London.

The ILEA works through an Education Committee of sixty-nine persons, the fifty-three members of the authority and sixteen added members chosen from "people experienced in education who are familiar with the needs of schools and other educational establishments in inner London (ibid.)."

The authority's administrative unit, which is headed by the Education Officer (roughly comparable to the superintendent of schools in the United States), is situated in the County Hall and has nine administrative branches, ten divisional offices, and an inspectorate.

The ILEA administers 1,107 nursery, primary, and secondary schools with a teaching staff of 18,780 for 406,970 pupils (see table 12:1). These schools include boarding institutions and a wide variety of schools for the handicapped. Its educational services extend beyond this range to include nine colleges of education, fifty-one colleges of further education, such as commerce, art, and technology, eight recreational institutes, thirty-eight literary and adult education institutes, and twenty youth centers (ibid., pp. 34, 35). The primary

FIGURE 12:1. THE GREATER LONDON AREA, SHOWING THE JURISDICTIONS OF THE ILEA AND OF OTHER LOCAL EDUCATION AUTHORITIES

Local Education Authorities (LEAs)

A	Waltham Forest	K	Kingston-upon-Thames
B	Redbridge	L	Richmond-upon-Thames
C	Havering	M	Hounslow
D	Barking	N	Hillingdon
E	Newham	O	Ealing
F	Bexley	P	Brent
G	Bromley	Q	Harrow
H	Croydon	R	Barnet
I	Sutton	S	Haringay
J	Merton	T	Enfield

Source: Great Britain, Department of Education, "The Local Education Authorities," *Reports on Education* 31 (October 1966).

TABLE 12:1. SOME STATISTICS OF THE ILEA

Nursery, primary, and secondary schools (including 360 special agreement and aided schools, mostly denominational)	1,107
Teaching staff	18,780
Pupils	406,970
Colleges of Education	9
Colleges of Further Education	51
Recreational Centers	8
Literary and Adult Education Centers	38
Youth Centers	20
Expenditures, 1968/69	$303,214,200

Source: Inner London Education Authority (1968), pp. 22, 34, 35.

and secondary schools include 360 "special agreement and aided schools, most of which are denominational (ibid., p. 8)." The governors have certain financial responsibilities for the external repair and improvement of buildings, but all other costs are borne by the authority.

Each primary school is grouped with two or three neighboring schools under a managing body comprising twelve persons, eight of whom are appointed by the ILEA and four by the local borough. Each secondary school has its own governing body, members of which are called governors. Both bodies are charged with the "oversight of the conduct and curriculum" of the school (Inner London Education Authority 1967 *b*, p. 3, *c*, p. 16).

Each school is administered by a head, and each school is best described by the ungrammatical yet probably precise term *relatively autonomous*. Certainly the ILEA schools are autonomous to an extent not dreamed of in a system such as that of New York City, yet the authority "shall determine the general educational character of the school and its place in the Authority's educational system (Inner London Education Authority 1967 *b*, p. 16)." Each school is quite free to go its own way, but its path is monitored and indirectly controlled by persuaders in the forms of the inspectorate, examining boards, the National Union of Teachers (NUT), and a host of others. This autonomy produces schools that cause educational administrators to complain of diversity and to seek for a degree of conformity. (Particular reference is made to discussions among some forty educational administrators in a seminar series conducted in the winter of 1969 at the University of London's Institute of Education.)

The budget at the time of this study (1968/69) called for the expenditure of £126,339,500 ($303,214,800), with the major contributions being £80,797,500 from the inner-London borough councils and £27,197,000 from the national government (Inner London Education Authority 1968, p. 22).

The ILEA is part of the national system of education in England and Wales. Having said this, one needs to define what is meant in England by the term *educational system,* since it might vary from the American's meaning. The Department of Education and Science (DES) is under the Secretary of State (a position not comparable to the one with a similar name in the United States) and is charged with the responsibility of implementing educational policies of Parliament. These responsibilities extend to making financial grants, setting minimum standards for school buildings and health, defining national policies, and the like. Under this broad and rather vague mandate, the DES, among other things, participates in negotiating the national salary scale and retirement and other benefits for teachers, approves building plans, asks for and reviews plans of Local Education Authorities (LEAs), prods authorities towards comprehensive secondary schools, and provides Her Majesty's national inspectorate. The creation in 1964 of The Schools Council for Curriculum and Examinations, financed by the national government, may be considered a step towards systematizing education. The council's role is to "promote and encourage curriculum study and development . . . and to sponsor research and enquiry where this is needed to help solve immediate and practical problems (Great Britain, Department of Education and Science 1966 *a*)." The department's almost complete detachment from what is taught in the schools must be noted; this is an essential aspect of the English system. The editorial comment of *The Manchester Guardian Weekly* for the week ending 4 July 1970, which describes English lower education in these words: "It is anarchy licensed by the DES. It is no system at all" would appear to be a realistic appraisal by a critical observer. However, it might be more appropriate to say that there is a system that *provides* for education than to say that there is a national education system or that there is no system at all.

THE STRUCTURE OF THE ILEA

The Inner London Education Authority is a creature of the Greater London Council, which has overall responsibility for planning, roads, traffic, housing, parks, licensing, sewage, land drainage, refuse collection and disposal, civil defense, building construction, entertainment, and, through the ILEA, education.

ILEA Membership and the Education Committee

The forty members of the Greater London Council and the thirteen borough and city representatives who sit on the Inner London Education Authority augment their number with sixteen persons for the Education Committee. The added members are chosen from people interested in and knowledgeable about education. They are generally selected in proportion to the representation of each party although some are chosen without regard to political affiliation. Lady Plowden, director of the study that led to the highly influential Plowden Report, is an added member who illustrates the idea behind the added member concept.

The Report of the Committee on the Management of Local Government (a departmental committee set up and reporting to the Minister of Housing and Local Government) contains a description, an analysis, and a set of recommendations for added members. It points out that:

> Under the Education Act, 1944, the education committee must "include persons of experience in education and persons acquainted with the educational conditions prevailing in the area." This does not necessarily mean that these persons should not be members of the council (1967, p. 103).

In reviewing evidence presented to it, the Committee on the Management of Local Government concluded that abuses, such as appointing defeated councillors, relatives, and unsuccessful political aspirants, constituted only 2 or 3 percent for each case and were of no great consequence. The value to local committees of knowledgeable and experienced people could not be denied. The committee recommended that local committees should make greater use of the co-option of added members and allow them to vote. At least 2/3 of each committee should, however, be elected members of the local authority.

In 1969, the ILEA included for the first time three teachers among their added members, although it has been common since 1904 to have as many as four teachers in Local Education Authorities in other parts of the country. According to Sir Ronald Gould, the General Secretary of the National Union of Teachers, the three teachers were nominated to the ILEA Education Committee by the Joint Consultative Committee, a body to which teachers are elected and which meets with the Education Officer of the ILEA. Their ILEA selection gave rise to considerable controversy, as it was felt that it was impossible for the three to represent all factions among the teachers. Because the teachers sat with the Education Committee for the first time on 18 June 1969, there was no evidence at the time of this study of how well they function.

Membership on the Education Committee is viewed differently; some see it as a stepping stone to Parliament, others as a public service, others as a status symbol. During the spring of 1969, Christopher Chataway, the Leader of the Education Committee, was elected to Parliament by the Conservative Party, thus demonstrating to a degree the validity of some people's perception.

Members serve without compensation; only the Leader receives travel funds. The Leader is given an office and a secretary by the authority and one by his party. The chairman and vice-chairman are also provided with secretaries.

Functioning of Education Committee

The Education Committee elects a chairman and a vice-chairman who conduct meetings. The chairman is selected as a person who can be objective and impartial. He must abstain from party politics while holding the chair. He rarely votes, although he may as a member and he must in case of a deadlock.

The basic unit in the structure of the committee is the political party. The Conservative Party was in power in London in 1969 and had a majority of seats on the committee. The chairmanship of each of the subcommittees was in the hands of the Conservative Party. The Schools Subcommittee has twenty-three members; the Further and Higher Education Subcommittee, twenty-one members; the Finance and Administration Subcommittee, fourteen members (all elected); and the Policy Coordination Subcommittee, nine members.

The Policy Coordination Subcommittee is composed only of members of the majority party and meets fortnightly with the Education Officer to attempt to integrate policy making; however, all decisions must be cleared with the respective subcommittees.

In keeping with Parliamentary tradition, the Labor Party has appointed a shadow chairman for each of the committees. It would appear that their major function is to keep fully abreast of the work of their committees and to raise questions during meetings.

The ruling party elects the Leader of the Education Committee. He is provided with a clerical staff and represents the committee at all times. It should be noted that it is the Leader and not the chairman who is the effective head of the committee. The party out of power elects an Opposition Leader.

Most of the actual work of the committee is carried on through the first three subcommittees listed above. Members of the Education Officer's staff are assigned to each subcommittee, and they prepare the reports on which the subcommittee acts.

An examination of the agenda of the Education Committee meeting of 18 June 1970 illustrates the activities of one subcommittee: the Schools Subcommittee recommended the acquisition of a site for a primary school, the acquisition of land to increase the size of another school site, the acquisition and alteration of a piece of property for a new school for maladjusted boys, and the partial refurbishing of a school. These recommendations all require a vote of the Education Committee. It also announced appointments to seven headships, the acquisition of a site, the results of an evaluation of French teaching in primary schools, the naming of a school, and a reiteration of their unwillingness to force the consolidation of a grammar and a comprehensive school.

While four subcommittees might appear to be a very small number to do the business of the authority, the fact that the subcommittees join on problems of mutual interest enables the structure to encompass all problems. The Policy Coordinating Subcommittee monitors the decisions of subcommittees functioning separately to determine their consistency and adherence to the purposes of the authority.

Dynamics of the Education Committee Meeting

The ordinary meetings of the committee are held monthly. Copies of the agenda are sent to members well in advance of the meeting. The agenda consists of reports of the four subcommittees; it is printed and is typographically attractive. The agenda for the meeting described here ran to twenty letter-size pages, set in 8-point type. Questions on the agenda must be submitted by 5 p.m. on the day before the meeting. Answers to these questions are prepared by members of the Education Officer's staff, reviewed by the appropriate subcommittee chairman, and read by him at the meeting. Meetings are held at 3 p.m. in The County Hall, London.

I arrived early at The County Hall for the meeting and proceeded to the meeting room. Although it was nearly 3 p.m., the hall was virtually empty. A few representatives of the press were in place asking one another if "anything exciting" was in store and, "Are the teachers going on strike?" The public section was occupied by an elderly gentleman, who informed me that he used to sit "down there," pointing to the floor of the meeting room and he expressed grave concern over a threatened teacher walkout. (The subject of a strike or walkout never was discussed by the committee, even though one had been announced previously by the NUT and later materialized.) Several members of the Education Officer's staff wandered in and out of the public seating area. Very few people attend meetings of the Education Committee; in fact, the public section would seat only twenty or thirty people at the most. One reason for the lack of attendance is probably that, under the organization of the ILEA, most of the issues of interest to the public or to teachers are handled either locally at the school or division level or nationally, as in the case of salaries. For example, the later walkout was a salary protest and was directed against 10 Downing Street and the Secretary of State, not against the ILEA.

The meeting was opened and conducted by the chairman according to strict Parliamentary procedures. As the meeting progressed, it was apparent that the committee members were highly sophisticated, with "point of order," "point of interpretation," "point of personal preference" being heard frequently. In spite of the great show of formal courtesy (a member on arriving late or leaving early would always stand, face the chairman, and execute a bow, which would be returned), speakers were heckled, and there were interruptions and gentle demonstrations of support or rejection.

Of the sixty-nine members of the Education Committee, fifty-five were present at one time or another. The leadership of the Conservative Party sat in the front row to the right of the chairman, the Opposition Leader and shadow chairman to his left (see figure 12:2). The backbenchers, as is the English custom, sat where they could. Members would frequently leave only to be summoned back by the Whip for a division (recorded vote). A division was mandatory if any eight members would stand in place following the presentation of a motion. Attention appeared to be rather strict, although one member fell asleep during a lengthy speech by another member.

The order of business followed the agenda. The chairman handled the reports of each subcommittee, reading the questions from the Opposition and the answers, which had been prepared by members of the Education Officer's staff. There were often additional questions and comments to which the chairman of the appropriate subcommittee would respond, generally asking for further comments by members of the subcommittee. The members seemed to be well informed and articulate. They appeared to be very sensitive and intelligent about the attitudes of their communities,

FIGURE 12:2. PLAN OF EDUCATION COMMITTEE MEETING

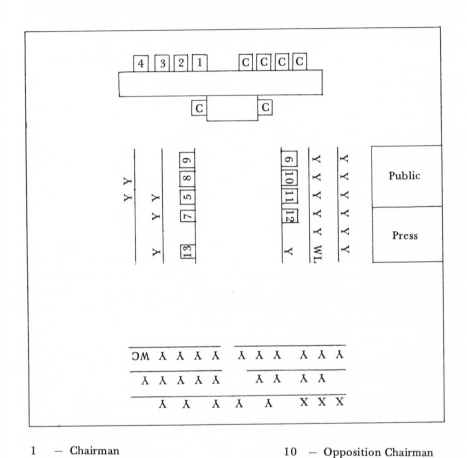

1	— Chairman	10	— Opposition Chairman
2	— Vice-chairman	11	— Opposition
3	— Education Officer	12	— Opposition
4	— Finance Officer	13	— Lady Plowden
5	— Leader	C	— Clerks
6	— Opposition Leader	X	— Teacher members
7	— Chairman, Schools	Y	— Backbenchers
8	— Chariman, Finance & Administration	W_C	— Conservative Party Whip
9	— Chairman, Further & Higher Education	W_L	— Labor Party Whip

particularly the point of view of the parents. Two of the three teacher members spoke eloquently on two of the issues, evidencing particular interest in the matter of the final year for those leaving school at age sixteen. They sided with Labor in opposing a flexible law that would let children elect to enter colleges of further education and advocated keeping them in their secondary schools.

Neither the Education Officer nor any other professional spoke during the meeting, nor do they ever speak. There are always two high-ranking officials sitting on the dais; when one leaves, another, who has been in the public section during the whole meeting, takes his place. While teachers speak as members of the Education Committee, no administrator or other professional educator ever speaks.

Other than the teachers, the members seemed to represent a broad spectrum of the community: many women, some retired persons, young businessmen, and a few lawyers. Six members of the committee I observed held titles and many of the members were of the working class. There was one West Indian member, but there appeared to be no other immigrants on the committee.

Throughout the debates, the difference between the parties was very clear. All divisions were on a strict party basis and, if a member did not vote with his party, he abstained. There were two divisions during the meeting: one on the amalgamation of the St. Marylebone Grammar School and the Rutherford School, which would combine a boys' school with a coeducational one, the basic issue being whether these schools would become a comprehensive secondary school; the second, putting the committee on record in favor of allowing pupils in the last year of compulsory education the right to attend an establishment of further education. The Schools Subcommittee saw fit to recommend in opposition to the Secretary of State on the first, and all three subcommittees recommended in opposition to the Education Officer on the second. When a division was in order, a bell rang, followed by a four-minute intermission. The Whips left the chamber to round up members. After four minutes, the reading of the names began and each motion was carried on strict party lines.

The ideological positions of each party appeared to be reflected in the rhetoric. The Conservatives used such terms as *freedom, flexibility,* and *local option* in their speeches and, whenever the opportunity arose, favored selective entrance to secondary schools. Laborites favored strong national legislation and expressed the belief that one cannot trust local authorities. They took every opportunity to support comprehensive secondary education and were opposed to selection.[1]

Politics and the Committee

It appeared that all decisions were made on the basis of political parties; however, when I raised this point with the Leader, university professors, the Education Officer and his staff, the General Secretary of the NUT, and with educational administrators, they strongly denied this conclusion, indicating that rhetoric was part of the game being played and that there was frequent concurrence on basic educational issues. The facts would seem generally to support their contention. While, for instance, the Labor Party has made the conversion of the multiple system of secondary education to comprehensive schools part of their national platform, the London Education Service (the predecessor of the ILEA) had pioneered the development of comprehensive schools long before the Labor Party recognized the issue. Further, outside London, the only major authority to go completely comprehensive is Leicestershire, which is Conservative. Musgrave (1968, p. 26) supports the contention that the political parties are quite similar in their educational outlook because "increasingly, both Labor and Conservative councillors tend to be former grammar school pupils and hence tend to have common norms and values about many educational matters."

It is the opinion of the Education Officer that the ILEA made more progress toward comprehensive education before the Labor Party made it a political issue. The Association of Education Committees (a national organization of LEAs) issued a call for greater freedom from direct political control at the national level (*The London Times* 19 June 1969). No mention was made, however, of the political constitution of the education committees in the association.

When the question of politics in education was raised with Mrs. Townsend, the ILEA Education Committee Leader, she responded that party politics did not enter into education and that the differences between parties were more apparent than real. (Sir Ronald Gould concurred in this, adding, "Politicians like to talk about abstractions.") Mrs. Townsend felt strongly, however, that there were definite values in the political basis for the governance of education. First, she contended, the two parties often overstate their position on a particular issue. This tends to clarify the issue, since the extremes are clearly stated. The result is a decision that is better than one arrived at by a nonpartisan group because the issue has been clarified, positions taken, and the consequences of each position predicted by the other side. The second value is that the parties are made responsible for the condition of education. If, for instance, the people of London were to feel that education is being poorly handled, the ruling party can be voted out. Each party, therefore, considers that it is responsible for improving the condition of education. This is reflected in extremes ranging from the determination of broad educational policies at the highest national levels to the efforts of councillors to get a better school building for the children in a sector of their borough.

Influences on the Committee

There were not many clues as to who influences the Education Committee or how they do it. Mrs. Townsend listed several factors, most of which are the same as those that exert influence on any democratically elected body. Members must stand for election every three years, so they are held accountable on rather short terms. The constituency was claimed to be the most influential of all of the bodies seeking to move the committee to do their bidding. While the mails and telephone are the ordinary ways of getting to a member, an additional one called "Surgery" is employed. (This is the British term for the doctor's being in his office to receive patients.) The members hold "Surgery" once a week or fortnightly and talk face-to-face with their constituents.

There is also the usual lobbying by neighborhood associations and organizations of parents, consumers, rate-payers, and the like. The role of the NUT *vis-à-vis* the committee was not clear. It would appear that there are strong ties between the NUT and the administrative structure, with the committee being influenced through the Education Officer and his staff.

The national parties also appeared to me to influence at least the rhetoric of the local parties. In actuality, it would be difficult in most education authorities to determine the political party in power by examining either the schools or the administration of the authority.

ADMINISTRATION

The British use of the term *administration* is at considerable variance with the American usage. The term is never applied to those who work in a school, except for the school secretary, even though each school has a number of people performing what Americans call administrative functions. English administrators are, rather, people in executive positions at The County Hall or in divisional offices. It should be noted, however, that senior administrators have generally had teaching experience. Administrators provide services that enable others, called *teachers* (regardless of whether they are actually teachers or headmasters, housemasters or department chairmen), to conduct the education of others. Administrators generally do not concern themselves with the substance of education; in fact one gets the feeling that they are absolutely barred from any involvement with it. Teachers, the whole range of them, keep education to themselves.

There is, however, one position that stands between administrators and teachers, and this is that of the inspector, so it can be said that the administration of the ILEA consists of the staffs of the Education Officer, the divisional officers, and the Inspectorate.

Education Officer's Department

At the time of this study the Education Officer was Sir William Houghton and his deputy was Dr. E. W. Briault. There are nine branches of the Education Officer's Department covering the administrative work of the authority; seven of the branches being headed by an Assistant Education Officer, as shown in figure 12:3.

One should not assume that the Education Officer merely provides services to the schools. His leadership and planning roles are probably more significant. Not only do the Education Officer and his staff plot the direction of the ILEA, but also, because of the size and status of inner London, they are very influential at the national level. They prepare papers and appear before national study groups such as the Plowden Committee and committees of Parliament.

Since the staff work for the Education Committee is done by the Education Officer's staff, they influence the committee's every action. Major policies, such as the introduction of the secondary comprehensive school, take form because of the leadership of the Education Officer, even though the implementation of such a policy awaits the approval of the Education Committee.

Divisional Offices

Much of the administrative work that directly concerns the schools is done in the divisional offices. The ILEA is divided into ten geographic divisions for administrative purposes, the boundaries of which are coterminous with those of the inner-London boroughs (two divisions contain two boroughs each). Each division has a divisional officer, a deputy, and a staff located in a conveniently situated office. Others, such as inspectors, are housed in divisional offices but they do not report to the divisional officer.

I interviewed Mr. H. W. Wales, Divisional Officer for Islington, a

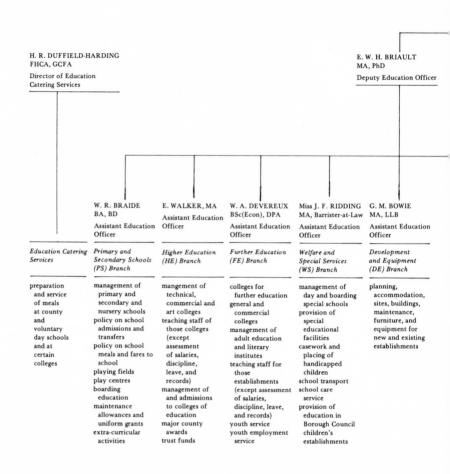

H. R. DUFFIELD-HARDING
FHCA, GCFA

Director of Education
Catering Services

E. W. H. BRIAULT
MA, PhD

Deputy Education Officer

W. R. BRAIDE BA, BD	E. WALKER, MA	W. A. DEVEREUX BSc(Econ), DPA	Miss J. F. RIDDING MA, Barrister-at-Law	G. M. BOWIE MA, LLB
Assistant Education Officer	Assistant Education Officer	Assistant Education Officer	Assistant Education Officer	Assistant Education Officer

Education Catering Services	*Primary and Secondary Schools (PS) Branch*	*Higher Education (HE) Branch*	*Further Education (FE) Branch*	*Welfare and Special Services (WS) Branch*	*Development and Equipment (DE) Branch*
preparation and service of meals at county and voluntary day schools and at certain colleges	management of primary and secondary and nursery schools policy on school admissions and transfers policy on school meals and fares to school playing fields play centres boarding education maintenance allowances and uniform grants extra-curricular activities	mangement of technical, commercial and art colleges teaching staff of those colleges (except assessment of salaries, discipline, leave, and records) management of and admissions to colleges of education major county awards trust funds	colleges for further education general and commercial colleges management of adult education and literary institutes teaching staff for those establishments (except assessment of salaries, discipline, leave, and records) youth service youth employment service	management of day and boarding special schools provision of special educational facilities casework and placing of handicapped children school transport school care service provision of education in Borough Council children's establishments	planning, accommodation, sites, buildings, maintenance, furniture, and equipment for new and existing establishments

THE EDUCATION OFFICER'S DEPARTMENT

SIR WILLIAM HOUGHTON
Education Officer

L. W. H. PAYLING, MA, PhD
Chief Inspector

Inspectorate

Inspection of educational
establishments and advice on
their work and organization

H. A. RUGGLES
Head of Branch

L. G. A. SAUNDERS Assistant Education Officer	R. M. GORDON, MA Assistant Education Officer	R. T. TIMSON MA, PhD Establishment Officer	J. C. WYKES, MA Director of Educational Television Service	A. N. LITTLE BSc (Sociology), PhD, JP Director of Educational Research and Statistics Group	*Finance* *(F) Branch*
Teaching Staff *(TS) Branch*	*General Purposes* *(GP) Branch*	*Establishment* *(Estab) Branch*			
teaching staff policy and control of staff numbers, discipline, welfare, assessment of salaries, leave, and records of teachers recruitment, appointment, and allowances for teachers in schools and colleges of education lectures and classes for teachers, in-service training	general policy new legislation and coordination enquiries publications libraries and museums use of educational premises outside normal hours lectures for pupils various examinations official openings visits to schools use of school organization road safety consultative committees nature study scheme carol festivals	administrative, professional, and clerical and all other nonteaching staff staffing questions of general application to all staff schoolkeeping organization and methods, work study and other management services accommodation and office equipment and materials training			finance, including estimates and accounts, and control of expenditure payment of wages and teachers' salaries, and heating, lighting, window cleaning, and chimney sweeping accounts security (The Finance Officer and certain members of his staff are seconded from the Treasurer's Department of the GLC)

Source: Inner London Education Authority, "Welcome to London Schools."

depressed section of London, studied the office, and talked to a number of the staff. The functions performed, the staff, and the method of operation of the Islington division are similar to those of the other nine. The Islington division has 106 schools from nursery through secondary, 1,650 teachers, and 34,000 pupils. It is considered a difficult division because of the large number of immigrants there, including Greek Cypriots, Turks, Africans, West Indians, Asian-Africans, and Pakistanis. Some schools have now reached 60 to 70 percent immigrant population. The area is depressed socially, and there are severe housing shortages. There is, for England, a considerable amount of violence.

The divisional office is situated in a garden-apartment building in a business area of Islington. It is across the street from an underground station, and buses run past its doors.

Mr. Wales described the functions of the divisional officers: general administration, application of the Authority's policies, conveyance of local problems and needs to the Authority, keeping the schools running—seeing that there are teachers, materials, and equipment, and that the children go to school, and maintenance of accessibility to the people. According to R. M. Gordon, an Assistant Education Officer of the ILEA, the divisional officers do not report to anyone in particular. They have a monthly conference over which the Deputy Education Officer presides and which is attended by heads of administrative branches, or their representatives, if the business of the conference concerns them. The divisional officers are the representatives of the Education Officer in the divisions and they work with the head of whatever branch is dealing with the subject in question. Most of their dealings would probably be with the Schools Branch and with the Development Branch, but all the Assistant Education Officers have dealings with the divisional officers.

The Islington divisional office is divided into six sections, and two district inspectors and a Children's Care Organization are housed in the office, but these people do not report to the divisional officer. A chart of the office (see figure 12:4) indicates the sections and relationships.

Mr. Wales is among the last of a vanishing breed of English school administrators—a nongraduate. The trend in the ILEA is toward the employment of university graduates for administrative positions, while the general practice elsewhere in the country is to recruit graduates with teaching experience. Of the ten divisional officers in the ILEA, none has had teaching experience, and five have no university degree. Mr. Wales commented that he, and others with similar qualifications, "wouldn't stand a chance outside London." He

FIGURE 12:4. CHART OF DIVISION OFFICES

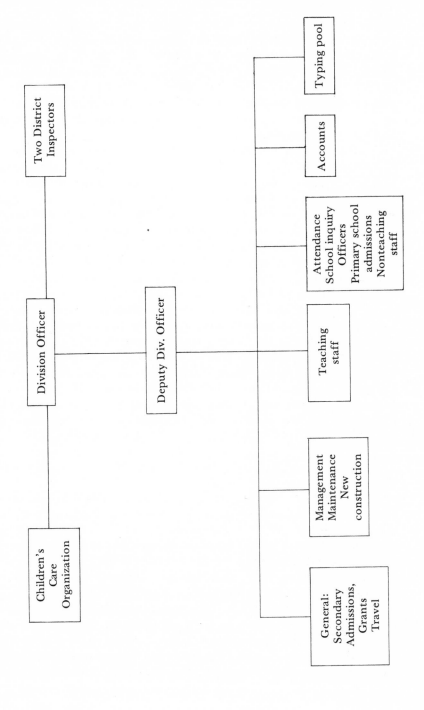

also made the point that fewer and fewer were coming into educational administration in the ILEA through the backdoor. A study of graduate administrators in the LEAs would seem to bear him out. Fewer than 10 percent of the graduate administrators surveyed did not have teaching experience (Rendel 1968, p. 21). Since the study was restricted to graduates, no conclusions can be drawn from it as to the numbers of nongraduates in educational administration throughout the country.

Mr. Wales entered the Education Department of the London County Council at the age of eighteen, starting as a clerk in an office that handled the paper work on children from other authorities. By individual study, enrollment in LEA courses, and passing exams, he worked his way up through the ranks. He worked in school building maintenance, administered a program for children evacuated from London during World War II, and headed an emergency teacher-training program after the war. He was the Education Officer's personal secretary (administrative assistant) for several years before becoming a divisional officer.

In talking with Mr. Wales and others of similar background, one feels that the fear of administrators who lack educational and/or teaching experience that one hears expressed in America are groundless. These men seem to have a slightly exaggerated view of the importance of professional education training and, as a result, are probably too subservient to the heads and teachers. Regardless of the reasons, it appears that the ILEA is shutting off a source of excellent manpower in restricting itself to graduates for administrative positions.

The Inspectorate

The Inspectorate is the cement that holds the educational system together (to the extent that there is a system). There is no American counterpart of the English inspector, so it is very difficult to define the post by reference to American education. While it is felt in England that the title *inspector* is misleading, attempts to find a more descriptive term have failed. Edinburgh and Glasgow, for example, now call their inspectors *advisors,* yet this would certainly be a misnomer for the ILEA inspector. Although ILEA inspectors do not inspect in the old sense, they are far more than advisors. They are a combination of examiners (such as those in New York City), consultants for both subject and grade levels, supervisors in the American pattern of elementary school supervisors, and inspectors in

the English tradition. An anonymous chief inspector is credited with
the following description of the inspector:

> An inspector is a collaborator, an organizer, an in-
> spirer, a consultant, a cross-fertilizer, a stimulator of
> slackers, a conductor of classes and conferences for
> teachers, a composer of quarrels, a selector of poten-
> tial heads, a prompter of initiative, a provoker of
> thought, a disturber of unthinking routine, a philos-
> opher, a friend. He is an interpreter of schools in the
> office and the office in schools, with a view to pro-
> moting fuller mutual understanding.

While this is a rather glowing and overly enthusiastic description,
ILEA inspectors have the reputation of living up to it. They are
university graduates with honors degrees, highly professional, and
well up in their fields. They are an indispensible element in the
English system. Without inspectors there would be no educational
system, just a loose management arrangement.

There are seventy-seven ILEA inspectors headed at the time of
our study by Dr. L. W. H. Payling, responsible for coordinating the
work of the Inspectorate and advisor to the subcommittees of the
authority and to the Education Officer. In addition, the Inspectorate
includes the schools' psychological service, with a senior educational
psychologist, a liaison office, and twenty-six psychologists.

The ILEA is divided into nineteen inspectorial districts, each
having a district inspector, who is responsible for the general oversight of primary, secondary, and special schools in the area. The fact
that the ILEA is divided into ten geographical divisions for administrative purposes but nineteen districts for educational supervision,
should be kept in mind. (It is, apparently, one of the many ways in
which the two aspects of the ILEA are kept separate.) Fifteen of the
inspectors hold the rank of district inspector, while the other four
hold the rank of staff inspector and have the additional responsibility
of being in charge of their subject for all of the ILEA. Each of the
fifteen district inspectors also has a specialty and is a member of a
specialist subject team under a staff inspector. These teams make one
full inspection of a school each term—the inspection normally lasts
for a week, but may last two or three weeks in a large school. Each
school is inspected once every twelve years. These inspections are
similar to the cooperative studies of school districts performed by
the New York State Education Department or the accreditation visits
of such organizations as the Middle States Association of Colleges

and Secondary Schools. There are four inspectors of special education, who have general oversight of all day and boarding schools, home tuition groups, hospital schools, primary schools attached to the large homes for children, and for special education in approved schools and foster homes. There are twelve inspectors of further and higher education and forty-one inspectors of art, drama, handicraft, housecraft, music, physical education, infants' education, and nursery education, and there have been added inspectors of English, math, science, modern languages, primary education, and secondary education, who are termed pure specialists, since they devote their entire time to their subject and have no responsibility for a district.

The functions of inspectors are:

1. To give professional advice on the staffing requirements of each school and on the appointment of staff, in particular to headships and other posts of responsibility.
2. To assess the potentialities of young and inexperienced teachers and to assist and encourage their development. To assess the potentialities of more experienced teachers for promotion, leaves of absence for courses and interchange, reduced fee places, interviews of applicants for the ILEA service, and so on.
3. To organize and conduct courses and discussions for in-service teachers and for those returning to the profession or entering it for the first time (induction courses, advisory panels, refresher courses, and so on).
4. To keep abreast of current educational thinking in both general and particular areas of study; to contribute to such thinking and to act as a cross-fertilizer of ideas (the Nuffield Foundation, the Newson Commission, teaching machines, language laboratories, French in primary schools, teaching of immigrants, local centers— new examinations, supply of evidence for the committee's consideration for submission to national bodies, commissions, or study groups, such as Newsom, Crowther, Plowden, Albermarle, and so on).
5. To act as a professional adviser on the provision made by the authority whether in buildings, facilities, equipment, or in organization and arrangements.
6. To appraise critically but with understanding the strengths, weaknesses, and problems of individual schools and colleges and to advise on measures necessary for future progress (visits and full inspections in which detailed local knowledge of individual schools and colleges is necessary).
7. To act as a channel of communication between the administration on the one hand and schools on the other.

In a system designed to maximize the independence of individual schools and the autonomy of the heads, the inspectors are the major moderating influence. They develop the educational philosophy of the authority and spread it, through persuasion and other indirect means such as appointment of heads, content of in-service courses, and the like. They are probably the major influence on the professional behavior of heads, approached in this role only by the headmaster's teachers and his peers. In a system that has no syllabi, no list of approved texts, and no inclination toward them, the inspectors manage to bring a degree of similarity of educational offerings and methodology. In Mr. Brown's opinion, the inspectors have succeeded to the point where "there is not too much diversity." (The major source for this section is his speech on the Inspectorate [1969] and an interview given by C. W. A. Brown, Staff Inspector, Secondary Education.)

THE SCHOOLS

In order to understand the organization and administration of individual schools, I studied and wrote cases on three schools; collected and examined handbooks, research reports, and other documents; and interviewed administrators, teachers, and professors.

The schools studied had been recommended as typical of the three most common types in the ILEA: primary, comprehensive secondary, and grammar. While as types they may have been typical, they appeared to be above average in quality. The Sullivan School is a primary school in the West End that draws on a heterogeneous population ranging from dustmen to professionals and foreign ambassadors. Mallory is a comprehensive secondary whose catchment area is a public housing development. Isleworth is a grammar school situated just west of the ILEA in Hounslow. (Isleworth is not an ILEA school; its use in this study is minimal and illustrative.) Five aspects of the organization and administration of individual schools are probably significant for this study: the governing boards, the selection and role of the headmaster, the selection of teachers, the administrative structure, and the social and tutorial organization.

Governing Boards

Each secondary school has a board of governors; primary schools are grouped so that a board of managers governs three or four schools. Although the names differ, there appear to be few if any differences between the formal functioning of the two types of boards. A close examination of two booklets, *The Government of County Secondary Schools* (Inner London Education Authority 1967 *b*) and *The Management of County Primary Schools* (Inner London Education Authority 1967 *c*), both published by the ILEA for the guidance of members, reveals that the contents differ only in size of type and the appropriate use of such words as *governor* and *manager, primary* and *secondary*. Any differences in operation among boards appear to be a function of the personality and style of headmasters and members. The method of appointment of members was recently changed by the Education Committee so that:

> The managers shall, unless the Authority decides otherwise, be constituted as follows: Not less than fourteen persons of whom not less than ten shall be appointed by the Authority, two on the nomination of the University of London Institute of Education, and not less than four by the minor authority or authorities concerned.

The role of the governing board in the ILEA was perhaps best put by Sir William Houghton:

> Under the general direction of the Authority it is upon the governors that responsibility rests for the smooth running of the school with the headmaster as agent. In the first place, it is to the governors that the headmaster should explain and, if necessary, justify his plans, his organization and the general conduct of the school. Equally, it is to the governors that he should look for support in the first instance in cases of difficulty.

> Government by a local committee is in the English democratic tradition of decentralization. Governors have a very clear share of the responsibility for the smooth running of the school organization, and on the cooperation between governors, headmasters, staff, and parents, the development of secondary education will depend (Inner London Education Authority 1967 *b*, pp. 1-3).

The so-called representative members of governing boards are selected by the party whips at The County Hall, generally in line with party strength on the authority; most are recruited at the constituency level. The university members are generally nominated by the University of London Senate, while most of the added places are filled through party channels. In general, the chairman is a member of the majority party although he may be, on occasion, a university representative (Baron and Howell 1968, pp. 130-131). In their study of secondary school government in the ILEA, Baron and Howell found that most heads accepted the need for a political element on governing bodies. Most heads said, however, that party politics never obtruded at governors' meetings, but that "disquiet was often voiced about the very variable calibre of individual governors (ibid., p. 131)." Heads' comments on their boards ranged from "sincere and interested, but ignorant" to "on the whole satisfied with a body of exceptional quality (ibid., p. 132)." The central thrust of the Baron and Howell report would seem to be that the quality of board membership could be improved and that the political basis for appointment was the major obstacle to getting suitable people.

Boards meet at least three times a year, once each term. A clerk from the division office sits in at each meeting and prepares the minutes, copies of which are sent to the Education Officer at The County Hall and to the other interested parties. (This method of communication to the division office and The County Hall should be noted.) A review of two agendas from the board of managers for the Sullivan School and the three primary schools with which it joined revealed the following items of business: reprinting program, minor repairs, school allowance, note from Education Officer containing information of the [new] Race Relations Act, fuel economy, prize days, school hours, visits by managers, accidents to pupils, meals and milk, election of board officers, staffing, suspension or expulsion of students, enter/wait sign provided for a headmaster's office, school holidays, and the headmasters' reports. A review of reports by the four headmasters to the board supported the contention of one that "I jolly well don't tell them anything about education . . . I'm a law unto myself." The headmasters' reports included comments on: the Road safety campaign, Redecoration, Staffing changes, Illness of the schoolkeeper, Fire drill, Sports day, Road accidents, Roll and attendance, Music teaching, Silver medal won in London Flower Lovers' League Competition, Prize day, End of term concert, Equipment, Dramatic presentation, Publication of the history of Isleworth School, and the Foreign exchange program.

While the comment of one headmaster, who said, "You'd have to be stupid to tell them anything about education" would seem to reflect the point of view of English professional educators, one should not feel that only conflict exists between heads and the boards. Mrs. Townsend, the ILEA Leader at that time, who was also chairman of a secondary school board, reported that heads turn to boards for help when they are in trouble. In fact, she spent the morning of the day of our interview counseling a head who was in deep trouble. Very probably Baron and Howell's statement typifies the attitude of ILEA heads most precisely: "Apart from the one headmistress who thought her governors were useless, and the head-master who was at odds with his, there was no suggestion that the schools would be just as well off without governors, even though the university governors might be critical of the lack of executive powers and the narrow composition and poor quality of some governing bodies (ibid., p. 137)." (The two heads were in a sample of twenty.)

There seems to be general agreement on what the boards ac-tually do and do not do. It is clear that they have little or no effect on the curriculum, even though they are charged with "the general oversight of the school and its curriculum." Baron and Howell say, "There has been no suggestion that they ever try to influence the curriculum directly, and heads report that the governors simply noted what they chose to tell them (ibid., p. 134)." The financial activity is likewise limited: "It is unanimously agreed that the gov-ernors' financial powers are purely formal (ibid., p. 133)." While these are the two sets of proscribed activities, it does appear that the major functions of boards are to participate in selecting the head-master and "assigned teachers," put pressure on the Authority to improve school plant, equipment, maintenance, and the like, perform ceremonial functions and relate to the public (one headmaster thought the illiterate board members did this best because they lived with the people).

Administrative Staffing of the Schools

While the English contend that there are no administrators at the school level, each school does have a number of people perform-ing functions that Americans call administrative. As a matter of fact, administrative duties are assigned to over half of the full-time teach-ers in secondary schools and to a sizable number of primary school teachers—each of whom receives an additional salary allowance. Table 12:2 gives typical data for moderate-sized ILEA comprehensive secondary schools. The administrative positions for which these al-lowances are paid are illustrated by the three schools studied. Mallory School, with 1,350 students, had a headmaster, a deputy head who taught 6 to 10 periods a week (the school has a 35-period

TABLE 12:2. NUMBERS OF STAFF MEMBERS
AND ALLOWANCE HOLDERS

School	Full-time equivalent staff	Full-time staff	Allowance holders
Parliament Hill	78	60	44
Brooke House	53	45	29
Forest Hill	84	67	46
Dick Sheppard	65	47	33

Source: Inner London Education Authority. *London Comprehensive Schools 1966*, p. 36.

week), a senior master who taught 10 periods a week, 15 department chairmen, and 8 housemasters, all of whom taught full-time. Isleworth School had only six hundred students, but it had a headmaster who taught five periods a week (an "easy" class, he confided), a deputy head who taught more, and the department chairmen. Sullivan School, with 350 pupils, had a full-time head and a deputy.

There is also a sizable number, ranging from 50 to 100 (roughly the same number as the total number of teachers), of nonteaching staff in the comprehensive schools (Inner London Education Authority 1967 *a*, p. 43). Notable among these is the school secretary, who is an administrative officer drawn from the Education Officer's department, which means that he will have had experience in several branches and often in a divisional office. He enjoys a status comparable to that of the teaching staff, attends governors' meetings, advises on administrative problems, deals with all financial matters, supervises clerical workers, and receives a salary approximately double that of a beginning teacher (ibid., p. 44).

The English headmaster is quite comparable to his American counterpart, the principal, except that he is apparently more independent and exercises more power. The autonomy of the head was stressed by everyone with whom the question was raised, and references to autonomy appear frequently in the literature. The heads constantly refer to their authority. One head, for instance, reported that he set the hours of attendance (9 a.m. to 4 p.m. with an hour and a half for lunch), allocated money to departments for books, materials, equipment, and the like (£10,000 a year), appointed chairmen, approved the curricula and syllabi (but he stressed that he always relied heavily upon the department chairmen), selected teachers, and concluded our interview by making the point that, when the authority appointed him, it gave him a free hand to run the school.

The primary school head talked about the use of the per capita allocation for supplies and materials as a way of increasing his power; he can spend the money as he pleases but must report expenditures to the board of managers after the fact. The grammar school head's authority extended to the selection of students for admission, where he is also supreme. He made his decisions on the basis of grades, scores on the 11-plus tests, and recommendations of primary school headmasters. He did not use interviews. He, as is typical, used funds for teachers' salary supplements to get personnel in scarce supply. For example, he employed a physics teacher as chairman of the department and paid a supplement of £750 (the basic salary was approximately £1,020).

The method by which comprehensive secondary school heads are selected appears to be as follows:

1. The authority advertises the vacancy in the *London Times* and other prestigious papers and publications.
2. Candidates apply to the authority.
3. A committee composed of the heads of primary and secondary schools, inspectors, and the chairman of the board of governors reviews the applications and prepares a short list (six or eight names).
4. The short list is referred to the board of governors, which interviews applicants in the presence of an inspector and recommends a minimum of three (in order of preference) to the authority.
5. The Schools Subcommittee of the Education Committee, with the inspector and chairman of the governing board sitting in, select the head.

Heads are not certified, and there is no program of studies that they must pursue. No use is made of written examinations in the selection process, although confidential reports on the candidate's work are submitted by inspectors if the candidate is from the ILEA, or by others if from outside. Most of the heads of comprehensive schools are from the ILEA even though the authority advertises nationally (ibid., p. 41). Once appointed, a head virtually has life tenure. There is a process for relieving heads of their positions, but it is rarely employed.

Selection of Teachers

There are two types of teachers in the ILEA, and the method of selection differs for each. The more common category is that of *assigned teacher*. When there is a vacancy in a school, an advertisement is placed in the same places as were mentioned in the section above on the headmaster. Candidates are interviewed by the head, and those getting through the screening are then interviewed by the board of governors. In practice, this interview is generally conducted by the chairman, and the vote of the board is a formality.

For the second category, that of *divisional staff*, teachers form a pool from which the schools can draw. The procedure is for the divisional office and an inspector to interview prospective teachers (generally new graduates of colleges of education) and appoint them to the divisional staff. Heads then request a teacher to fit a particular need. A divisional staff teacher must be made a member of an assigned staff before being appointed to a position of responsibility beyond teaching.

Social and Tutorial Organization

Among the inventions of the comprehensive schools, the social and tutorial structures must rank high. It was felt from the beginning of the comprehensive school movement that it was necessary to develop a structure apart from the academic, a structure in which children could be viewed as individuals while at the same time they would learn to accept the responsibilities of community life. A number of structures were developed, some horizontal and some vertical in nature. (For discussions and illustrations of various structures, see Inner London Education Authority 1967 *a*, pp. 49-55.)

The horizontal structures are based upon the year, or form (class), and social, physical, and recreation activities, and school trips take place under its auspices. Generally the clubs, dances, pupil records, and pastoral care (guidance) are also handled in the horizontal structure.

Mallory School exemplifies use of the opposite type of structure, the fully developed vertical organization called the *house*. Mallory was opened in September 1958, and contained, for the first time in the ILEA, facilities built especially for the house plan. The school has eight house blocks, each with house rooms, dining facilities, lockers, cloakrooms, toilets, and a room for the housemaster. As the concept of the house is used at Mallory, it means a division of the school containing about 180 students who are fully representative of the school according to age, ability, and sex. Pupils attend a house assembly each week and have dinner each day with the staff. Houses compete with one another in athletics, music, drama, verse speaking, and debating. The houses also have numerous student officers called prefects, with functions ranging from team captaincies to the performance of duties such as milk distribution. Representatives from the houses make up the school council, which has jurisdiction over certain school funds. Although the head and two teachers are officers, they do not vote. The houses are subdivided into tutorial groups of about thirty pupils, who meet daily for registration and other administrative tasks. The house tutor is assigned to a group of children when they enter the school and both he and they stay together until the children leave. Since it is the tutor's job to be the guide, counselor, and friend to each member of his group, all matters that concern a child are first referred to the tutor. As the academic day of the student is divided among many teachers, it is the tutor who gets to know the student as an individual.

The housemaster and deputy housemaster are always chosen from opposite sexes, are selected for personal characteristics, and are responsible for the general oversight of house organization, development of activities, discipline, the detailed records of the welfare and progress of pupils, and for involving parents in the school.

Although the house plan has been judged to be very successful at Mallory School, a shortage of money for school construction has meant that more recent buildings do not have Mallory's special house facilities (ibid.). Other comprehensive schools have developed variations on the house concept with varying degrees of success.

CONCLUSION

The comparison between English and American practices takes the form of a table of statements. I have no intention of saying that the American approach is absolutely wrong and London's absolutely right, but rather, that "here is something different, let us talk about it."

TABLE 12:3. HOW THE ILEA DIFFERS FROM STANDARD AMERICAN PRACTICE

1. **Its relationship with the national government:**

   a. Teachers are paid on a national pay scale and receive a London supplement.
   b. Building grants are made on a national basis.
   c. The inspectors are members of the civil service.
   d. There is a tie between national and local political parties on educational issues.

2. **On the city level:**

   a. The ILEA does not include all of London.

b. The Education Committee has a political basis.
c. The Education Committee has the status of a special committee of the Greater London Council.
d. The relationship between the Education Office and the schools has no parallel in America.
e. The existence of the Inspectorate.
f. Its divisional structure.
g. The presence of teachers and added members on the Education Committee.
h. The administrators are not always members of the school's particular community.
i. The parochial schools are in local educational authorities.

3. **On the school level:**

a. The school is autonomous.
b. The headmaster's role has no parallel in America.
c. The selection of the headmaster and staff differs entirely from American practice.
d. The individual schools are small.
e. The social and tutorial organization is not to be found in American schools.
f. The existence of a governing body for each secondary school and for groups of three or four primary schools is a characteristic unique to the English school system.
g. Parents may choose the particular school they prefer.

Propositions for Discussion

Since the purpose of this study was to develop alternatives to the American approach to organizing and administering education in large cities, I conclude with a number of propositions for discussion. Some are being proposed because the practice is not only different and exciting, but also because it appears to be working well; the added member concept is one of these. Others are offered as pure concepts, which, while they appear to be useful, have not worked particularly well in London; the boards of governors and managers illustrate these. The purpose of these propositions is to stimulate public discussion that will revitalize school districts in the United States.

1. American city school districts should move in the direction of separating management and education so that they approach a "system that provides for education" rather that being an "educational system."

This is a key concept that is fully accepted in England, but is not even talked about in this country. The separation of management and education should occur before any attempts to decentralize take place. This recommendation would decentralize schools educationally but would keep management functions, such as the recruitment of personnel, purchasing, maintenance, planning and construction of school buildings, in the central office where they can be done more efficiently.

2. Each individual school should have educational autonomy with its educational philosophy and curriculum determined by its board of governors, teachers, and principal.

3. Each city should be divided into an appropriate number of divisions, each with a divisional officer so that necessary services can be provided to schools with an absolute minimum of delay.

4. There should be a unit of educational advisors attached to the central office who would perform part or all of the functions of the ILEA Inspectorate.

Assuming that the argument for proposition one is accepted, propositions two, three, and four implement the concept of educational autonomy for the schools.

5. All schools—public, private, parochial, vocational—from nursery through junior college should be under the jurisdiction of the city or central board.

In essence, this proposition calls for all schools through the two-year junior college to be combined in a single public school system. This becomes feasible and its acceptability increased by private school owners and the churches since the above propositions, particularly proposition two, guarantee the educational autonomy of each school. The spirit of this proposition is to make more efficient the management of all schools, personnel recruitment, selection, and promotion, the procurement of materials and equipment, the construction, maintenance, and operation of school buildings, and the provision of such services as health care, social work, and food. The benefits of implementing such a concept might well be an increase in the democratization of American schools, since all schools would have the same financial support and all pupils in a given jurisdiction would have the same per capita expenditure, which would mean comparable facilities. Also, all teachers would be on the same salary schedule.

6. Each school district should be very large, and each school should be very small.

In light of the British experience, the total population of a school district should not be smaller than five hundred thousand with no maximum stated. With the function of the district restricted to providing for education, there is no evidence as to how large it can grow since, in all probability, managerial efficiency is directly proportional to size. However, schools should be severely restricted in their enrollment, since size is probably inversely related to educational efficiency and to the pupils' social development. Elementary schools should probably range from two hundred to three hundred pupils, while secondary schools should not exceed twelve hundred. Secondary schools should employ the house plan for internal organization, with each house not exceeding 150 pupils.

7. Each district should create a semiautonomous research and development center.

The research and development centers would be funded by the federal government and be as independent as possible. They would develop improved methods and materials for instruction and involve teachers in the development of new curricula. The use of such products would not be mandatory, but schools would be urged constantly to upgrade their programs.

8. The governance of American schools should move from "nonpolitical" to "political."

People might be elected to governing boards as members of a political party or certain members of the city common council might be members of the school board concurrently. As a result, the governing party would be held responsible for the state of education. Further, the partisan nature of boards would cause arguments to be stated in extreme forms, so that the public would be able to see the issues more clearly and be able to forecast consequences more precisely.

9. American boards of education should adopt the "added members" concept.

Whether other propositions are adopted or not, American boards of education should make use of the added member concept and include in their membership teachers and other persons who have a high degree of skill and knowledge in education.

NOTES

Data for this study were gathered in the spring of 1969 while I was a Visiting Scholar at the Institute of Education, University of London. The research was supported by a Ford Foundation Study Grant. I wish especially to acknowledge the help of Dr. George Baron and D. A. Howell of the Department of Educational Administration, University of London; Tobias Weaver, Deputy Secretary, Department of Education and Science; and R. M. Gordon, Assistant Education Officer, Inner London Education Authority. I give special thanks to D. A. Howell for his detailed analysis of the first draft of this chapter, but retain responsibility for any errors that may remain.

1. The term *comprehensive secondary education* has different meanings in

England and the United States. In England it is used to designate a school to which all types of students would go but, once in school, they would be put into "streams." Students of different academic and social backgrounds meet for social, athletic, and cultural activities in house or year groups. In addition, students may change streams after the age of eleven, something virtually impossible in other types of English secondary schools.

REFERENCES

Baron, George, and Howell, D. A. "School Management and Government." *Research Studies 6.* Royal Commission on Local Government in England. London: Her Majesty's Stationery Office, 1968.

Brown, C. W. A. "The Function of the Inner London Education Authority Inspectorate." A speech made at the Inner London Education Authority teachers' residential center, Stoke D'Abernon, England, Spring 1969.

Great Britain, Department of Education and Science. "The Schools Council." *Reports on Education* 29 (February 1966) *a.*

——— . "The Local Education Authorities." *Reports on Education* 31 (October 1966) *b.*

Great Britain, Ministry of Housing and Local Government, Committee on the Management of Local Government. *Management of Local Government.* London: Her Majesty's Stationery Office, 1967.

Inner London Education Authority. *London Comprehensive Schools 1966.* London: Inner London Education Authority, 1967 *a.*

——— . *The Government of the County Secondary Schools.* London: Inner London Education Authority, 1967 *b.*

——— . *The Management of County Primary Schools.* London: Inner London Education Authority, 1967 *c.*

——— . *ILEA Guide.* London: Inner London Education Authority, 1968.

——— . *Welcome to London Schools.* London: Inner London Education Authority, 1968-69.

Musgrave, P. W. *The School as an Organisation.* London: Macmillan, 1968.

Reller, Theodore L. "The Greater London Council and the Education Service." *Educational Administration Quarterly* 4 (Spring 1968): 5-18.

Rendel, Margherita. "Graduate Administrators in LEAs." Mimeographed. London: University of London, Institute for Education, Appointments Board, 1968.

part IV

Future Options for Metropolitan Schools

The crisis of the metropolitan problem demands clear and precise description and rigorous analysis of metropolitan school organization. In chapter thirteen, Reller elaborates on the metropolitan scene. He stresses that a more thoroughgoing analysis of the history of present concepts and purposes is essential before options can be developed to meet the educational needs of a pluralist society more appropriately. We should seek knowledge of how present structures came into being and under what conditions. Certainly our present condition is unsatisfactory and, as our beliefs change, some of what we discarded in the past may now be more appropriate. There is a further need to examine educational structures other than our own, and to increase our research and development activities to this end. Future study should be accomplished by highly motivated research teams who combine the resources of the university and its disciplines, industry, and government at all levels.

Many problems still confront the development and implementation of metropolitan structures. Some elements and concepts do not apply to the notion that bigger is better and quantity is quality. To differentiate between the elements and concepts to be decentralized and those to be centralized is the problem that confronts all who are interested in an improved educational system. Educational structures are in need of reform. Cooperative efforts are needed to seek new relationships and to develop the concepts derived from rigorous study and research.

13

Options for the Future

Theodore L. Reller

In recent years my experience with the study of metropolitanism has focused on metropolitan units in other nations and on the San Francisco metropolitan area. I mention this because the reader must be aware of the possible introduction of bias, for each one of us tends to look at metropolitanism in terms of his own experience.

THE CHALLENGE TO RESEARCH AND DEVELOPMENT

We have in recent years come to realize the future problems of education in our society. Werner Hirsch's *Inventing Education for the Future* (1967), Daniel Bell's *Toward the Year 2000* (1968), Alvin Toffler's *Future Shock* (1971), and Walter Hack's *Educational Futurism 1985* (1971) are examples of writings that have stimulated thinking about the future and its implications for individuals and the society in which they will live. The metropolitan problem moves rapidly toward crisis. Many of us are not able to see the big picture, which includes the inner city, the peripheral city, and the suburbs as a totality. Most of us view the metropolitan scene from the perspective of where we live. The picture of the inner city is blurred when viewed by affluent suburbanites, as is that of the suburb when viewed by the inner-city poor. This inequity of perception and belief structure creates the crisis. We need more knowledge, obtained through more rigorous analysis of both the macrometropolitan problem and its elements, such as education, about the crisis we face.

While metropolitan educational systems have been discussed, relatively little hard analysis of the basic background, the history, the attitudes, and the proposals themselves has been made. Few attempts have been made to base the analysis on a theoretical foundation or to test a conceptual framework against an operational metropolitan unit (Kaplan 1967). Such study may help the development of tough minded proposals for the problems and issues of metropolitanism. The problem involves finance, administrative behavior, organizational structure, and the educational process itself, to which we have given too little attention. It seems by now that we should have developed an understanding that the more we know the less we know. In recent years so many problems have unfolded about which we have so little to offer that has been tried and has worked.

We should emphasize more that we need to look at history simply because we have a tendency today, perhaps because most of our society is under thirty years old, not to look at past experience to the degree we should. We should ask: How did we get where we are? How can we avoid error? Why did we throw out some of the things that, it is proposed, we should return to, such as, for example, the ward election of school board members? At the moment we may not be adverse to going back to it but, if we do, let us see why we gave it up and avoid some of the things that caused us to give it up. A description of the London model should lead us to questions such as: How did London get to be the way it is? What is its history? Many additional questions should arise from the magnificent controversy in Parliament over the question of whether London should turn entirely to borough control of education (Reller 1968). Why, when the Conservative government was holding hearings on its proposal to turn totally to the borough plan and to have no Inner London Education Authority—keep in mind that the proposal of the Conservative government was to eliminate the London County Council and the Inner London Education Authority entirely—did Parliament retreat? Why did the last Churchill government have to retreat? It had to retreat it seemed because nobody seemed to be unhappy with the London County Council. It is astounding that a great city like London, with a magnificent educational structure that operated from 1902 to 1963, would change its educational system when no one seemed averse to it, not even parents or teachers. The government had to accept this and for that reason. The Inner London Education Authority is looking two ways and has an interesting plan. In the inner part of Greater London there is essentially an *ad hoc* independent organization for education, in all the other parts of the authority's territory the boroughs run education, and the two systems operate within the same government unit. I think the concepts in the London model are magnificent and should be tested in this country.

As we study metropolitan organization, we need to study other organizations, other structures, not just those in the United States. It has been worthwhile to look at Toronto, to look at London, to look at some of our large cities. I think also that a study of the struggles of the university reorganization would be an interesting contribution. My own interest in metropolitan development has been influenced more by working in international community development than by any other way. Beginning some ten years ago, we slowly learned that, in general, our efforts in international community development were not successful because each profession decided it was going to do the job on its own. The educators went in and said, "Oh, what they need is literacy." The road builders went in and said, "What they need is roads." So they built roads and the jungles took them back. The health people went in and said, "What they need is health." Thus they aggravated the population problem and are partly responsible for upsetting its balance. It never occurred to any of these professionals that, if they were going to function significantly in underdeveloped areas, they were going to have to change their professional roles and learn to function in a different way. This chapter does not permit the examination of the question whether we have achieved much more from the various professions in the inner cities than we did from them in foreign countries. It does seem clear that a major breakthrough in our knowledge concerning metropolitan school organization will be made through at least the coordination of several disciplines if not by an interdisciplinary team of researchers and developers. Research and development needs should be organized, especially in newer universities because there we can most readily break the separation of other disciplines from educational administration. The metropolitan problem cannot be dealt with effectively by any one discipline. We are depending upon other disciplines much more than we did fifteen or twenty years ago but, in our universities, the schools of education still live too much in isolation for us to grapple with the problem of creating appropriate models for metropolitan education.

I would ask: Are we preparing personnel, for management, educational leadership, or research and development, who will attack the problems of the metropolitan community? Many accept pretty much the opinion of those from the inner city who say, "We've been researched enough. If you have a commitment to working through our problems, help us work through them, bring assistance to us, come back. But if you are just talking about coming and collecting some more data about us, the door is closed." How do we respond? Are we preparing people with a larger vision and the competence to assist the inner city and the surrounding suburbs? Universities must no longer emphasize only certain kinds of research. For example we can learn from anthropology to describe a city holistically, using a team of ethnographers. Such studies and methods can be helpful in advancing our understanding of cultural mechanisms and internal and external integration (Price 1972).

Simulation for planning, forecasting, and the building of models has been used by other disciplines (Hamilton et al 1969). To what extent may the technique of simulation be used to test a metropolitan delivery system before it is implemented? Universities need to face the problem of becoming involved with a subdistrict in an inner city without being swallowed up by it. We have watched the attempts of universities and subdistricts at a distance with interest and concern, but we have not provided direct assistance by way of substantive knowledge or leadership. Much of the lack of responsiveness on the part of the university is due to its inability to define the purpose of the university and its rights and responsibilities. We are encountering today increasing demands that the university adopt new criteria for determining how it serves society (Graubard 1970). Can the university rise to the challenge for reform that comes both from within and without? The debate is dividing university faculties. Can the university in times of strife provide leadership in social, political, and educational issues so apparent in metropolitan areas?

THE EMPHASIS ON PLURALISM

Many concepts come to mind as one considers experiences in other societies, the history of education in this country, past or present cultural drives in our own society and metropolitanism. As educators and as citizens we have not really examined two central questions about pluralism. What do we mean by pluralism in our society? What kind of pluralism do we wish to achieve?

One danger of pluralism is that it drives you toward conformity. For example, I spent a year in England some thirty-five years ago studying local city administration. Englishmen would say to me,

"Well, you are so busy making Americans. Thank God we are all Englishmen, we do not have to worry about building Englishmen." Our lack of tolerance for diversity in the past drove us toward conformity and now in an attempt to escape from it we are having a lot of difficulty. At present we are uncertain about what conformity should be promoted. For example, I do not think the "Americaniza-tion" of Italians necessitated the reduction of the importance of music in their lives to the extent that it probably produced this result.

We are a diverse nation and I think this diversity is one of the great treasures of our society. The diversity of the San Francisco Bay Area where I reside is magnificent. It is striking that when the Berkeley school system decided that it was going to have the same percentage of Caucasians in each school, it also stated proportional percentages for Blacks and Asiatics. I recall going into a school in a nearby community, just three or four years ago, and noting the teachers who were Caucasian, Black, American-Indian, Asian-Indian, Chinese, Japanese, Filipino, Mexican-American, and Latin American. Is this pluralism or have we rubbed out all the differences and made ours a conformist society? We should give a lot more thought to pluralism because we could easily move toward more conformity, rather than toward the more desirable diversity. I think that it is possible to build common values and at the same time accept the particular values of the various groups in our society. Can the society move toward the acceptance of diversity? Can we rid ourselves of our excessive concern about the melting pot? Such questions need to be kept in mind as one develops educational delivery systems in metro-politan areas with diverse cultural groupings.

SOME CHARACTERISTICS OF METROPOLITAN MODELS

What are some facets, some elements of models that we ought to be talking about? Each situation is going to have its own model because of history, because of a notable creativity or a lack thereof, because of the many forces and factors that have evolved in any particular community.

There is going to have to be much more state and federal action in the metropolitan areas. This action is long overdue, and objections to the idea must be overcome. Probably even more important is the establishment of machinery through which we can provide a thorough consideration of metropolitan areas and their organization. A serious study is needed to identify the kinds of alternatives that might be employed to increase this consideration and action in terms of metropolitan areas.

In Ontario, metropolitan Toronto was created as a result of problems pertaining to certain services and after considerable discussion by the Municipal Board. It was not created by having each of the units vote. In London also they did not turn to a vote of the people. After collecting data, discussing things extensively, and calling upon the people to present their views, Parliament made the decision. We have to get rid of this idea that voting is the only key to participation on any issue. I think we need to become organized so that we get some much needed leadership from the states on the metropolitan problem.

Metropolitan units are desirable in many instances. Only through a metropolitan structure will we get a unit that will coordinate the efforts of all the people. Only in this way would it be possible to have the fusion on a broad scale that we need in order to concentrate upon educational issues. There are many things that even a limited metropolitan government unit can do in education. There are many things that a metropolitan government unit can do, for example, in research and development. A real metropolitan organization might work with its subunits, organize them, and provide some of the resources to help them test selected alternatives. There is a real demand for educational improvement in the community and it has a lot of strength and a great deal of action associated with it. But we are not capitalizing on the resource. We are not encouraging subunit participation to find answers. The whole matter of research and development, which goes so relatively untouched in our society, could be fostered by a metropolitan unit. This is a limited power, but an enormously significant one. Take the problem of personnel development—an enormous issue, which is not going to be solved from the outside by the colleges and universities. Universities and colleges have a role to play, but someone within the structure must do much more and it could be the metropolitan unit. The new technology provides another example. If we are really going to use technology effectively, the usual small unit, of eight or ten thousand students, is not going to have the resources to give the required leadership. A metropolitan unit could, and the central city could move back into our society in the position of leadership it held fifty years ago. The cities are in ferment at the moment, they are a dynamic part of our society, and we ought to be working with them. No way of doing that is more promising than by having a metropolitan unit of limited but highly significant powers.

Concurrently with the development of a metropolitan unit or

authority, it would be necessary to develop significant subunits that would be the operational units and would be encouraged to be different from one another. These operational subunits would be quite aware of the need for greater involvement of the people. The subunits of a metropolitan school system should have a vitality and a dignity of their own. Diversity would be sought and encouraged by the metropolitan board. We are not going to overcome the drive toward conformity unless we consciously plan to move against it and value individuality and uniqueness. We could break up the core city, but no one knows the best way to do it. One of the more striking systems is found in the city of Belgrade where the commune is the local unit of government, the equivalent of a county in our government system. Marx apparently said that you would need a heterogeneous commune if it is going to be good. Belgrade is cut into nine pie-shaped pieces, each extending well out into the country so that each commune has core-city territory, suburbs, and rural areas. These communes together create the metropolitan authority, but the power lies in the commune. Here is federation. The Yugoslavs broke with the Russians about twenty years ago on this local power issue and the fact that decision making should be at the local level and should involve not only members of the party. This program of decentralization occurred in substantial part because of the leadership of the party, but each of the units or subdistricts seems to have a life, a quality of its own. New York is struggling toward decentralization now, and struggling is the word. One is not sure that the overall principles have been established. Surely, New York does not have much that has been tested to go on.

I have made these comments often, during a good many years when meeting with groups and trying to convince them that we ought to get large units. They always said, "Give us some real evidence that significant decentralization will then follow. Tell us where it has been effective in our society." We do not have the answers to these questions. We are not able to find the places where we really have decentralization. That is why many have come to believe that we move toward centralization and conformity in large units. We are not leading the way toward decentralization and that is why the development of the subunits is one of the most important elements in the concept of metropolitanism. We should not be interested in a metropolitan unit if we are unable to build significant subunits within it, units that will have the power of organization to be creative, to move forward educationally, and provide for wide differences in educational practice. Many would say we have not been at all successful. All too often, and partly because of our attitudes, when a community grows and builds a new high school, everyone wants to be sure that it is going to be like the other schools. The people should be saying, "Let's make this school excellent but different from our other schools." The great beauty of England educationally, is that it still has institutions that were established four hundred years ago functioning alongside those that were created ten years ago. This enormous maze, scarcely understandable, gives it diversity.

About three years ago while making a study in England, I was told by the headmaster of an elementary school from which ninety-two children were graduating that year, that the children were going to thirty-one different secondary schools, for all kinds of sound and unreasonable reasons. "Some of them," he said, "are going to skip the nearest comprehensive secondary school because their parents know too much about it; they are going to the second one down the road—they don't know as much about it."

Diversity was a great strength of the London County Council. What made the Inner London Education Authority a reality was that the members of the London County Council accepted variety. For example, a request would be made for a single-sex school and the Labour party contingent, which dominated the Council for thirty-five years, would say, "Well, we do not believe in single-sex schools but, if some of the people want them, why shouldn't they have them?" This concept is important to the success of a metropolitan unit.

In England, some thirty years ago, I visited a most exciting upper elementary boys' school, run by an unmarried man who had worked out with the London County Council an arrangement that, whenever any teacher got married, he would be transferred to another school because the headmaster would only have single men on his staff. The beautiful thing was that this school was in the slums of London. It had captured the swimming championship of London for seven consecutive years. Ninety-five percent of the parents were coal hawkers. Practically all the parents appeared when their children were going to have a physical examination. You would see the coal hawker teams, fathers and mothers, in front of the school while the parents came in to meet the nurse, the social worker, and the doctor to discuss the health of their children. You could go down the street—not very far—and find a principal who still wore a celluloid collar, with all that it implied. Diversity is one of the things that we must seek and we have not encouraged it sufficiently.

It is at the subdistrict level that the real coordination of education and the related public services must be effected. We must encourage a rethinking to develop such diversity for its absence is one of the most central problems. Education has been removed from general government services—this is related to the politics of education in a sense—and a remarriage must be made. The place to bring about such a remarriage is not at the metropolitan area level, except in broad principle, but at the subdistrict level. Here, we can find a realignment with all of the other community services. This realignment may take widely different forms in different subdistricts. The viable subunit provides a mechanism through which we can escape the isolation that has characterized the whole educational service in our society. This isolation is related to the tendency to regard schooling and education as the same thing, when they are very different. We have tended to confuse the two terms because of our commitment to schooling, and because of the great contribution of education to our society and our great faith in it. An increased commitment must be made to unite education and other community services. Community life has to be remade and it must be at the subdistrict level. We cannot direct this development in detail from any central office but we can create a climate in which it can flourish in different ways in each of the subdistricts.

One of the things that we have not done and that we must do is to delineate carefully the powers of the metropolitan board and of the subdistrict boards. The metropolitan board has limited powers; the subdistrict board has operational powers. This operational power concerns such matters as personnel, curriculum, instruction. A subdistrict board can call upon and use the services of the metropolitan board while still operating independently. There are some places where this has been worked out. The New York City struggle in 1968 between teachers and "community control" was not wholly necessary. When two great forces each seek large or new powers in the same area confrontation can be predicted. Some would argue that we may need confrontation at times. The avoidance of severe confrontation is one of the things that we must plan for much more carefully in the future. We need to answer the questions: What are going to be the powers of the subdistricts? What are going to be the powers of the metropolitan board? How are they going to work together? What is the plan for cooperation and coordination? We have not yet spelled out the process of power sharing, in a way that would show that we are ready to test it or to give any community leader much confidence in what we are proposing. We just have not grown enough in our thinking. The problems now associated with the metropolitan concept have been explored, but we have not probed these problems and analyzed them in a hard-fisted manner so that we are really ready to make and defend proposals for metropolitan school organization. The elements of a model should be explored through a variety of efforts. We should consciously be seeking participation by the people in many ways, and move toward diversity. This is a major challenge. If we are going to develop a model, it is going to have a number of components, not always of the same number because the metropolitan areas are very different.

Are we going to implement the models incrementally or in one great leap? There does not seem to be an answer to this question. If the change is to be immediate, it will come out of a major crisis. Many recall the depression and the days when North Carolina had no schools operating because the local districts failed to function. The state stepped in to provide six months of school throughout the state. Many remember the shock when the state of West Virginia abolished the existing school systems and created new ones under a politically elected and unprepared county superintendent of schools. These are but two examples of major crises and the immediate changes that followed. Metropolitan authorities may develop as a result of these kinds of situations. Growth comes out of crisis and it may very well happen in some of our metropolitan areas. I would hope that education in the metropolis will not get that bad. But, even if change is immediate, much of the work will remain to be done. We must still build the confidence in the people of subdistricts. We must still get people really involved and this is a tough job because they are easily alienated. One of the striking things about the Toronto Metropolitan Board was that it maintained, or it retained, or it developed, the ability to change even after it got under way. It started on relatively simple terms compared with those that would probably characterize a similar organization in any of our metropolitan areas.

Therefore, a lot of our efforts are much more likely to be in the direction of incremental change based upon court decisions, upon ideas, individual and group insights, and upon educating the metropolitan citizen. One of the striking things of the San Francisco Bay Area is that no one belongs to the Bay Area—no one is a citizen there. The people perceive themselves to be citizens of some city or village somewhere around it, and of the state of California. Smog is beginning to make them think that perhaps they are citizens of the metropolitan area. But education falls short of the smog crisis. The Bay Area citizen is almost more ready to believe that the education of people in Mississippi is of greater concern to him than that of people in the district next door. California's state system of education has encouraged our looking to the state for answers and this is undesirable. State mandated formulas finance the educational enterprise; some of them work against the development of metropolitanism. A school district in the metropolitan area that is poor by state definition sometimes gets financial aid when it is not really poor. The core city, by state definition, may not be poor. We did not consciously develop a finance system that is not defensible in terms of impact on metropolitan organization, but we have one. Some say that educators are as isolated and localized as laymen in their thinking about metropolitanism. Citizens and educators are concerned about the problems of their own community, their own district, and in councils, see how they can get the assistance to advance their own little unit. They do not get together very much to see what they can do to improve education for the entire metropolitan area. Most of us are going to be living in metropolitan areas and it is time that we begin to get concerned about metropolitan citizenship.

SOME OPTIONS

As I consider the conclusion of this statement and the options open to us, I note the points of concern and offer the following suggestions.

We must increase our efforts to gain more knowledge of metropolitan areas and units, their purposes, functions, and problems.

We must broaden our present knowledge of the history of metropolitan development and the projected strategies for implementation.

We must increase efforts to support new approaches to the study of metropolitan areas and the identification of new concepts.

Strategies for the study and development of metropolitan areas must use the resources of several disciplines simultaneously.

Concepts accepted as desirable for a viable society must be studied further in order to insure their inclusion in the development of future metropolitan education models.

We must fuse institutions in the study and development of metropolitanism if we are to accept the concept of metropolitan citizenship.

We must develop strategies and processes that will educate citizens, as individuals, as groups, and as institutions, to a new tolerance for diversity.

We must, with renewed effort, expand our study of social institutions beyond our own boundaries to determine the utility of operating systems and institutions for this society.

We need to stress the invention, testing, and implementation of metropolitan models for the future as well as to assist with present educational problems and issues.

Continued lifelong learning for all citizens should be the overriding goal of educational planning development in metropolitan educational delivery systems.

REFERENCES

Bell, Daniel, ed. *Toward the Year 2000: Work in Progress.* Boston: Houghton Mifflin, 1968.

Hack, Walter G.; Briner, Conrad; Knezevich, Stephen J.; Lonsdale, Richard C.; Ohm, Robert E.; and Sroufe, Gerald. *Educational Futurism 1985: Challenges for Schools and Their Administrators.* Berkeley, Ca.: McCutchan, 1971.

Hamilton, H. R.; Goldstone, S. E.; Milliman, J. W.; Pugh, A. L., III; Roberts, E. B.; and Zellner, A. *Systems Simulation for Regional Analysis: An Application to River-Basin Planning.* Cambridge, Mass.: M.I.T. Press, 1969.

Hirsch, Werner Z. *Inventing Education for the Future.* San Francisco: Chandler, 1967.

Graubard, Stephen R. Preface. *Daedalus* 99, no. 3 (Summer 1970): v-xiv.

Kaplan, Harold. *Urban Political Systems: A Functional Analysis of Metro Toronto.* New York: Columbia University Press, 1967.

Price, John A. "Reno, Nevada: The City as a Unit of Study." *Urban Anthropology* 1, no. 1 (Spring 1972): 14-28.

Reller, Theodore L. "The Greater London Council and the Educational Service." *Educational Administrative Quarterly* 4 (Spring 1968): 5-18.

Toffler, Alvin. *Future Shock.* New York: Random House, 1970.

Bibliography

Abrams, Charles. *The City Is the Frontier.* New York: Harper and Row, 1965.

Agger, Robert E., and Goldstein, Marshall N. *Who Will Rule the Schools: A Cultural Class Crisis.* Belmont, Ca.: Wadsworth, 1971.

Alkin, Marvin. *Challenges in Municipal-School Relations.* Washington, D.C. and Chicago: American Association of School Administrators, and International Association of City Managers, 1965.

American Association of School Administrators. *The American School Superintendent.* Washington, D.C.: The Association, 1971.

American Institute of Planners. "The Role of Metropolitan Planning." *Background Paper.* Mimeographed. Washington, D.C.: The Institute, September 1965.

Ardrey, Robert. *Territorial Imperative.* New York: Atheneum, 1966.

Austin, Allan G., and Lewis, Sherman. *Urban Government for Metropolitan Lima.* New York: Praeger, 1970.

Bailey, Stephen K.; Frost, Richard T.; Marsh, Paul E.; and Wood, Robert C. *Schoolmen and Politics: A Study of State Aid to Education in the Northeast.* Syracuse, N.Y.: Syracuse University Press, 1962.

Banfield, Edward C. *Big City Politics: A Comparative Guide to the Political Systems of Nine American Cities.* New York: Random House, 1965.

_____ . *The Unheavenly City: The Nature and Future of Our Urban Crises.* Boston: Little, Brown, 1970.

Banfield, Edward C., and Wilson, James Q. *City Politics.* Cambridge, Mass.: Harvard University Press, and MIT Press, 1963.

Banovetz, James M. *Perspectives on the Future of Government in the Metropolitan Areas.* Chicago: Loyola University, 1968.

Baron, George, and Howell, D. A. "School Management and Government." *Research Studies No. 6.* Royal Commission on Local Government in England. London: Her Majesty's Stationery Office, 1968.

Baron, Harold N., ed. *The Racial Aspects of Urban Planning.* Chicago, Ill.: The Urban League, 1968.

Bebout, John E. "State Constitutions and Constitutional Revision 1965-67." *The Book of the States 1968-69.* Chicago: Council of State Governors, 1968.

Bebout, John E., and Bredemier, Harry C. "American Cities as Social Systems." *Journal of the American Institute of Planners* 29, no. 3 (May 1963): 64-76.

Bell, Daniel, ed. *Toward the Year 2000: Work in Progress.* Boston: Houghton Mifflin, 1968.

Bendiner, Robert. *The Politics of Schools.* New York: Harper and Row, 1969.

Benson, Charles S. *The Cheerful Prospect: A Statement on the Future of Public Education.* Boston: Houghton Mifflin, 1965.

Berke, Joel S.; Campbell, Alan K.; and Goettel, Robert J. *Financing Equal Educational Opportunity.* Berkeley, Ca.: McCutchan, 1972.

Billingsley, Andrew. *Black Families in White America.* Englewood Cliffs, N.J.: Prentice-Hall, 1968.

"Black Power 1968." *Phi Delta Kappan* 49, no. 8 (1968): 447-52.

Bloom, Benjamin; Davis, Allison; and Hess, Robert. *Compensatory Education for Cultural Deprivation.* New York: Holt, Rinehart and Winston, 1965.

Blum, Virgil. *Freedom in Education: Federal Aid for All Children.* Garden City, N.Y.: Doubleday, 1965.

Blumenfeld, Hans. *The Trend to the Metropolis: Bibliography.* Monticello, Ill.: Council of Planning Librarians, 1970.

Bollens, John Constantinus, and Schmandt, Henry J. *The Metropolis: Its People, Politics, and Economic Life.* New York: Harper and Row, 1970.

Booth, David A. *Metropolitics: The Nashville Consolidation.* East Lansing, Mich.: Institute for Community Development and Services, Michigan State University, 1963.

Bottomly, Forbes. "Some Notes on City School Tensions." *Compact* 2, no. 2 (April 1968).

Brameld, Theodore. *Education as Power.* New York: Holt, Rinehart and Winston, 1965.

Brazer, Harvey. "Some Fiscal Implications of Metropolitanism." Brookings Institution Reprint 61. Washington, D.C.: Brookings Institution, 1962.

Breese, Gerald. *Urban Australia and New Zealand: A Selected Bibliography to 1966.* Monticello, Ill.: Council of Planning Librarians, 1969.

Brown, Claude. *Manchild in the Promised Land.* New York: Macmillan, 1965.

Burkhead, Jesse. *Input and Output in Large City High Schools.* Syracuse, N.Y.: Syracuse University Press, 1967.

Burns, Leland S., and Harman, Alvin J. *The Complex Metropolis.* Housing, Real Estate and Urban Land Studies Program, Research Report no. 9. Los Angeles: University of California, 1968.

Callahan, Raymond E. "The History of the Fight to Control Policy in Public Education." In *Struggle for Power in Education,* edited by Frank Lutz and Joseph Azzarelli, pp. 16-34. New York: The Center for Applied Research in Education, 1966.

Campbell, Alan K. "Educational Policy Making Studied in Large Cities." *The American School Board Journal* 154, no. 3 (March 1967): 18-27.

Campbell, Alan K., and Meranto, Philip J. "The Metropolitan Education Dilemma: Matching Resources to Needs." *Urban Affairs Quarterly* 11, no. 1 (September 1966): 42-63.

Campbell, Alan K., and Sacks, Seymour. *Metropolitan America: Fiscal Patterns and Governmental Systems.* New York: The Free Press, 1967.

Campbell, Alan K., and Schuman, H. *Racial Attitudes in Fifteen American Cities.* Supplemental Studies. National Advisory Commission on Civil Disorders. Washington, D.C.: U.S. Government Printing Office, 1968.

Campbell, Roland F. *School-Community Collaboration in Our Cities.* White House Conference on Education: Consultants' Papers, pp. 144-51. Washington, D.C.: U.S. Government Printing Office, 1965.

Campbell, Roland F., and Layden, Donald H. *Policy Making for American Education.* Chicago: University of Chicago, Midwest Administration Center, 1969.

Carlton, Patrick W., and Goodwin, Harold I. *The Collective Dilemma: Negotiations in Education.* Worthington, Ohio: Charles A. Jones, 1969.

Cease, Ronald C., and Saroff, Jerome R., eds. *The Metropolitan Experiment in Alaska: A Study of Borough Government.* New York: Praeger, 1968.

Clark, Kenneth B. *Dark Ghetto: Dilemmas of Social Power.* New York: Harper and Row, 1965.

_____ . "Alternative Public School Systems." *Harvard Educational Review* 38, no. 1 (Winter 1968): 100-103.

Cleaveland, Frederic N., ed. *Congress and Urban Problems.* Washington, D.C.: The Brookings Institution, 1969.

Cohen, David K. "Policy for the Public Schools: Compensation and Integration." *Harvard Educational Review* 38, no. 1 (Winter 1968): 114-37.

Coleman, James E. et al. *Equality of Educational Opportunity.* Washington, D.C.: Superintendent of Documents, U.S. Government Printing Office, 1966.

Coleman, James S. et al., eds. *Equal Educational Opportunity.* Cambridge, Mass.: Harvard University Press, 1968.

Committee for Economic Development. *Guiding Metropolitan Growth.* New York: The Committee, 1960.

_____ . *Reshaping Government in Metropolitan Areas.* New York: The Committee, 1970.

Committee on Educational Finance. "Financial Status of the Public Schools." *Negotiation Research Digest.* Washington, D.C.: National Education Association, 1968.

Community Services Commission. *A Future for Nashville.* Nashville, Tenn.: The Commission, 1952.

Conant, James B. *Shaping Educational Policy.* New York: McGraw-Hill, 1964.

Coons, John E.; Clune, William H.; and Sugarman, Stephen D. "Educational Opportunity: A Workable Constitutional Test for State Financial Structures." *California Law Review* 57, no. 2 (April 1969): 305-421.

Cornell, Francis G. "A Comprehensive Survey of the Metropolitan School System: Nashville and Davidson County, Tennessee." Mimeographed. White Plains, N.Y.: Educational Research Services, 1963.

Cox, James L. "Federal Urban Development Policy and the Metropolitan Washington Council of Governments: A Reassessment." *Urban Affairs* 3, no. 1 (1967): 75-94.

Crain, Robert L. *The Politics of School Desegregation.* Chicago: Aldine, 1968.

Cunningham, Luvern L.; Dykes, Archie; Kincheloe, James; and Ostrom, Vincent. "Report on the Merger Issue." Mimeographed. Louisville and Jefferson County School System, 1966.

Cunningham, Luvern L. "Hey, Man, You Our Principal? Urban Education As I Saw It." *Phi Delta Kappan* 41, no. 3 (November 1969): 123-128.

Daly, Charles U. *The Quality of Inequality: Urban and Suburban Public Schools.* Chicago: University of Chicago Press, and the Center for Policy Study, 1968.

Danielson, M. N. *Metropolitan Politics.* Boston: Little, Brown, 1966.

Davidson, Helen H., and Greenberg, Judith W. *School Achievers from a Deprived Background.* New York: The City College of the City University of New York, 1967.

Dentler, Robert A. "Community Behavior and Northern School Desegregation." *The Journal of Negro Education* 34, no. 3 (Summer 1965): 258-67.

Dentler, Robert A.; Mackler, Bernard; and Warshauer, Mary Ellen. *Urban R's: Race Relations as the Problem in Urban Education.* New York: Praeger, 1967.

Derr, R. L. "Adaptive Strategies of Urban Schools." *Intellect* 101, no. 2344 (November 1972): 88-90.

Doll, Russell. *Varieties of Inner City School: An Investigation into the Nature and Causes of their Differences.* Kansas City, Mo.: Center for the Study of Metropolitan Problems in Education, 1968.

———. "Categories of Elementary Schools in a Big City." Mimeographed. Chicago: Department of Education, University of Chicago, 1969.

Donovan, John C. *Politics of Poverty.* New York: Pegasus Press, 1967.

Downs, Anthony, Jr. "Alternative Futures for the American Ghetto." *Daedalus* 97, no. 4 (Fall 1968): 1331-78.

Doyle, Patricia Jensen. "The Pittsburg Public Schools." In *Social Planning in Pittsburg: A Preliminary Appraisal,* Appendix 4, pp. 93-110. Kansas City, Mo.: Institute for Community Studies, 1969.

Dror, Yehezkal. "Urban Metapolicy and Urban Education." *Educational Technology* 10, no. 9 (September 1970): 15-21.

Duncan, Beverly, and Lieberson, Stanley. *Metropolis and Region in Transition.* Beverly Hills, Ca.: Sage, 1970.

Earle, Valerie. *Federalism: Infinite Variety in Theory and Practice.* Itaska, Ill.: Peacock Press, 1968.

Edwards, T. Bentley, and Wirt, Frederick M., eds. *School Desegregation in the North.* San Francisco, Ca.: Chandler, 1967.

Egner, J. R.; Lowe, W. T.; and Stutz, F. H. "Regional Educational Development in New York State. A Project Report Submitted to the New York State Education Department." Mimeographed. Albany, N.Y.: State Education Department, 1970.

Eldredge, Hanford Wentworth, ed. *Taming Megalopolis.* New York: Praeger, 1967.

Faltermayer, Edmund K. *Redoing America.* New York: Harper and Row, 1968.

Fanon, Frantz. *The Wretched of the Earth.* New York: Grove Press, 1967.

Fantini, Mario D., and Weinstein, Gerald. *The Disadvantaged: Challenge to Education.* New York: Harper and Row, 1968.

Fantini, Mario; Gittell, Marilyn; and Magat, Richard. *Community Control and the Urban School.* New York: Praeger, 1970.

Fantini, Mario D., and Young, M. A. *Designing Education for Tomorrow's Cities.* New York: Praeger, 1970.

Farquhar, Robin H. "The Public School Administrator Views the Catholic School—Or Does He?" *Educational Administration Quarterly* 4, no. 3 (Autumn 1968).

Feldman, Lionel D., and Goldrick, Michael D. *Politics and Government of Urban Canada.* Toronto: Methuen, 1969.

Finlayson, Judith. "Councils of Governments: What and Why Are They?" *American County Government* 32, no. 4 (1967): 20-25.

Fitzwater, C. O. *State School System Development: Patterns and Trends.* Denver, Colo.: Education Commission of the States, 1968.

Fox, David J. "The Controversy over More Effective Schools." *The Urban Review* 2, no. 6 (May 1968): 17-23.

Gans, Herbert J. *The Levittowners: Ways of Life and Politics in a New Suburban Community.* New York: Pantheon Books, 1967.

Gardner, John W. *Self-Renewal: The Individual and the Innovative Society.* New York: Harper and Row, 1964.

Garvey, John, Jr. "What Can Europe Teach Us about Urban Growth?" *Nation's Cities* 7, no. 4 (1969): 13-18, 31.

Gitchoff, G. Thomas. *Kids, Cops, and Kilos: A Study of Contemporary Suburban Youth.* San Diego: Malter-Westerfield, 1969.

Gittell, Marilyn, ed. *Educating an Urban Population.* Beverly Hills, Ca.: Sage, 1969.

Gittell, Marilyn, and Hevesi, Alan G., eds. *Politics of Urban Education.* New York: Praeger, 1969.

Goldwin, R. A. *A Nation of States.* Chicago, Ill.: Rand McNally, 1963.

Gottman, Jean. *Megalopolis.* New York: Twentieth Century Fund, 1961.

_____ . *Economics, Esthetics, and Ethics in Modern Urbanization.* New York: Twentieth Century Fund, 1962.

Grant, W. Vance. "A Statistical Look at American Education." *American Education* 5, no. 8 (October 1969): 24-25.

Graubard, Stephen R., ed. "The Negro American." *Daedalus* 94, no. 4 (Fall 1965): 773-1168, and 95, no. 1 (Winter 1966): 1-454.

Great Plains School District Organization Project. *Guidelines for School District Organization: A Project Report.* Lincoln, Neb.: Nebraska State Department of Education, 1968.

Greeley, Andrew M., and Rossi, Peter H. *The Education of Catholic Americans.* Chicago, Ill.: Aldine, 1966.

Greenfield, T. D.; House, T. H.; Hickzox, E. S.; and Buchanan, E. H. *Developing School Systems, Planning, Organization, and Personnel.* Toronto, Can.: Ontario Institute for Studies in Education, 1969.

Grottman, Jean, and Harper, Robert A. *Metropolis on the Move.* New York: John Wiley, 1967.

Hack, Walter; Briner, Conrad; Knezevich, Stephen J.; Lonsdale, Richard C.; Ohm, Robert E.; and Sroufe, Gerald E. *Educational Futurism 1985.* Berkeley, Ca.: McCutchan, 1971.

Hal'asz, D., ed. *Metropolis: A Selected Bibliography.* The Hague: M. Nijhoff, 1967.

Hamilton, H. R.; Goldstone, S. E.; Milliman, J. W.; Pugh, A. L., III; Roberts, E. B.; and Zeller, A. *Systems Simulation for Regional Analysis: An Application to River Basin Planning.* Cambridge, Mass.: MIT Press, 1969.

Hansen, Carl F. *Danger in Washington.* West Nyack, N.Y.: Parker, 1968.

Hanson, Royce. *Metropolitan Councils of Governments: An Information Report.* Washington, D.C.: Advisory Commission on Intergovernmental Relations, 1966.

Hartley, Harry J., and Holloway, George E. *Focus on Change and the School Administrator.* Buffalo, N.Y.: State University of New York at Buffalo, School of Education, 1965.

Havighurst, Robert J., ed. *Metropolitanism: Its Challenge to Education.* Sixty-Seventh Yearbook of the National Society for the Study of Education, Part 1. Chicago: University of Chicago Press, 1968.

———. "The Reorganization of Education in Metropolitan Areas." *Phi Delta Kappan* 42, no. 6 (February 1971): 354-58.

Havighurst, Robert J., and Levine, Daniel U. *Education in Metropolitan Areas.* Rockleigh, N.J.: Allyn and Bacon, 1971.

Havighurst, Robert J., and Neugarten, Bernice L. *Society and Education,* 3d ed. Boston: Allyn and Bacon, 1967.

Hawkins, Brett William. *Nashville Metro—The Politics of City-County Consolidation.* Nashville, Tenn.: Vanderbilt University Press, 1966.

Hawley, Amos Henry, and Zimmer, Basil G. *The Metropolitan Community: Its People and Government.* Beverly Hills, Ca.: Sage, 1970.

Hearld, James E., and Moorell, Samuel A. *The Teacher and Administrative Relationships in School Systems.* New York: Macmillan, 1968.

Heikoff, Joseph M. *Urban Politics: Selected Readings Related to Planning.* Monticello, Ill.: Council of Planning Librarians, 1971.

Hentoff, Nat. *Our Children Are Dying.* New York: Viking, 1966.

Herman, Harold. *New York State and the Metropolitan Problem.* Philadelphia: University of Pennsylvania Press, 1963.

Hickrod, G. Alan, and Sabulao, Cesar M. *Increasing Social and Economic Inequalities Among Suburban Schools.* Danville, Ill.: Interstate, 1969.

Hill, Roscoe, and Feeley, Malcolm. *Affirmative School Integration.* Beverly Hills, Ca.: Sage, 1968.

Hirsch, Werner Z. *Inventing Education for the Future.* San Francisco: Chandler, 1967.

Hodge, Patricia Leavey, and Hauser, Phillip M. *The Challenge of America's Metropolitan Population Outlook—1960 to 1985.* Research Report no. 3, prepared for the consideration of the National Commission on Urban Problems. Washington, D.C.: U.S. Government Printing Office, 1968.

Hughes, Larry W.; Achilles, Charles M.; Leonnard, James; and Spence, Dolphus. *Interpretive Study of Research and Development Relative to Educational Cooperatives.* Knoxville, Tenn.: College of Education, University of Tennessee, 1971.

Iannaccone, Laurence. *Politics in Education.* New York: The Center for Applied Research in Education, 1967.

Inner London Education Authority. *The Government of Secondary County Schools.* London: The Authority, 1967.

_____ . *London Comprehensive Schools 1966.* London: The Authority, 1967.

_____ . *Management of County Primary Schools.* London: The Authority, 1967.

_____ . *ILEA Guide.* London: The Authority, 1968.

_____ . *Welcome to London Schools.* London: The Authority, 1968.

Isika, Daniel. *Urban Growth Policy in the United States: A Bibliographic Guide.* Monticello, Ill.: Council of Planning Librarians, 1972.

"Jacksonville and Its New Government." Symposium. *Negro Education* 21, no. 1 (April 1970): 50-78.

Jacoby, Susan. "New Power in the Schools." *Saturday Review,* 18 January 1969, p. 49.

James, Thomas E.; Kelly, James A.; and Garms, Walter I. "Determinants of Educational Expenditures in Large Cities of the United States." Cooperative Research Project #2339. Mimeographed. Stanford, Ca.: Stanford University, School of Education, 1966.

Jencks, Christopher; Acland, Henry; Bane, Mary Jo; Cohen, David; Gintis, Herbert; Heyns, Barbara; and Michelson, Stephan. *Inequality: A Reassessment of the Effect of Family and Schooling in America.* New York: Basic Books, 1972.

Johns, Roe L.; Goffman, Irving J.; Alexander, Kern; and Stoller, Dewey H. *Economic Factors Affecting the Financing of Education.* Gainesville, Fla.: National Educational Finance Project, 1970.

Johns, Roe L.; Alexander, Kern; and Rossmiller, Richard, eds. *Dimensions of Educational Need,* vol. 1. Gainesville, Fla.: National Educational Finance Project, 1969.

Johns, Roe L.; Alexander, Kern; and Jordan, K. Forbis, eds. *Planning to*

Finance Education. Gainesville, Fla.: National Educational Finance Project, 1971.

Johns, Roe L.; Alexander, Kern; and Stoller, Dewey H., eds. *Status and Impact of Educational Finance Programs.* Gainesville, Fla.: The National Educational Finance Project, 1971.

Johnson, Carroll F., and Usdan, Michael D. *Decentralization and Racial Integration.* New York: Teachers College Press, 1968.

Johnson, Lyndon B. Problems and Future of the Central City and Its Suburbs (Message to the Congress, First Session, U.S. House of Representatives, Document no. 99). Washington, D.C.: U.S. Government Printing Office, 1965.

Joint Center for Urban Studies. *The Effectiveness of Metropolitan Planning.* Washington, D.C.: U.S. Government Printing Office, 1964.

Jones, Victor. *Metropolitan Government.* Chicago: University of Chicago Press, 1942.

Kain, J. F. "Housing Segregation, Negro Employment, and Metropolitan Decentralization." *Quarterly Journal of Economics* 82, no. 2 (May 1968): 175-97.

Kaplan, Harold. *Urban Political Systems: A Functional Analysis of Metro Toronto.* New York: Columbia University Press, 1967.

Kent County Michigan Planning Commission. *Grand Rapids Metropolitan Area: Development Plan.* Grand Rapids, Mich.: The Commission, 1969.

Keppel, Francis. *The Necessary Revolution in American Education.* New York: Harper and Row, 1966.

Kerber, August, and Bommarito, Barbara. *The Schools and the Urban Crisis.* New York: Holt, Rinehart and Winston, 1965.

Kerner, Otto, ed. *The Kerner Report.* National Advisory Commission on Civil Disorders. New York: Bantam Books, 1968.

Keyes, Scott. *Urban and Regional Studies at U.S. Universities.* Baltimore, Md.: Johns Hopkins Press, 1964.

Klotsche, Martin J. *The Urban University.* New York: Harper and Row, 1966.

Kohn, Sherwood D. *Experiment in Planning an Urban High School: The Baltimore Charette.* New York: Educational Facilities Laboratories, 1969.

Kozol, Jonathan. *Death at an Early Age.* Boston: Houghton Mifflin, 1967.

Leach, Richard. "A Leadership Crisis." *National Civic Review* 54, no. 5 (May 1965): 244-52.

Levin, Henry M., ed. *Community Control of Schools.* Washington, D.C.: The Brookings Institution, 1970.

Levine, Daniel U. "Cooperation in an Age of Interdependence." In *Partners for Educational Progress,* edited by Frank W. Markus, pp. 7-22. Kansas City, Mo.: Metropolitan School Study Group, and Mid-Continent Regional Educational Laboratory, 1967.

Levine, Daniel U., and Clayner, Jerry B. *Multi-Jurisdictional Metropolitan Agencies and Education.* Kansas City, Mo.: Center for the Study of Metropolitan Problems in Education, 1967.

Levine, Naomi. *Ocean Hill-Brownsville: Schools in Crisis.* New York: Popular Library, 1969.

Lowe, William T.; Egner, Joan Roos; and Stutz, F. H. "Strategies for Metropolitan Cooperation in Education." Mimeographed. U.S. Department of Health, Education, and Welfare, 1971.

Maguire, Louis M.; Temkin, Sanford; and Cummings, C. Peter. *An Annotated Bibliography on Administering for Change.* Philadelphia: Research for Better Schools, Inc., 1971.

Malcolm X. *The Autobiography of Malcolm X.* New York: Grove Press, 1965.

Marando, Vincent L. "Inter-Local Cooperation in a Metropolitan Area." *Urban Affairs Quarterly* 4, no. 2 (1968): 185-200.

Markus, Frank W., ed. *Partners for Educational Progress (PEP): An Analysis of Cooperation: Importance, Status, Principles, Examples, and Action Programs.* Kansas City, Mo.: University of Missouri, School of Education, 1967.

Martin, Roscoe C. *The Cities and the Federal System.* New York: Atherton Press, 1965.

_____ . "Government Adaptation to Metropolitan Growth." In *Politics in the Metropolis,* edited by Thomas R. Dye and Brett W. Hawkins, pp. 404-18. Columbus, Ohio: Charles E. Merrill, 1967.

Martin, Roscoe C. et al. *Decisions in Syracuse.* Bloomington, Ind.: Indiana University Press, 1961.

Martin, Ruby, and McClure, Phyllis. *Title I of ESEA: Is it Helping Poor Children?* Washington, D.C.: Washington Research Project, and NAACP Legal Defense and Education Fund, 1969.

Masotti, Louis H. *Education and Politics in Suburbia.* Cleveland: Case-Western Reserve University, 1967.

Massachusetts, Commonwealth of. "An Act Providing for the Elimination of Racial Imbalance in the Public Schools." 1965.

Masters, Nicholas A.; Salisbury, Robert H.; and Eliot, Thomas H. *State Politics in the Public Schools.* New York: Knopf, 1964.

McCandless, Carl Albert. *Urban Government and Politics.* New York: McGraw Hill, 1970.

McConnell, Grant. *Private Power and American Democracy.* New York: Knopf, 1966.

McGuiness, Lewis J. "The Role of the Public School in Organizing, Coordinating, and Financing Community Action Programs." In *Partnership in School Finance: Proceedings of the Ninth National Conference on School Finances,* pp. 137-58. Washington, D.C.: National Education Association, 1966.

McKelvey, Troy V., ed. *Metropolitan School Organization,* Volume 2: *Proposals for Reform.* Berkeley, Ca.: McCutchan, 1973.

McKelvey, Troy V., and Swanson, Austin D., eds. *Urban School Administration.* Beverly Hills, Ca.: Sage, 1969.

Memphis and Shelly County Planning Commission. *Metropolitan Memphis: Its Facilities, Its Services. Existing Community Facilities and Future Requirements for Metropolitan Memphis.* Memphis, Tenn.: The Commission, 1968.

Midwest Administration Center. "Cincinnati School Survey." Supplementary Papers. Mimeographed. Chicago: University of Chicago, Midwest Administration Center, 1968.

Miles, Simon R., ed. *Metropolitan Problems: International Perspective.* Toronto: Methuen, 1970.

Morphet, Edgar L., and Jesser, David L., eds. *Emerging Designs for Education: Program, Organization, Operation, and Finance.* Denver, Colo.: Designing Education for the Future, 1968.

Morphet, Edgar L., and Ryan, Charles O., eds. *Designing Education for the Future:* No. 2. *Implications for Education of Prospective Changes in Society.* No. 3. *Planning and Effecting Needed Changes in Education.* New York: Citation Press, 1967.

Morphet, Edgar L., and Jesser, David L., eds. *Designing Education for the Future:* No. 5. *Emerging Designs for Education,* 1968. No. 7. *Preparing Education to Meet Emerging Needs,* 1969. New York: Citation Press.

Mueller, Van D., ed. "The Educational Research and Development Council of the Future." Mimeographed. Minneapolis: The Educational Research and Development Council, 1968.

Mumford, Lewis. *The Urban Prospect.* New York: Harcourt, Brace and World, 1968.

Munger, Frank J., and Fenno, Richard F., Jr. *National Politics and Aid to Education.* Syracuse, N.Y.: Syracuse University Press, 1963.

Musgrave, P. W. *The School as an Organization.* London: Macmillan, 1968.

Nam, Charles B., and Powers, Mary G. "Variations in Socio-Economic Structure by Race, Residence, and Life Cycle." *American Sociological Review* 30, no. 1 (February 1965): 97-103.

Nashville Chamber of Commerce. "Metropolitan Government for Nashville and Davidson County." Mimeographed. Nashville, Tenn.: Nashville Chamber of Commerce, 1956.

Nashville City Planning Commission, and Davidson County Planning Commission. "Plan of Metropolitan Government for Nashville and Davidson County." Mimeographed. Nashville, Tenn.: Metropolitan Planning Commission, 1963.

National Advisory Commission on the Education of Disadvantaged Children. *Title I—ESEA, A Review and a Forward Look—1969.* Washington, D.C.: U.S. Government Printing Office, 1969.

National School Public Relations Association. "Industry Steps Up School Role." *Education U.S.A.,* 13 May 1968, p. 205.

Netzer, Dick. *Economics of the Property Tax.* Washington, D.C.: The Brookings Institution, 1966.

New York State Commission on the Quality, Cost, and Financing of Elementary and Secondary Education. *The Fleischmann Report on the Quality, Cost, and Financing of Elementary and Secondary Education in New York State.* Volume 1. New York: Viking Press, 1973.

Odell, William R. "Educational Survey Report on the Philadelphia Schools." Mimeographed. Philadelphia: Philadelphia Board of Education, 1965.

Passow, A. Harry. *Education of the Disadvantaged.* New York: Holt, Rinehart and Winston, 1967.

_____ . "Summary of a Report on the Washington, D.C. Public Schools." Mimeographed. New York: Columbia University, Teachers College, 1967.

_____ . *Toward Creating a Model Urban School System: A Study of the Washington, D.C. Public Schools.* New York: Columbia University, Teachers College, 1968.

_____ , ed. *Education in Depressed Areas.* New York: Columbia University, Teachers College, 1963.

Pell, Claiborne. *Megalopolis Unbound.* New York: Praeger, 1966.

Pettigrew, Thomas F. "Racially Separate or Together?" *Journal of Special Issues* 25, no. 1 (1969): 43-69.

Phi Delta Kappan 41, no. 3 (November 1969). Special issue on school finance.

Phi Delta Kappan 53, no. 9 (May 1972). Special issue on busing.

Prentice, Justus A. "A Cooperative Board Provides Regional Service." *Educational Leadership* 24, no. 6 (1967): 553-59.

Price, John A. "Reno, Nevada: The City as a Unit of Study." *Urban Anthropology* 1, no. 1 (Spring 1972): 14-28.

Purdy, Ralph D., ed. *Planning for School District Organization: Selected Position Papers.* Lincoln, Neb.: Great Plains Organization Project, 1968.

Ranney, David C. "The Impact of Metropolitanism on Central City Education." *Educational Administration Quarterly* 5, no. 3 (Winter 1969): 24-36.

Reller, Theodore L. "The Greater London Council and the Educational Service." *Educational Administration Quarterly* 4, no. 2 (Spring 1968): 5-18.

Rendel, Margherita. "Graduate Administrators in L.E.A.s." Mimeographed. London: University of London, Institute for Education, and Appointments Board, 1968.

Roberts, Joan, ed. *School Children in the Urban Slum.* New York: Free Press, 1967.

Roberts, Wallace. "Can Urban Schools Be Reformed?" *Saturday Review*, 17 May 1969, pp. 70-72, 87-91.

Rochester Center for Governmental and Community Research. *Target: The Three E's.* Rochester, N.Y.: The Center, 1969.

Rodwin, Lloyd. *Urban Growth Strategies of Nations: A Comparative Analysis.* Monticello, Ill.: Council of Planning Librarians, 1969.

Rosenthal, Robert, and Jacobson, Lenore. *Pygmalion in the Classroom.* New York: Holt, Rinehart and Winston, 1968.

Rouse, James W. "Major Issues of Metropolitan Development." *Regional Planning News* 81 (February 1966): 7-8.

Sandberg, John, ed. *Schools and Comprehensive Urban Planning.* Portland, Ore.: Northwest Regional Educational Laboratory, 1969.

Sargent, Cyril G.; Ward, John B.; and Talbot, Allan R. "The Concept of the Educational Park." In *The Schoolhouse in the City,* edited by Alvin Toffler, pp. 186-99. New York: Praeger, 1968.

Saxe, Richard W. *A Report of a Survey of the Mayors of the Fifty Largest Cities Concerning Their Role in Educational Issues.* Toledo, Ohio: University of Toledo, Department of Educational Administration and Supervision, 1969.

Schmandt, Henry J. *Metropolitan Reform in St. Louis: A Case Study*. New York: Holt, Rinehart and Winston, 1961.

Schmid, Calvin F., and Nobbe, Charles E. "Socioeconomic Differentials Among Non-White Races." *American Sociological Review* 30, no. 6 (December 1965): 909-22.

Schnore, Leo F. "The Growth of Metropolitan Suburbs." *American Sociological Review* 22, no. 2 (April 1957): 165-73.

Schuchter, Arnold. *White Power/Black Freedom*. Boston: Beacon Press, 1968.

Serrano v. Priest, 5 C3d 584, 96 CR 601 (1971).

Sexton, Cayo. *Education and Income*. New York: Viking Press, 1961.

Silberman, Charles E. *Crisis in the Classroom: The Remaking of American Education*. New York: Random House, 1970.

Sizer, Theodore R. *Religion and Public Education*. Boston: Houghton Mifflin, 1967.

Sofen, Edward. *The Miami Metropolitan Experiment*. Garden City, N.Y.: Anchor Books, 1965.

Starr, Rodger. *The Living End*. New York: Coward-McCann, 1966.

Sufrin, Sidney C. *Issues in Federal Aid to Education*. Syracuse, N.Y.: Syracuse University Press, 1962.

Suttles, Gerald D. *The Social Order of the Slums*. Chicago: University of Chicago Press, 1968.

Swanson, Austin D. *The Effect of School District Size Upon School Costs*. Buffalo, N.Y.: Western New York School Study Council, 1966.

_____ . "The Cost-Quality Relationship." *The Challenge of Change in School Finance*. Proceedings of the Tenth National Conference on School Finance. St. Louis, Mo., 1967.

Thomas, Piri. *Down These Main Streets*. New York: Knopf, 1967.

Toffler, Alvin. *Future Shock*. New York: Random House, 1970.

_____ , ed. *Schoolhouse in the City*. New York: Praeger, 1968.

Tunnard, Christopher, and Pushkarev, Boris. *Man-Made America: Chaos or Control? An Inquiry into Selected Problems of Design in the Urbanized Landscape*. New Haven, Conn.: Yale University, 1963.

Tussman, Joseph, and tenBroek, Jacobus. "Equal Protection of the Laws." *California Law Review* 37, no. 3 (September 1949): 341-81.

United States Advisory Commission on Intergovernmental Relations. *Alternative Approach to Government Reorganization in Metropolitan Areas*. Washington, D.C.: U.S. Government Printing Office, 1962.

_____ . *Metropolitan America: Challenge to Federalism*. Washington, D.C.: U.S. Government Printing Office, 1966.

_____ . *Urban and Rural America: Politics for Future Growth*. Washington, D.C.: U.S. Government Printing Office, 1968.

United States Commission on Civil Rights. *Civil Rights Under Federal Programs: An Analysis of Title VI*. CCR Special Publication No. 1. Washington, D.C.: U.S. Government Printing Office, 1965.

_____ . *Racial Isolation in the Public Schools*. Washington, D.C.: U.S. Government Printing Office, 1967.

_____ . *Educational Parks.* Clearing House Publication, no. 9. Washington, D.C.: U.S. Government Printing Office, 1967.

United States Department of Commerce. *Statistical Abstract of the United States, 1972.* Washington, D.C.: U.S. Government Printing Office, 1972.

United States Department of Education and Science. "The Schools Council." *Reports on Education* 29. Washington, D.C.: U.S. Government Printing Office, 1966.

_____ . "The Local Education Authorities." *Reports on Education* 31. Washington, D.C.: U.S. Government Printing Office, 1966.

United States Department of Health, Education and Welfare, Office of Education. *Successful Compensatory Education Programs.* Washington, D.C.: U.S. Government Printing Office, 1969.

_____ . *Interpretive Study of Research and Development Relative to Education Cooperatives.* Washington, D.C.: U.S. Government Printing Office, 1971.

United States Department of Housing and Urban Development. *Cooperative Ventures in Urban America: The Urban Development Inner Governmental Awards Program.* Washington, D.C.: U.S. Government Printing Office, 1967.

United States Department of Labor. *The Negro Family: The Case for National Action.* Washington, D.C.: U.S. Government Printing Office, 1965.

Valentine, Charles. *Culture and Poverty.* Chicago: University of Chicago Press, 1968.

Van der Berghe, Pierre L. *Race and Racism: A Comparative Perspective.* New York: John Wiley, 1967.

Vendiner, Robert. *The Politics of Schools: A Crisis of Self Government.* New York: Harper and Row, 1969.

Verdi, Ralph, and Hutchinson, David, eds. *Planning for School District Organization.* Lincoln, Neb.: Great Plains School District Organization Project, 1968.

Virginia Metropolitan Area Study Commission. *Metropolitan Virginia: A Program for Action.* Richmond, Va.: The Commission, 1967.

Walsh, Annmarie Hauck. *The Urban Challenge to Government: An International Comparison of Thirteen Cities.* New York: Praeger, 1969.

Warner, S. B. *Planning for a Nation of Cities.* Cambridge, Mass.: MIT Press, 1966.

Warren, Robert O. *Government in Metropolitan Regions.* Davis, Ca.: University of California at Davis, Institute of Governmental Affairs, 1966.

Warren, Roland L., ed. *Perspectives on the American Community.* Chicago: Rand McNally, 1966.

Watson, Bernard C. "Rebuilding the System: Practical Goal or Impossible Dream?" *Phi Delta Kappan* 42, no. 6 (February 1971): 349-53.

White, Anthony G. *A Selected Bibliography: City-County Consolidation in the United States.* Monticello, Ill.: Council of Planning Librarians, 1972.

Wilcox, Preston. "The Controversy Over I.S.201." *The Urban Review* 1, no. 3 (July 1966).

Williams, Oliver P. "Life Style, Values, and Political Decentralization in Metropolitan Areas." *The Southwestern Social Science Quarterly* 48, no. 3 (1967): 299-309.

Wilson, James Q. *The Metropolitan Enigma: Inquiries into the Nature and Dimensions of America's Urban Crisis.* Cambridge, Mass.: Harvard University Press, 1968.

———. "The Urban Unease: Community versus City." *The Public Interest* 12 (Summer 1968): 25-29.

Wise, Arthur. *Rich Schools, Poor Schools.* Chicago: University of Chicago Press, 1968.

———. "Is Denial of Equal Educational Opportunity Constitutional?" *Administrator's Notebook* 13, no. 6 (February 1965): 1-4.

Wolf, R. "The Measurement of Environments." In *Proceedings of the 1964 Invitational Conference on Testing Problems*, pp. 93-106. Princeton, N.J.: Educational Testing Service, 1965.

Wood, Robert C. "The Challenge of Metropolitan Growth." *Metropolitan Viewpoints* 3, no. 2 (1968): 1-4.

Wurster, Stanley R. "The Intermediate Administrative Unit." *ERIC/CRESS Newsletter* 3, no. 2 (1968): 1-4.

Zimmerman, Joseph F. *1967 Metropolitan Area Annual.* Albany, N.Y.: Y B Printing, 1967.